COUNTRY PERSPECTIVES IN
CLASS AND SOCIETY

Caste Culture and Society Series—2

Country Perspectives in Class and Society

Edited by

Virendra Prakash Singh

COMMONWEALTH PUBLISHERS
NEW DELHI (INDIA)

Country Perspectives in Class and Society

ISBN 81-7169-239-7

First Published 2024

Published by :
COMMONWEALTH PUBLISHERS (P) LTD.
4831/24, Govind Lane,
Ansari Road, Darya Ganj,
New Delhi - 110002
Ph. : 23242541, 23272541
e-mail : commonwealthpublishers2016@gmail.com

Distributed by :
ARJUN PUBLISHING HOUSE
4831/24, Govind Lane,
Ansari Road, Darya Ganj,
New Delhi - 110002
Ph. : 23242541, 23272541
e-mail : arjunbooks2001@gmail.com
arjunpubhouse@gmail.com

Laser Typesetting by :
Dimple Computers
Delhi

Printed at :
Milan Enterprises
Delhi

"Dedicated to the people's
Who lost their lives in
The struggle against
Caste System."

Preface

The dynamics of the much discussed caste system in India has had profound and far-reaching effects on the very ethos and character of development efforts in the country. The division of society into four castes on inherently religious grounds is a theory of class which, on deeper insight, contains many more levels of reasoning related not only to an understood order in nature but also the mechanics of occupation, place in the hierarchy, the ordained structure of human endeavour and, not the least, the economic viability of the entire social and economic structure of nations. The caste system in relation to class structure and cultural change has over the years become the subject of a vast amount of literature, a large part of which can be termed as the Sociology of the Caste System.

The division of people into distinct classes with understood functions and place in overall society are not a phenomenon peculiar to India. The Japanese have their *bura-kumin*, the "untouchables", and ethnicity in South-East Asia has also bred many so-called sub-cultures and race distinctions. It is accepted, nonetheless, that in traditional society, particularly villages such as those in India and other Asian countries, there are even more subtle variations of the easte system. In fact, "caste" is, in other contexts, a purely social division based on such misconceptions as racial superiority, the arrogance of wealth and the much-vaunted educational advantage. But, at this point we may take a quick look at the dynamics of the caste system in India.

The ancient Hindu pattern of social organisation aimed at the value of *Dharama*, *Artha*, *Kama* and *Moksa* by the individual through his physical, psychological and social evolution. This evolution was calculated to be effected through the process of the Varna-asrama system. It was a comprehensive scheme of individual fulfilment with social purpose through concrete institutions. It has been regarded as the basic concept of Hindu culture and the pivot of Hindu social structure throughout the ages. At the same time it cannot be denied that the Varna Dharma has been equally the target of vehement attack by saints and scholars alike from time to time.

It would be necessary to look into the meaning of the Varnasrama Dharma. The protagonists of this system maintain that the Varna Dharma aimed at the classification of society into four Varnas—the Brahmin, the Ksatriya, the Vaisya and the Sudra, respectively, in the order of precedence and on the basis of the element of Sattva, Rajas and Tamas in the nature of human beings to fulfil the multitudinous needs and purposes of society at large. The Asrama Dharma my be best described as the vision of normal life for the individual in his social mileau. It refers to the main stages of life through which the normal individual is expected to pass—student, householder and hermit (in two stages) in the process of evolution and fulfilment of his personality. So far as the Asrama Dharma is concerned, it has been appreciated by all but what is regrettable is that with the passage of time it has been observed more in breach than in practice.

As far as the subject of Varna Dharma, it has been the most controversial theme since long and particularly of late, scholars, sociologists and politicians have held diverse opinions about the origin and usefulness of this institution. Its advocates maintain that the genesis of this fourfold classification of society is to be found in the 'Purus Sukta' of the Rgveda. We also find similar references in the Satapatha and the Taittiriya Brahmana. The Puranas and the Smritis in particular give an elaborate account of it. The Mahabharata and the Gita are also full of several references about this institution. The other school of scholars maintain that there is no mention of the four Varnas in the Vedic literature. The Veda speaks only of the Arya and Dasa Varna. The third school of scholars stress that the concept of Varna Dharma is not only eternal but also universal and it does and did exist in one form or the other in all climes, times and species. They say that the classification of society on the basis of Guna-Karma (nature and work) exists not only in the human or animal world but also in the world of inanimate things. A peep into the ancient history of Egypt, China, Japan, Persia, Greece and Rome shows that there did exist three or four distinctive classes of the priests, the warriors, the businessmen and the artisans and the agriculturists or the slaves resembling more or less the Brahmins, the Ksatriyas, the Vaisyas and Sudras of ancient India.

The next important question, although a very controversial one, that engages our attention is: What is the basis of this fourfold classification of Varnas? Whether it is Janmona (by birth) or Karmana (by work or occupation)? The Sanatana (orthodox) school of Hindu theologists regard Janmana as the basis of the Varna classification while the scholars of the reformist school emphasise the Karmana aspect. The late Dr. Bhagwan Das propounded the Karmana theory. His three-volume study of Indian social organisation has been regarded as a pioneering work in the field of Hindu sociology in modern times. The progressive school of Indian sociologists maintain that the fourfold classification of Varnas was merely a poetic concept of the ancient Hindu sociologists and it did never have a practical existence. They say that it can be proved from history that the theory of the Varna Dharma remained divorced from practice. The name of Sardar K.M. Panikkar may be cited as a representative scholar of this school. His book *Hindu Society at Crossroads* deserves careful study by students of Hindu sociology. He has tried to prove that the Brahmins alone may be regarded as illustrations of the theory of Varna Dharma while the same thing cannot be said about the other three Varnas, *i.e.*, the Ksatriyas, the Vaisyas and Sudras. But at the same time, Sri Panikkar states that slthough the concept of four Varnas is merely an imaginary creation of ancient Hindu sociologists, yet the Hindu social life is inspired and pervaded by this concept. Thousands of castes and sub-castes that comprise the Hindu society try to establish their origin from one or the other of the four Varnas. So we may say that the original concept of the four Varnas either did never find a practical form or if it ever existed in the practical world, that must have been only partially evolved. With the passage of time the original concept might have degenerated into the practical form of the castes and sub-castes that we see with all their glaring absurdities even in the present day Hindu society.

What are the cardinal principles underlying the Varna concept? The following three principles are regarded as the quintessence of the Varna Dharma:

1. Unchangeable inequality based on birth.
2. Classification of occupations and their disparity.
3. Prohibition of marriage outside one's own Varna.

The first and the third may be noted to be prevalent even doday while the second has never been observed in practice. From the Vedic times upto the present day works of history and literature provide several illustrations which show that persons born in lower castes took up occupations theoretically belonging to the higher castes and *vice versa*. Example of inter-Varna or inter-caste marriages are also cited from the ancient literature. A certain class of scholars maintain that Varna is changeable but not caste. The principle underlying the Varna theory, according to them, is Guna-karma while that of caste is birth. So one may change one's Varna but not caste. They cite illustrations from the old literature to prove their contention. But whatever they might believe about the practicability of the Varna concept, it has to be conceded that it played an important role in the evolution and development of Hindu social organisation.

The principal underlying the religious and secular activities of the Hindus has been spirituality. That one cardinal value is the realisation of unity in diversity. Hierarchy will exist as long as diversity remains in the world and without diversity there can be no world; but spiritual equality was regarded by the ancient seers of India as a permanent safeguard against the hierarchy breaking up into an anarchy of ego-centric individuals. Except in periods, according to an eminent thinker, when it displayed a downward curve, Indian culture has been a harmonisation of the individual and the collectivity. In the Mahabharat it is said that if an untouchable happens to be virtuous, even the Gods would recognise him as a Brahmin. This harmonisation of the individual and the collectivity has been regarded by many as a marvel of Hindu sociology, but there are others who lay their accusing finger on the intolerant and exclusive priestcraft and petrified social hierarchy, and conclude that it has disfigured Indian history and caused the general impression of a repression of the individual under a system of hidebound orthodoxy. Prof. A.R. Wadia has taken this stand in his *Contemporary Indian Philosophy.*

A certain section of scholars maintain that the concept of fourfold Varnas was really a novel and useful device of the Hindu sociological brain to maintain the purity and solidarity of the society but later on what caused the decay and disintegration of society was not the Varna classification but its gradual degeneration into innumerable castes and sub-castes. Not only that but the caste system, despite their glaring drawbacks, did play a very significant part in maintaining the purity and solidarity of Hindu society at the time of external aggressions and alien rule. According to these scholars, it was the caste system of Hindus that saved their culture from the onslaughts of Islam and Christianity and kept undefiled the original content.

Now we come to a very perplexing problem that poses itself before every student of Hindu sociology and that is; What is the future of the Varna and caste system after the promulgation of the present constitution of India which does not recognise any sort of disparity or inequality on the basis of caste, colour, creed, sex or religion. The concept of the modern welfare or socialistic state with authorised powers to inerfere in every sphere of human activity and to make or amend laws to fulfil its declared aims has also posed a challenge before the Hindu society which must be answered.

Sardar K.M. Panikkar's approach deserve consideration in this respect. He proves by his penetrating analysis that the various social institutions of the Hindus are not a part of religion and that they are based on laws, customs and traditions and hence they are secular. Thus he tries to establish and conclude that since these social institutions are based on laws and customs, it is desirable that the constitution or the constituted authority should re-interpret or amend them whenever the necessity arises to do so. This he has tried to establish on the basis of the amendments and reforms made in the various Smritis from time to time.

This view is not very far from truth and carries much weight. Varna and caste have now outlived their utility. It is time when we should recast our social structure on the basis of complete equality. History has proved that man is a highly individualistic and group-minded creature who is apt to divide and separate even where perfect unity and equality is intended. A concept or a system based on a view to divide may only aggrevate the division. Man's natural separatism should not be assisted by social separatism; it should rather be fought by social equalism, on all levels and at all fronts. Then only we can hope to acquire the minimum equality needed to harness human energies for progress, material and spiritual.

The inspiration for this collection of papers, articles and comments, from a wide variety of both published and unpublished sources, is drawn from the character that has marked the Indian peoples-always hospitable, adapting, loyal yet not blind and most willing to be swept off by the tumultuous changes that mark the present age. It is hoped that the anthology of reference and source material, some as old and precious, as six decades, will be useful for the student and scholar as well as sociologist and economist. Class and culture are relative terms and caste is inherent. All interact and effect in various ways the economic and social development efforts of the government. This too has become a part of our planning process, evident from the special component for Scheduled Castes and Scheduled Tribes. The Mandal Commission and the Reservation issue are just behind us. Atrocities on a caste basis continue to hamper growth and development. Caste is also an integral part of our political ethos. One hopes for change and change brings pain and suffering. India is on the move and in the midst of change.

In this effort at compilation, the publishers and I wish to thank all the librarians, assistant librarians, research scholars and academicians who assisted in identifying and also at times providing copies of the papers and articles. Due thanks are due to all of them.

EDITOR

Contents

1

Evolutionary Thesis and Societal Change

S.F. ARNOLD

I. Introduction

The purpose of this paper is to examine the utility of evolutionary theory for the study of social change. Of course, the central concern is with those social changes that together constitute economic development. However, the study of social change *cannot* be theoretically differentiated according to the level of economic development of the units of observation. History does not end when the industrial revolution occurs. This observation may be one of the most important lessons to be learned from evolutionary thought. For surely there is no question but that societies change, and that social change is in some general sense evolutionary in character. Thus, the fact that societies constantly evolve is not problematic. The only alternative is to admit to special laws of social creation.

However, although the crude fact of societal evolution of some form and in some degree is not problematic, almost every other facet of the relationship between social change and evolutionary theory is open to question and profoundly problematic. Perhaps a list of the most salient questions or problems may provide an efficient outline for organizing this essay. (At least it provides some organization, and given the excessively broad and general title, any organization is to be avidly sought and jealously cherished).

In any case, the discussion will be oriented around the following three sets of questions:

1. What are some of the barriers preventing more adequate understanding of social change? Is it possible to suggest some ways of reducing these barriers?
2. What is understood by evolutionary theory? What elements containen in this body of thought seem most useful for studying social change?
3. What are the critical issues involved when the social changes encompassed by economic development are viewed as evolutionary? How may an evolutionary point of view contribute to our understanding of these social changes?

Of course, these questions are quite ambitious and pretentious, especially as they suggest that answers are forthcoming. Let me immediately disclaim any such aspiration. Rather, these questions can be "revived", and their importance for social science in either developing or developed societies can be indicated.

II. The Double Contingency of Order and Change

Human societies are always ordered. Human societies are always changing. The juxtaposition of these two elemental properties of social life represents a serious problem for those who would as scientists understand the nature of societies and the manner in which they change. For both order and change should be encompassed by any body of social research that claims the adjective scientific. On this norm there is universal although most often pious agreement.

Yet it is an exceedingly rare study that simultaneously examines the character of the social order and the course of social change. Rather still is the area of research that enjoys comparable growth and development in both of these respects. Rather, most sociological (and I suspect that one could have written "social") research displays a decided and perhaps understandable preference for one or the other of these elements as the problem for investigation. Such discretion may have been the better part of scientific valour and wisdom. However, what may have been wise scientific strategy shows signs of becoming ill-conceived doctrine, if not dogma.

The Initial Error. In sociology, the preferred strategy has been to defer the study of change until the mapping of the social order was relatively complete. This strategy is defended and justified on the grounds that one cannot adequately conceptualize social change prior to a relatively complete picture of what it is that experiences change.

The initial merit of this justification for separating social statics and dynamics is of late made dubious by the perserverance of statics and the almost total exclusion of dynamics. For this enduring separation has brought into being a theoretical and empirical apparatus ill-suited to and thus unable to cope with the crude facts of social change.

Indeed, it may be suggested that there was little initial advantage to be gained from this strategy of separation, and that perhaps the losses exceeded the gains. For if significant change is ubiquitous, any map of society that ignores change can hardly be accurate. Alfred Marshall expressed this view with typical although none the less remarkable lucidity, when he wrote: "I cannot conceive of any static state, which resembles the real world closely enough to form a subject of profitable study, and in which the notion of change is set aside even for an instance".

The extent to which the conceptual schemes derived from a concern with statics are ill-suited to dynamic analysis is most apparent when these schemes are applied to the analysis of change. Most of these applications share the following characteristics:

1. Change is always perceived as a consequence of some disturbance to some integrated status quo.

2. Thus, the source of the disturbance and therefore the

source of change is always exogenous to the social system experiencing change.

3. Change is a stimulus leading to the eradiction of the causing disturbance.

4. The process is completed when integration is once again achieved.

There is some ambiguity as to whether these characteristics are supposed to obtain for all social change, or whether they describe a specific kind of change. In any case, the use of statically based concepts has drastically limited the kinds of social changes that can be studied. In part this severely stylized view of social change results from an incautious over-commitment to the equilibrium concept. Change is perceived as those almost pathological periods of time when societies swing away from and then back to either the same or some other equilibrium state. It seems that when in doubt, the sociologist always imagines a pendulum.

Some Variations And Their Consequences. One common variation of the distinction between statics and dynamics is the corollary one between change within a social system and change in the system itself. This distinction is of course, between micro-dynamics and macro-dynamics. And it is argued that the former rather than the latter represents a more viable task.

As a consequence of this distinction, a considerable body of information about micro-dynamics has been amassed, while the systematic study of macro-dynamics is relatively neglected or deferred. Thus, there is increased information about such processes as the interaction within small groups, the mechanisms of childhood and adolescent socialization, the life-cycle of the family, the manner in which executives arrive at and carry through on business decisions. All of these micro-processes have come under concerted attack by various of the social sciences, and admirable theoretical and empirical progress has been recorded.

Unfortunately, the emphasis on micro-dynamics is in some degree oppositional to the study of macro-dynamics. For, the distinction between change within a social system and change of the system assumes a systems within systems conception of societies. Moreover, it also assumes that the relationship between system and sub-system is uniquely hierarchical, and in one direction autonomous, i.e.,—change in the sub-system does not necessarily depend upon nor necessarily stimulate change in the next higher system.

It is this hierarchical and partly autonomous view of the relationship between a societies component systems that gives rise to the incredible assertion that values do not change or that they change much more slowly than any other factor. And since values are located at the most general system level, this assertion alone almost precludes macro-dynamic analysis.

In any case, macro-dynamics typically assumes the stability of macro-systems and concentrates upon adaptive and/or adjustive mechanisms to the macro-system as constituted, i.e.,—changes in the means employed to achieve or maintain unchanging values.

As a consequence of its deferred status, the study of macro-dynamics enjoys a curious inflation. For like most postponed tasks, the difficulties involved multiply until they assume awesome proportions. Thus, macro-dynamic social theory is inflated to the status where nothing but an encompassing theory of history will satisfy. Such inflation either leads to continued avoidance on the part of potential students, or to an embarassed self-consciousness on the part of those who undertake to work in this area as a result of the supposed pretentious character of their specially. Of course, it can be all too easily demonstrated that the study of social change is quite as pedestrian as any other area of sociological inquiry.

Variation II. When macro-dynamics is attempted, it is usually in the form of comparative statics. This is the case for most of our current knowledge about industrialization. There are a number of excellent studies that compare the institutional morphology of pre-industrial societies with their analogues in industrial societies. The changes are deduced as the mechanisms required to get from the former to the latter. And even if one takes into account the problems intrinsic to generalizing from one version of an industrial revolution to other, possibly more exotic versions, it is clear that propositions derived in this manner are worthy achievements.

However, theory derived in this manner encounters a number of difficulties. The validity of this kind of theory rests upon the fragile assumption that processes may be inferred from static, cross-sectional relationships. Thus, while many theories of change arrived at through comparative statics incorporate attractive vocabularies of processes, in most cases, these processes are inferred from simultaneously static relationships. These theories invoke laws of change, but are devoid of direct observations of change.

The arch-type of this kind of theory is of course the theory of demographic transition. But there are other theories of change that assume the same form. For example, one might cite the theory that deals with the changing relationship between aspiration and achievement in the course of economic development.

The various changes in aspirations and achievement that accompany economic development are typically organized in terms of a three stage theory as is the case for demographic transition. Although it appears that no single writer has presented an exhaustive description of these stages, the following presentation attempts to make explicit the characteristics of each stage about which previous students seem to have achieved implicit consensus.

Stage of Social Lethargy

This stage is characterized by exceedingly low levels of both aspirations for and achievements of improved styles of life. It is argued that the low degree of both aspiration and achievement is a consequence of an exceedingly low level of economic development and therefore, levels of consumption that just barely satisfy subsistence requirements. Lethargy results from the absence of both physical and social energy.

Stage of Aspirations Explosion

The stage is characterized by slight economic development that minimally increase the opportunity for achievement but maximally stimulates aspirations. Thus, the slight initial development stimulates all kinds of desires, the bulk of which are disproportionate to the available opportunities for the satisfying of these new aspirations. The situation is often associated with the political instability and violence that occurs in these areas as a consequence either of the frustrated aspirations and/or the desire for power in order to participate more fully in the new order of things.

Stage of Balance

If and when the society is able to move on to more economic development and thus increase the rate of achievement, the latter is again brought into some balance with aspirations. Thus, this final stage is characterized by a high level of both aspiration and achievement and the result is a new form of political and social stability.

This "theory" (obviously patterned after demographic transition) is here stated most briefly and incompletely. The point, of course, is to illustrate the general form that comparative statics imparts to the study of social change. This form might be summed up as follows: too little—too much—just right. How ancient a formula!

Variation III. The errors involved in using macro-static observations as a basis for macro-dynamic processes are compounded by the temporal extension of these processes. Many of the hypotheses about the countinuing dynamics of industrial societies are the products of such temporal extensions, i.e.,—the extension of processes that are thought to accompany an industrial revolution.

Marx, of course, was an outstanding offender in this regard. Much of his theory of class formation and conflict founder on precisely these grounds; i.e.,—his most incorrect predictions of the increasing bifurcation, homogenization and polarization of social classes in mature industrial societies. And many share this problem with Marx. For example, the same problem is aptly illustrated by the somewhat naive convolutions of some demographers in their attempts to deal with recent and countinuing increase in fertility rates of industrial societies, without departing from their apparently unshakable belief in a high correlation between industrialism and low fertility rates.

I think that it is possible to argue that all of the errors described above can be attributed to the double dogma mentioned earlier in this section:

(*a*) that one can do static analysis without dealing with dynamics, and

(*b*) that the study of macro-dynamics must be deferred until knowledge of social form is relatively complete, until the whole social territory is definitively mapped.

These dogmas are so firmly entrenched in current theory, that many hesitate to make the obvious point, (if our critics are correct, such failure to deal with the obvious is rare), that it is virtually impossible to make these distinctions are preserve contact with the empirical world.

III. Some Principles of Social Evolution

In the preceeding section, an attempt was made to indicate the illegitimacy of any enduring distinction between statics and dynamics. But, the illegitimacy of this distinction cuts two ways. If it be true that the scientific validity of social research is proportional to the extent to which dynamic factors were taken into account (whether explicitly or not), then valid social research should contain much information about social change. Re-stating this notion, if static and dynamic analysis cannot be separated in the collection of valid empirical knowledge, then the considerable fund of apparently valid knowledge about social systems that has been collected should contain much information about social change.

What appears to be lacking, is the presentation of research results in a manner that would bare its content re-social change, and the means of making such a presentation. It may now be suggested that evolutionary thought, when carefully culled, provides social science with such means.

Of course, not all of the components of evolutionary thought prove equally useful for the study of social change. It is precisely this problem that has aroused the widest and most intense controversy. For all too often the literature on social evolution takes the form of wholesale attacks upon or defenses of the totality of evolutionary thought as it was stated in nineteenth century biology. Indeed, quite frequently both parties to the controversy make the surprising assumption that evolutionary thought itself has failed to evolve beyond its original nineteenth century statement.

Now, there is no single, stable theory of evolution in either the biological or the social sciences. Rather, there is a magnificent set of ideas and conceptions that have themselves experienced change, and that have been applied most fruitfully to the study of a wide range of phenomena, including social change. For, although there is little to be gained from playing the stately game of scholarly exegesis at this point, an evolutionary tone can easily be located in many theories of social change. This is especially true of what one might call the classic theories of change, e.g.,—Gemeinschaft to Gesellschaft, mechanical to organic solidarity, traditional to rational-legal systems of authority, folk to urban, sacred to secular. All of these approaches to social change involved some evolutionary principles either explicitly or implicitly. This is to say that an evolutionary tone is present in the very same conceptions of social change that were previously criticized, since they are, in many ways, quite derivative from the aforementioned "classics".

Thus, it may be efficient to begin the search for some tenable principles of social evolution by re-stating in summary fashion the elements of the approach to the study of social change previously described.

1. Social systems are viewed as sets of hierarchically arranged formal, static structures.
2. Social changes are viewed as transition periods during which one variety of static structures is succeeded by another.
3. Thus, social changes are perceived as discreet incidents rather than continuous processes.

4. The specific processes or mechanisms of change are at least phrased in terms of a vocabulary of pathology, if not actually conceived as socially pathological.

5. Social differentiation, the common denominator of all theories of social change, is conceived in terms of stages (usually three-fold) and the final stage typically consists of a new static integration of the now more differentiated structures.

I think that it can be argued that a tenable scheme of social evolution involves the reversal of all of these characteristics. Thus, social evolution involves a view of social systems and the manner of their change that encompasses the following elements:

1. Systems are, in Steward's phrase, "to be viewed as culminations of predominant processes, rather than as static, formal structures".

2. Since, as Veblen put it, systems are to be defined by their processes, change is incessant and not to be perceived as either temporary periods of disequilibrium or as discreet incidents.

3. Systems are perceived as experiencing permanent strains and persistent tensions. Thus, social change and social conflict are associated by definition, and the association is permanent.

4. Evolution clearly involves differentiation. However, it is not a stage theory (although its vocabulary often is unfortunately) and there is no automatic assumption of the functional integration of differentiated structures.

It is now possible to use these elements of social evolution, and combine them into a theoretical posture viz-a-viz social change. This theoretical posture may be briefly and summarily stated as follows:

(*a*) All social systems contain persistent social strains which generate social conflict.

(*b*) The order characteristic of any social system consists of those institutions that control, ameliorate and/or cannalize the conflict produced by persistent social strains. Thus, a society encompasses both conflict and its associated change as well as a social order; that is, essentially a set of tension-management devices or systems.

(*c*) Tension-management systems are inherently dynamic in that the persistent social strains that they manage offer most hospitable environments for social change. Although profoundly social strains may never be completely solved, they are also quite unlikely to endure unaltered. Thus, social change is ubiquitous.

(*d*) Any given social change is potentially both conflict-producing and conflict-reducing in its own right. In any case, social change and social conflict are highly correlated in some narrow sense by definition. New social norms that result from any change will necessarily be in conflict with some existing norms and will necessarily adversely affect some existing interests, even though the same change may complement still other previously existing norms and interests.

It now remains to be seen if this theoretical posture can be informative for the study of social change. Thus, the following section of this chapter will examine the character of social change at the level of the firm during the course of economic development. And while the exposition is not as "tight" as it might be, I believe that the relevance of the view of change outlined above is clear.

IV. The Evolution of the Firm

Most theories of the firm fail to distinguish between the firm as exclusively a membership unit and the firm as the point at which a number of analytical social systems intersect and thus interpenetrate. The membership unit is one of the intersecting social systems and in its own right worthy of investigation. Indeed, membership systems are precisely the unit of observation of general administrative theory. However, when the membership system is the exclusive theoretical concern, difficulties result from the effort to "stuff" the almost infinite variety of concrete phenomena taking place within the firm into a single analytical social system with a consistent set of norms: the norms of the primary work group in the case of those who view the firms as a village and the norms of the market place in the case of those who view the firm as an actor-entrepreneur.

It will be argued here that the social boundaries of the firm are never coterminus with any single analytical social system. Thus, the firm neither has a single, all-powerful goal, nor a consistent set of norms.

The firm is more than a place of work. It is a market for both labour and commodities. It is an arena for the different occupational and union groups. The norms of the communal and societal status system are also present, and influence, in varying amounts, the behaviour of the firm's membership.

In specific firms, elements from the different analytical systems may be so closely connected as to appear indistinguishable, thereby masking the multiplicity of systems that are present. For example, the line supervisor may also be the hiring agent, and thus the norms of the work place and the norms of the labour market may be combined into a single status position. But it is an error to deduce, from this empirical fact, the theoretical proposition that these norms must be so integrated or combined. Indeed, the norms that the line supervisor is most anxious to inculcate into his work subordinates (commitment to the job, stability, indentification with the unit's task, etc.) are least like and most competitive with the norms of the labour market, (mobility, affective neutrality, universality, etc.). Thus, when these two systems are combined into a single position the person occupying that status will be performing in terms of competing norms. When these two systems, work and the market, are separated into two different positions (a special case of the separation of line and staff) the competing norms will manifest themselves as organizational conflict.

The Fragmentation-Pervasion Hypothesis

The image of the firm, projected in the preceding discussion, is the inter-section and interpenetration of a number of potentially conflictual social systems. This view is quite similar to Professor Friedmann's conclusion that as technological change rationalizes the production procedures of the manufacturing firm, the result is a number of internally conflicting levels of rationalization. Thus, one social consequence of technological change within the firm is an increase in the number of conflicting levels of rationalization.

It is possible to apply Friedmann's position to the image of the firm stated above, and derive the following proposition. Technological change increases the number of analytical social systems that intersect and interpenetrate at the concrete firm. The separation of certain staff from line functions are, of course, illustrations of this process.

It was previously argued that these emergent analytical social systems are naturally conflictual, in some degree. For example, it was previously pointed out that the separation of the labour market system from the production system encouraged the overt manifestation of conflict between their respective norms.

In this sense, an increase in the number of intersecting social systems is likely to be accompanied by an increase in the salience of the particular social system to which a norm belongs. For example, "rational" selection of personnel as a labour market norm may be relatively in-operative as long as the line supervisor does the hiring. He is subject to other norms (e.g., low rates of labour turnover) that are more important for his primary social system, line production. However, once the breed of personnel men make their appearance, a "party" is formed that is precisely devoted to presumably rational techniques of hiring, partly motivated by a desire to establish a professional self-image, perhaps as a sincere belief in the value of such procedures. In any case, the salience of the particular system to which a norm belongs is increased by the very emergence of that system within the firm.

Technological change, then, increases the number of social systems that intersect at the firm by creating a larger number of more specialized social systems. The normative content of each of the emergent social systems is more limited in scope and in that sense narrower. In the previous illustration, the personnel department is narrowly concerned with labour market considerations, while the line supervisor is narrowly concerned with maintaining production schedules.

It is important to note that the narrowing of the normative scope of the intersecting social systems has a relative, as well as an absolute connotation. Thus, the duties assigned to either the personnel department or to the line supervisor are a more limited segment of the firm's total duties than were previously assigned to their unitary ancestor. The specific tasks for which the line supervisor or the personnel man is responsible within his own social system may have increased, in part as a consequence of specialization. Nevertheless, such increases will now come within the narrower confines of the particular analytical social system.

The Process of Fragmentation. The preceding discussion identifies three interrelated processes that result from technological change within the firm. They can now be stated in summary form. Technological change within the firm:

1. increases the number of analytical social systems that intersect and interpenetrate at the firm,
2. increases the salience of the particular analytical social system to which a norm belongs, when attempting to explain its operation within the firm,
3. decreases or narrows the scope of social action (the normative content) that constitutes any one analytical social system.

Taken together, these three processes are aspects of a more general social change. The general social change will be subsequently called *fragmentation.*

The Process of Pervasion. Up to this point the process of

fragmentation has been illustrated within the firm. Fragmentation may also begin within the wider society. Regardless of the point at which fragmentation initially takes place, the firm and the society interpenetrate each other in regard to the emergent analytical social systems. Thus, the firm as a labour market is part of a wider labour market that extends into the society.

While only one segment of the firm is narrowly concerned with the labour market, the remaining employee's have a labour market status. For example, the line supervisor, while not a part of that system within the firm that is focussed upon the labour market, is a member of the wider labour market. In this manner, the labour market, as one analytical social system intersecting at the firm, interpenetrates both firm and society.

Interpenetration also may be expressed in the following manner. The newly formed analytical social systems are bases of status allocation both within the firm and within the wider society. Within any particular firm, an employee will have a primary status. There is a particular analytical social system to which his position belongs, e.g., the production system in the case of the line manager, the labour market system in the case of the personnel man. But the total position of each of these cases will also contain elements of the other analytical social systems. Thus, the line supervisor has a status in the labour market, while the personnel man has a status in firm's authority system, no matter how marginal this status may be. Both positions will have a status in the wider occupational prestige system.

Since each total position is in this manner *pervaved* by the several analytical social systems, status comparisons within any single system are possible. Thus, positions can be separately ranked in regard to their status in the labour market, the flow of work and organizational authority, the occupational prestige hierarchy, the community, etc., etc, Moreover, the narrowness of fragmented social systems increases the accuracy of any single status comparison. However, the accuracy with which total positions may be compared decreases as fragmentation proceeds. The various possible combinations and permutations of ranks in the several fragmented systems make the global comparison of positions increasingly difficult.

Rationalized, technological changes are responsible for both of these social consequences, i.e., the fragmentation of social systems and their simultaneous pervasion throughout the society. As the bases of status allocation are fragmented into highly differentiated systems, the statuses within any single fragmented system achieve a higher degree of comparability.

2

Collective Action as Cultural Evolution

The study of organised human effort, termed in the socio-political area as "Social movements", is regarded as part of the subject-matter of collective behaviour. The field of study with collective behaviour in focus, however, has been a neglected area in sociology and consequently we find very little systematic work on sociology of movements before 1930.[1] In the study of social change also, the study of social movements resulting from, contributing to or resisting social change have received relatively little emphasis. Probably because of a positional bias, individuals and groups have so often been regarded by most sociologists as the creatures rather than the creators of social change. By and large sociologists have looked at blind social forces in their search for dynamics of change, and not at the actions and interactions of willful goal-seeking active subjects. An implicit premise of vulgar determinism in sociology could not but result in developing blind spots, wherein ideologies, purposive human actions and goal-governed collectivitious remained out of sociologists' sight.

The term "movement" was first used in early nineteenth century. But during that period it was used in a specific sense, i.e., the movement of the new industrial working class. Later, in due course of time, the denotation expanded and the term took a more general sense subsuming unrest, upsurge and disturbance aimed at full or partial change in the existing institutions involving small or big groups of people working towards a consciously desired commonly shared future. The narrow definition, writes Haberle, of social movement, meaning the movement of the industrial working class is no longer possible in view of the peasants' and farmers' movements, of Fascism and national Socialism and of the independence movements in colonial countries to name only the most important instances.[2]

A movement may be developed around either a detailed rational plan for a new society—an utopia—or as in the case of Marxism, a theory, of history which predicts the inevitable coming of a new society.[3] The main characteristic of some of these ideas is their claim of logical consistency and their belief in casual explanation of problems. At the same time their tendency to believe that changes in certain social institutions will bring about final solutions to the problems is no less important. It cannot be said that social movements have received no attention of social scientists. Traditionally historians and political philosophers tried to study social movements. As a result of that consciously arrived at professional collective effort and sociological frame of reference, in the analysis of social movements, has been missing. Heberle, while talking about social movements, noted that "These were interpreted and analysed as if they were systems of philosophy; they were submitted to critical evaluations in terms of empirical truth, logical consistency and ethical standards. Not much attention was paid to the meaning of these groups, nor to other problems of sociological relevance."[4]

The relationship of social movements with social and cultural changes is a complex one. A changing social order or changing values and norms in a society might result in a diverse set of responses leading to phased orientation and coordinated action, often in conflict with each other. Alternatively collective goal-oriented concerted actions may themselves be causing structural, behaviourial and cultural changes. In the words of Sherif and Sherif, "A social movement . . . is a formative stage of interaction in human relations. It expresses an ongoing process".[5] Furthermore, "a social movement is always possessed by a sense of mission".[6]

Hence, attention has to be focussed on the interaction of consciously striving human beings as part of an emergent collectivity. This is to be distinguished from the study of stable groups or established institutions. Here we focus on groups and institutions in process of becoming. The changes which take place in the culture are important as end-products of past social movements and as features of the new milieu which gives rise to new movements. Change is the law of nature and a normal aspect of culture, and social movement is one of the most important ways through which social change gets manifested as a process involving conscious striving human actors in unison and in opposition to such other actors.

Two features of social movements have been explicitly noted:

(*a*) the effort of men to intervene in the process of social and cultural change, and

(*b*) the goal of bringing into being new social and cultural forms.[7]

But in either case, men are viewed as actors, not as passive responders to the flow of cultural or the homeostatic tendencies of the social system. Also essential to these ideas is the notion that sometimes human actions are collective which include opposition to other such collective actions seeking incompatible goals. This conceptualisation of social movements logically leads to a recognition of the following four characteristics present in all social movements:

(*a*) A sense of membership of participation—a "we-ness", and more or less a clear distinction between those who are seen to be for and those who are seen to be against.

(*b*) The existence of shared values—a goal or an objective, sustained by an ideology.

(*c*) A set of definite norms—shared understanding as to how the joiners should act and definitions of out-groups and how to behave towards then.

(*d*) A structure—a division of labour between leaders and followers and between different classes of each.[8]

Bruce Cameron discusses four familiar types of social movements viz., reactionary, conservative, revisionary and revolutionary. In its essence Communist movement is revolutionary in character because it rejects the existing social structure as inadequate and wishes to supplant it with socialistic pattern which is considered to be more suitable. This structural change has sometimes been called 'radical'. But one may be radically reactionary or radically revolutionary. The distinction between revisonary and revolutionary is a matter of scope or degree.

Approaches to the Study of Social Movement

In the various studies of social movements a variety of theoretical perspectives having their relative limitations and advantages have been applied. Broadly speaking, historians, psychologists and sociologists of different schools have theorised social movements in different ways but barring a few they have fallen victim to weaknesses inherent in their respective disciplinary approach.

Historical Approach

The most common and fairly large number of studies of social movements have presented the details of biographies and events in chronological sequence. In such sequential studies causal explanations of the events and action are seldom attempted and structures of social movements do not get any explicit attention. In such studies we find free use of the word 'movements' without discussing any theory of social movements or specific contribution of the particular movement study to any theory. It would be erroneous to say that in this approach only a chronological description of the emergence and growth of the movement is attempted. Some vague conceptualization, eclectic theorization, unstated psychological assumptions, in-implicit structural and functional analysis and in most cases muted philosophy of history are not ruled out. What earns the historical approach a reproach is the absence of any articulated conscious theorization.

No doubt, before going into the historical presentation, they give account of ideology, conducive situations which help the formation and growth of movement, and because of this reason such studies are interesting as well as useful. But generally studies of this kind centre round political or individual history of the leaders of movement.[9] Historians study may be both synchronic and diachronic. Some historians while describing dramatic events and powerful personalities do study the development of social structural conditions leading to a movement and contributing to its typicality. On the other hand sociologists may feel satisfied to superficially deal with the problem in more abstract and general terms taking into account only short-term historical changes in economic and social structure before the formation of the movements. Inherently there is nothing that separates historical from sociological approach. There are several documents relating to India's past which are now attracting the attention of social historians and which are of no less interest to sociologist.[10] A thorough study of any social movement should embrace ideally both history and sociology, drawing freely from each other methodological kit without abandoning its own historically acquired methodological advantages.

Psychological Approach

The emphasis on personalities, psychological adjustment and frustration of the individuals in the movement which are largely personality dispositions projected as having no relationship with sociological dimension, such as social bases of the movement and structural foundation of social mobilization, are the principal attributes of psychological studies of movements. The assumption is that the persons because of their personality type join the movement, rather than because of conducive prevailing social conditions. The movement as such is depicted as a kind of sublimation in the Freudian sense, i.e., an individual is a victim of his unconscious desires and the source of these unconscious desires is not sought in interaction with the social structural milieu.

Broadly speaking, individual personality has been conceptualized as of two types, viz., political and social. The political type is related to power attainment and thereby gives inspiration of social movement.[11] Similarly a radical mind possesses an intense element of negation and thus characterises a man who criticises and negates everything. A radical is an activist as well as visionary.[12]

A fairly large number of psycho-analytic theories stress frustration and repression born out of failure to reach goals that lead to aggressiveness which finally may find release by participating in social movements. This kind of idea finds expression in Lasswell's study in which he discussess the motivations of individuals who are oriented politically and relate them directly to childhood repression and adolescent paranoia.[13] Here the movement is not conceptualized in relation societal arrangements and changes in them but as a solution to the personality problems of its constituents.

The serious shortcoming of this approach is that it does not explain the societal causes of social movements and movement's consequences for the society; rather onesided attention is paid toward personality aspect of the revolutionaries. It asks essentially the question "who are the revolutionaries?"[14] McLaughlin opines that the main flow of this form of study is that it "fails to provide the total explanation of the origin of such movements".[15]

Another variant of the psychological approach to the study of social movements reduces the study to problems of techniques of propaganda, mobilization and ideological manipulation. Thus, context and consequence of the movement are neglected to emphasize personality and persuasive techniques as the sole constituents of social movements.

Functional—Ist Approach

Functionalism views society as a system. The various institutions of society are understood primarily in terms of their relationship to the whole and particularly with reference to the contribution they make to the system as a whole. Thus, functionalist analysis is focussed on the question of how soical systems are maintained.

"A social system", writes Parsons, "is a mode of organisation of action elements relative to the persistence or ordered processes of change of the interactive patterns of a plurality of individual actors".[16] These interactive patterns are not chaotic but governed by norms which have a common standard what Parsons calls "value-orientation standards".[17] Further, according to Gouldner, 'Basic to Parsons' analysis of the social system is his focus on equilibrium and on the conditions from which this derives.[18]

Endogenous change comes about due to dysfunction, tension and deviance. They "tend to resolve themselves or to be institutionalised in the long run through built-in mechanisms of adjustment and control".[19]

Since the focus is on the maintenance of the social system, it has tended to result in a positive evaluation of all the parts of society. Hence, change in the social system is seen as a departure from normaley. If there is no consensual absorption of value patterns then instability in the social system arises. Manifested process of this type in a movement continues till consensus is reached.

With regard to change and conflict the functionalist position can hardly be supported. Dahrendorf has criticised the idyllic stable portrait of a homeostatic society.[20] The static functionalist have not tried to see the continuties between everyday behaviour and routine social process.

Crane Brinton recognises the possibility of conflict and finds it healthy and beneficial, but arrives at an erroneous conclusion by not believing that conflict, revolution or movement can change society. He says that it will remain basically the same.[21]

With regard to structural strain functionalists have talked about the rise of new power-class, structural weaknesses, disintegration and relative deprivation. According to Lipset, fascist movements are caused by the threat of extinction which the middle class faces from big capitalists.[22]

Similarly, if attachements between persons are weakening then totalitarian movements arise. Such movements attract their leaders from among those who are not well integrated in the system. Kornhanser says that democratic societies are vulnerable to penetration and control by totalitarian movements when they lack strong secondary organisations or associational groups capable of mediating between elites and non-elites.[23]

Even Durkheim had agreed that the old order could not be restored; therefore the new one had to be integrated. "This was essential to avoid the recurring economic and political crises, the chronic mood of exasperation, and discontent, and finally, the 'disintegration' of society."[24] Durkheimian conception of classes[25] cannot be digested in Indian context. "Each people today", he writes, "forms a homogenous whole, not because it acquired the habit of identifying itself with such and such a function or class, but because it is a system of functions inseparable from one another and mutually complementing each other".[26] Thus, classes are termed as "functions" and are regarded as co-ordinative co-operative, and unifying never as conflictive. Whereas class forms the bases of consciousness which ultimately results into class antagonaism. Durkheim wanted to pose the social question in a manner entirely different from the way Marx did. This resulted in a conservative and authoritarian ideology that dominated his entire sociological system. In all Durkheim' reification of society we find an expression of his ideological concerns. "Society" becomes for him, as for the conservatives generally, a polemical concept and value with which to counter critical revolutionary theses.

The functionalist approach, with its emphasis on homeostatics, integration and normative consensus and continuity, sweeps under the carpet social change in general and self-conscious collective goal-oriented transformative action in particular. The neglect of historical development propelled by human efforts is inherent in this approach. It does not posit active human subject and consequently 'social movements' become routine social process with no lasting consequences in terms of directions and irreversibility towards achievement of desired goals.

Dialectical Approach

Dialectic is the theory of the nature and of logic which is also the theory of the structure and development of the society.

It was devised by the post-Kantian idealists, starting with Fichte and reaching a culmination in the philosophy of Hegel. The dialectic of Hegel tremendously influenced the later philosophical speculations. "Hegelian dialectic of progress", writes Barnes, "had much influence on later historical thought, particularly through its partial adoption by Karl Marx and its exploitation by Marx in the service of the materialistic philosophy of history".[27] On the other hand, the question to which Emanuel Kant had addressed himself and which has preoccupied the modern theory of knowledge was "What are the conditions in the nature of the universe on which it depends?"[28]

Emmanuel Kant had distinguished two aspects within logic:

(*a*) analytic, or the logic of understanding, which applied to the data of sesnation, yields knowledge of the natural, phenomenal world; and

(*b*) dialectic, or the logic of reasoning, which operates independently of experience and purports, erroneously, to give knowledge of the 'transcendent' order of 'noumena'.

Taking reality to be of the nature of the mind or spirit, Hegel supposed its activities and development to be of an essentially rational or logical kind. Standard or analytic logic, on this view, is rigid and abstract, a matter of fixed connections and exclusive oppositions. Dialectical logic sees contradictions as fruitful collisions of ideas from which a higer truth may be reached by way of synthesis. But Engels writes: "Hegel had freed history from metaphysics—he had made it dialectic; but his conception of history was essentially idealistic; . . . now idealism was driven from its last refuge, the philosophy of history; now a materialistic treatment of history was propounded, and a method found of explaining man's "knowing" by his "being", instead of as heretofore his "being" by his "knowing".[29]

While discussing and refuting the priorities and procedures of Hegelian dialectic, Marx writes, "The mystification which dialectic suffers in Hegel's hands, by no means prevents him from being the first to present its general form of working in a comprehensive and conscious manner. With him (Hegel) it is standing on its head. It must be turned right side up again, if you could discover the rational karnel within the mystical shell".[30]

Dialectics is materialist because it insists that the material world alone possesses reality, and that the ideas are simply reflexes of the system of material production prevailing at any given time. But it is also dialectical in the sense that change in the sense of development or progress, is invariably the outcome of a conflict between two opposed or contradictory forccs or elements within reality, as thus conceived. These forces are respectively thesis and antithesis and the result of their conflict is that they become united in a higher synthesis. Further it regards every historically developed form as in fluid movement, and "therefore, takes into account its transient nature no less than its momentary existence, because it lets nothing impose upon it, and is in its essence critical and revolutionary."[31]

The dialectics is thus the law or principle in accordance with which change occurs either in nature or in society. Marx "adopted some of the negative-critical or radical aspects of Hegel's thought but rejected the others".[32]

The conception of dialectics, borrowed from Hegel, was consciously developed by Marx. For Hegel's conception of reality was an altogether different one. In his system reality is identified with the idea, which is reason or pure thought and developed by a process of unfolding until it arrives at complete consciousness of itself. Hegel sought, therefore, to show that this development was dialectical as it took the form of conflict and reconciliation. Marx wanted to end every kind of dualism which would sharply separate consciousness from reality, but at the same time wanted to maintain the independence of consciousness from external being. Marx was aware that idealism emphasized the activity of the subject in opposition to modern materialism.[33] "Marx adopted the dynamic framework of Hegel's historical philosophy but chese to reverse the priority of the dichotomous factors . . . making the external conditions or material forces the independent variable and ideas the dependent variable".[34]

Thus, dialectics is a method, an instrument of knowledge.

But "knowledge itself is not a phenomenon which is detached from the life and interests of humanity. It is a weapon in the conservation of the species, an instrument which enables humanity the better to dominate the forces of nature, to understand the origins of the 'social question' and the ways to solve it".[35]

Yogendra Singh has beautifully projected a comparative picture of dialectical and functional approaches in sociology. "Functionalism", he says, "assumes that society is a relatively persisting configuration of elements' and consensus is an ubiquitous element of the social system. The dialectical model, on the contrary, treats 'change' or tension to be ubiquitous in society. Since functionalism assumes social systems to be in a state of value consensus, it relegates the role of power in social relations to a secondary place, dialectical model, on the other hand, presupposes that value conflict is a universal reality of any stratified social structure. Functionalism treats change as a slow, cumulative process of adjustment to new situations. Dialectical model holds that most changes are revolutionary in significance and effect qualitative transformation in the social structure . . . and the major sources of change are immanent in the system itself".[36] The dialectical approach in sociology has undergone further refinements in concepts and propositions. Its speculative-philosophical elements have been replaced by genuine sociological formulation of categories".[37]

In the present thesis the interplay between caste, a traditional social institution with conservative ideas, and the communist movement, with its revolutionary message, has been examined through the help of dialectical approach. We agree with the position that it is theoretically sound enough and "it helps in comprehending reality in all its complexity including contradictions and does not leave man defenceless against alien existence".[38] How far our position is tenable can be seen only if its efficacy is examined in the context of the actual emperical analysis that informs this research piece.

Methodology

Methodology refers to the study of the scientific use of devices and procedures used by the researcher in course of his investigation. One characteristic, among others, which distinguishes sociology is its method, the manner in which it approaches its problems. As a method of approach to the investigation of any phenomenon whatever, science implies primarily an attitude of mind, an attitude distinguished by adherence to several explicit principles. Among these principles are objectivity, relativism, ethical neutrality, parsimony, skepticism and humility.[39] And from these principles emerge the basic features of sociology i.e., its being empirical, theoretical, cumulative and non-ethical. Thus, method of study is a means to an end: it is a process not a product.[40]

The argument that theory varies with the investigator and is mutable whereas method is universal and immutable does not withstand scrutiny today. However, it may be said that methodology changes by accretion, while theory often changes by complete substitution. With the identification of new areas of investigation methods may change gradually to provide better tools of enquiry. In social sciences we cannot necessarily compartmentalise the various complex social phenomena. Precisely because of this reason, one set of methods cannot be universally applicable. But it does not mean that we admit disunity and discontinuity about the methods.[41] The exercise of addition and modification in both theory as well as method goes on with the unabated advancement of knowledge.

The styles of inquiry of social scientist are revealed in the decisions and choices made from among various possible alternatives, that occur at each stage of the research process. Some important alternatives deal with the basic research objectives, the method used in the definition and selection of variables under investigation, the design for observing and analysing the data, and the rules of logic that determine the structure of arguments and conclusions. Clarence Schrag has succinctly projected these exercises in the following paradigm.[42]

Concepts are logical constructs created from sense impressions, percepts or even fairly complex experiences. The tendency to assume that concepts actually exist as phenomena may lead to the "fallacy of reification". According to Merton, "Conceptual analysis which is confined to the specification and clarification of key concepts, is an indispensable phase of theoretic work."[43]

Causal Observation	Informal theory	Formal theory	
		Empirical theory	Pragmatic theory
A. Common sense terms	A. Defined concepts	A. Theoretical concepts	A. Control objectives
B. Unorganized impression	B. Generalizations, law-like assumptions	B. Postulates, Theorems	B. Inferred programmes of control
↑	↑	↑	↑
Everyday observation	Systematic observation	Controlled experiment	Contrieved experience

Weber's suggestion of the conceptualization in the realm of nature's phenomena in terms of verstehen[44] requires high degree of comprehending capacity or else the whole exercise may become hazardous. This 'enlightened' paths may not lead us to our destination. The identification of techniques and tools are much more important. Suitability of devices depends on the nature and the level of phenomena to be studied. "Even in physics it seems possible that there are accepted laws which do not explain all the facts but which are accepted because they do enable the physicist to explain the vast majority of them".[45]

The conceptual knowledge presupposes the reality of corresponding ideal or abstract object. "As mere opinion it is not knowledge, since, even when it happens to be true, it cannot justify itself. Genuine knowledge, on the other hand, which is based on reason, can authenticate itself".[46] The philosophical problem of knowledge can be dissolved by dialectics. "A consequence of accepting the people", writes Nirmal Singh, "as the goal of social science is to take the fact as it appears at a particular moment in history as problematic and to look for its transcendence in its dialectical potentiality".[47]

Concretization of Methods

The identification of the problem, the field and the method was done through extensive discussion. Since too many questions are being asked about the communist movement, a macro level survey of the available literature, which constituted the secondary source of data, was paid due attention, followed by macro level study of the problem. Because of the intermingling of several phenomena and the complexities involved therein a small district on Indo-Nepal border in an economically backward state Bihar was selected for intensive study. There were several reasons for the selection of Madhubani which we will discuss subsequently. For the time being it will suffice to say that the researcher hails from Darbanga: district of which Madhubani was a past till 1972. Secondly, communist movement has been very strong in this tradition—bound culturally rich but economically backward district. Thirdly, the local language which is a form of existence of thought and of its expression was not alien for the researcher. Fourthly, the pre-established personal contact with many local people was a positive asset in establishing further rapport with others. Fifthly, the general nature and the temperament of the people of the area was not entirely unknown to the author which helped in extracting information from them. These were some of the reasons for the choice of the field for empirical exploration.

NOTES

1. See, Jerome Davis, *Contemporary Social Movements* (New York, 1930), pp. 35-47.
2. R. Haberle, 'Social Movements', in D.L. Sills (ed.) *International Encyclopaedia of Social Sciences* (The Macmillan and Co. and the Free Press), 14, p. 439.
3. See, F. Engles, 'Socialism: utopian and scientific', Marx and Engles, *Selected Works*, Vil. II (Moscow, 1982), pp. 137-50.
4. R. Heberle, *Social Movements* (New York, 1951), pp. 1-2.
5. M. Sherif and C. Sherif, *An outline of Social Psychology* (New York, 1956), p 724.
6. *Ibid.*, p. 722.
7. See H. Blumer, 'Collective Behaviour' in A.M. Lee (ed.) *Principles of Sociology* (New York, 1951). pp. 190-195 and R. Heberle, *n. 4*, pp. 5-7.
8. For an initial thumb-nail description of the typology of movements see' W.M. Bruce Cameron, *Modern Social Movements* (New York, 1966), pp. 22-24.
9. See, Antonio and Pike, *Religion, Revolution and Reform* (London, 1964), pp. 21-25,, and Geoffrey Pridham, *Hitlar's Rise to Power: The Nazi Movement in Bavaria* (New York, 1973), pp. 86-109.
10. Ramakrishna Mukherjee, *Sociology of Indian Sociology* (New Delhi, 1979), p. 11.
11. R. Heberle, *n. 4*, pp. 102-3.
12. Robert C. Tucker, 'The Deradicalization of Marxist Movements' in *American Political Science Review*, Vol. LXI, No. 2, June 1967, pp. 343-58.
13. See, H. Lasswell, *Psychopathology and Politics* (Chicago, 1969), p. 39.
14. C., Johnson, *Revolution and the Social System* (Standford, 1964), p. 23.
15. McLaughlin (ed), *Studies in Social Movements* (New York, 1969), p. 10.
16. Talcott Parsons, *The Social System* (New Delhi, 1972), p. 24.
17. *Ibid.*, p. 38.

18. Alvin W. Goulder, *The Coming Crisis of Western Sociology* (New Delhi, 1971), p. 231.
19. Pierre L. Van, der Berghe, 'Dialectics and Functionalism' in Demerath and Peterson (eds) *System, Change and Conflict* (New York, 1967), p, 295.
20. R. Dahrendorf, *Class and Class Conflict in Industrial Society* (London, 1969), pp. 120-23.
21. Crane Brinton, *The Anatomy of Revolution* (New York, 1965), pp. 16-17.
22. S.M. Lipset Fascism—left, right and centre in Jospeh. R. Gusthi (ed), *Protest, Reform and Revolt*: Reader in Social Movements (New York, 1970), p. 36.
23. W. Kornhanser, *The Politics of Mass Society* (New York, 1968), p. 60.
24. Irving M. Zeitlin, *Ideology and the Development of Sociological Theory*, (New Delhi, 1969), p. 238.
25. Alwin W. Gouldner (ed), *Socialism and Saint-Simon* (London, 1959) pp. 130-139.
26. *Ibid.*, p. 148.
27. Harry Elmer Barnes (ed), *An introduction to the History of Sociology* (Abridged edition), (Chicago, 1967), p. 60.
28. Talcott Parasons, *n. 16*, p. 360.
29. F. Engles, 'Socialism: utopian and scientific', in Marx and Engles, *Selected Works, Vol. II* (Moscow, 1962), pp. 134-35.
30. Ka-I Marx, *Capital: A Critique of Political Economy*, Vol. I (Moscow, 1978), p. 29.
31. *Ibid.*, p. 30.
32. Irving M. Zeitlin, *n. 24*, p. 42.
33. Jorge Larrian, *The Concept of Ideology*, (New Delhi, 1980), p. 37.
34. Bill Harrell, 'Symbols, perception and meaning' in Llewellyan Gross (ed.), *Sociology Theory: Inquiry and Paradigms* (New Delhi, 1975) p. 106.
35. Ernest Mandel, *From Class Society to Communism—An Introduction to Marxism* (Secunderabad, 1983), p. 159.
36. Yogendra Singh, *Modernisation of Indian Trauition* (Faridabad, 1977), p. 4.
37. *Ibid.*, p. 18.
38. Nirmal Singh, *Education Under Seige* (New Delhi, 1983), pp. 33-34.
39. Robert Bierstedt, *The Social Order* (New Delhi, 1963) pp. 15-28.
40. See Abraham Kaplan, *Conduct of Inquiry* (California, 1964), pp. 13-14.
41. A.D. Ritchie, *Scientific Methods: An Inquiry into the Character and Validity of Natural Laws* (London, 19.0), p. 14.
42. Robert K. Merton, *Social Theory and Social Structure* (New Delhi, 1975), p. 143.
43. Clarence Schrag, 'Elements of Theoretical Analysis in Sociology'

in Llewellyn Gross (ed.) *Sociological Theory: Inquiry and Pardigms n. 34*, p. 251.

44. Max Weber, *The Methodology of Social Sciences,* (New York, 1949), pp. 16-17.
45. John Rex, *Key problems of Sociological Theory* (London and Henley, 1976), p. 18.
46. Frank Thilly, *A History of Philosophy* (Allahabad, 1984), p. 76.
47. Nirmal Singh, *n. 38*, p. 15.

3

Assessments in Social Mobility

In this paper, mobility has been analysed from the respondent's father to the respondent and from the respondent to his son. Usually, social mobility is studied in terms of the socio-economic status (SES) which in turn is determined by education, occupation and income. This is based on the assumption of a high degree of positive correlation between these factors, which is highly probable in more industrialised societies.

In developing societies like India which retain many craditional elements, the positive association between education, occupation and income is bound to be weak. This renders the analysis of social mobility as a composite function of these three factors extremely difficult. This difficulty is usually sought to be overcome by assigning values and weightages to each one of these factors and constructing a single index of status by summing them up. This procedure however has several limitations.

In any case it is necessary to relate these three factors, if at all we are to be justified in speaking about social mobility in general. Since we have in this study excluded income, the two factors to be interrelated are education and occupation. The procedure we propose to follow is to analyse each one of these in terms of the other.

Mobility has been classified in terms of direction into three categories, viz., upward, static and downward. The point of reference for ascertaining the direction is the concerned individual in the preceding generation. Accordingly an individual is classified as educationally upwardly mobile, if his level of education is higher than that of his father. The same is true in regard to occupation.

Accordingly, we have in this chapter tried to analyse occupational mobility and educational mobility in terms of each other separately for the respondent's fathers to the respondents' generation and for the respondents to their children's generation. This is bound to reveal the patterns of mobility among our respondents. The two dimensions and three directions of mobility jointly yield nine possible logical categories or patterns. But as we shall see the actual patterns are fewer than this which shows that some are more likely than others.

Respondent's Father's Generation to Respondent's Generation

Information on mobility in education is available for 834 out of the 921 or 90.55 per cent of the respondents. Of these 834 respondents, a majority of 52.04 per cent are educationally static when compared to their fathers. While 46.04 per cent of them are upwardly mobile, a small percentage of 1.92 are even downwardly mobile.

Information on mobility in occupation is available for 700 or 76.01 per cent of the 921 respondents. Of these 700 respondents, 44.43 per cent are occupationally static as compared to their fathers. While the percentage of those who are upwardly mobile is 46.28, the corresponding percentage for those who are downwardly mobile is as high as 9.29.

The fact that nearly a majority of the respondents are educationally static compared to their fathers is hardly surprising in the light of what we have observed in Chapter V. As far as upward mobility is concerned, the percentage is almost the same for both education and occupation. But what is striking is that the percentage of downward mobility is relatively higher for occupation than for education. This seems to suggest that some of those who are educationally static or upwardly mobile may have faced a downward trend in occupation, and conversely, among those who are occupationally downwardly mobile some may be educationally static or upwardly mobile. In other words, in inter-generational mobility among the Scheduled Castes, education seems to be a necessary but not a sufficient factor. We shall now see to what extent this is reflected in the combined analysis of mobility in the educational and occupational dimensions.

Comparative information on mobility in the education and occupation is available for only 682 or 74.05 per cent of the 921 respondents (see table 3.1). Of these 682 respondents, 27,27 per cent are educationally and occupationally static, and nearly an equal percentage of 25.07 respondents are upwardly mobile in both. The percentage of respondents who are both educationally and occupationally downwardly mobile is only an insignificant 0.73. The remaining respondents (i.e., 46.92%) have manifested other tendencies, the most important ones being educationally static and occupationally upwardly mobile (21.26%) and educationally upwardly mobile and occupationally static (15.98%). The percentage of respondents who are educationally upwardly mobile or static and at the same time occupationally downwardly mobile being only 4.40 and 3.96 respectively is not significant. On the other hand, the percentage of respondent who are educationally downwardly mobile and occupationally upwardly mobile or static is still more insignificant being only 0.29 and 1.03 respectively.

Thus, of the nine possible logical categories yielded by combining mobility in the educational and occupational spheres, as many as five are found to be either nearly vacuous or not of significance, and only four stand out markedly. These four in the descending order of importance are:

1. Educationally and occupationally static.
2. Educationally and occupationally upwardly mobile.
3. Educationally static and occupationally upwardly mobile, and
4. Educationally upwardly mobile and occupationally static.

TABLE 3.1

Educational and Occupational Mobility in Respondent's Father's to Respondent's own Generation

Educational Mobility	Occupational Mobility: Upwardly Mobile	Static	Downwardly Mobile	Total
Upwardly Mobile	171 (55.16) 55.77	109 (35.16) 36.09	30 (9.68) 48.39	310 45.45
Static	145 (40.50) 45.60	186 (51.96) 61.59	27 (7.54) 43.55	358 52.49
Downwardly Mobile	2 (14.29) 0.63	7 (50.00) 2.32	5 (35.71) 8.06	14 2.06
Total	318 (46.63)	302 (44.28)	62 (9.09)	682 (100.00) 100

It may be emphasized that the pattern of downward mobility in general is almost non-existent. This is easy to understand in the light of the fact that traditionally the Scheduled Castes were both educationally and occupationally most backward and also the probabilty is more for one to retain the status, however low it may be, than to go down further.

Another point that is brought out in the foregoing analysis is that education is a necessary factor in general social mobility, though it is not a sufficient one. It is seen that 52.34 per cent of the respondents are either educationally and occupationally upwardly mobile or static, and 37.24 per cent of the respondents are either educationally upwardly mobile and occupationally static or educationally static and occupationally upwardly mobile. The fact that 4.40 per cent of the respondents are occupationally downwardly mobile in spite of being educationally upwardly mobile may imply that educational mobility does not ipso facto mean occupational mobility. But the fact that the percentage of those who are occupationally upwardly mobile or static and educationally downwardly mobile is as low as 0.29 and 1.03 respectively would only suggest that either upward mobility or even retaining the occupational status inevitably involves educational mobility. We shall now see the extent of this relationship at each one of the three directions of mobility, viz., upward, static and downward, with reference to education and occupation separately.

Of the 310 respondents who are educationally upwardly mobile, a majority of 55.16 per cent are also occupationally upwardly mobile. While 35.16 per cent of them have remained occupationally static, as many as 9.68 per cent of them are occupationally downwardly mobile. Of the 358 respondents who are educationally static, a majority of 51.96 per cent are static occupationally also, 40.50 per cent of them are occupationally upwardly mobile and 7.54 per cent of the are downwardly mobile. Of the 14 respondents who are educationally downwardly mobile, only 5 are also occupationally downwardly mobile, the rest being either occupationally upwardly mobile (2) or static (7).

A columnwise reading of the Table reveals interesting points. Of the 318 respondents who are occupationally upwardly mobile, a majority of 53.77 per cent are also educationally upwardly mobile. While 45.60 per cent of them have remained educationally static, the percentage of those who are educationally downwardly mobile is as low as 0.63. Similarly, of the 302 respondents who have remained occupationally static, as many as 61.59 per cent are found to be static educationally also. The percentages of those who are educationally upwardly and downwardly mobile are 36.09 and 2.32 respectively. Finally, of the 62 respondents who are found to be occupationally downwardly mobile, only 8.06 per cent of them are also educationally downwardly mobile, the rest of them being either educationally upwardly mobile (48.39%) or static (43.55%).

While a majority of 52.49 per cent of the 682 respondents are educationally static, this tendency seems to be more pronounced among those who are also occupationally static (61.59%) than among those who are occupationally upwardly mobile (45.60%) or downwardly mobile (43.55%), 45.45 per cent of the 682 respondents are educationally upwardly mobile, and this tendency seems to be marked among those who are also occupationally upwardly mobile (53.77%), followed by those who are downwardly mobile (48.39%) and static (36.09%). While the percentage of those who are educationally downwardly mobile is as low as 2.06, this tendency seems to be relatively more marked among those who are also occupationally downwardly mobile (8.06%) than among those who are static (2.32%) or upwardly mobile (0.63%).

On the other hand, while 46.63 per cent of the 682 respondents are occupationally upwardly mobile, this tendency is most pronounced among those respondents who are also educationally upwardly mobile (55.16%), as compared to those who are educationally static (40.50%) or downwardly mobile (14.29%). The percentage of those who are occupationally static is 44.28 out of 682 respondents. This tendency seems to prevail among both those who are educationally static (51.96%) and those who are downwardly mobile (50.00%), while it is relatively less pronounced among the educationally upwardly mobile (35.16%) respondents. The percentage of those who are occupationally downwardly mobile is as high as 9.09 of the 682 respondents. But the tendency towards occupationally downward mobility seems to be most pronounced among those respondents who are also educationally downwardly mobile (35.71%), and it is more or less the same as in the subsample (i.e., 9.09, N=682) among those who are educationally upwardly mobile (9.68%) and static (7.54%).

In brief, these findings suggest that while upward mobility in education does not by itself guarantee upward mobility in occupation the prospects of upward mobility in occupation are very dim if mobility in education is downward. In the event of a lack of upward mobility in both education and occupation the chances are that those who are upwardly mobile in one will be static in the other. As noted earlier, as a general rule, combined down and mobility in education and occupation is totally insignificant. But it is observed that the percentage of those who are occupationally downwardly mobile is relatively high compared to those who are educationally downwardly mobile. However, most of the former are educationally upwardly mobile or static. On the other hand, the percentage of those who are educationally static is relatively high compared to those those who are occupationally static. However, the percentage of those who are downwardly mobile in the other respect is marginally high among the former. Finally, while the percentage of those who are upwardly mobile is seen to be almost the same in both education and occupation, the percentage of downward mobility in the other aspect is relatively very high among the educationally upwardly mobile compared to those who are occupationally upwardly mobile. In brief, the general trend seems to be that while educational upward mobility or staticness is necessary to ensure either retention of occupational status or upward mobility in it, it is not a sufficient condition.

We shall now see if the trends and patterns observed in mobility between respondent's father's generation and respondent's generation are found with reference to mobility between respondent's generation and respondent's son's generation.

Respondent's Generation to Respondent's Son's Generation

Of the 921 respondents in the sample, information on mobility in education from respondent' to respondent's son's*

* For analytical convenience only the maximum educated son of the respondent is taken into consideration.

generation is available for only 530 or 57.55 per cent. Of these 530 respondents, the sons of a majority of 56.98 per cent are educationally upwardly mobile, 31.32 per cent are static, and 11.70 per cent are downwardly mobile.

Information on mobility in occupational status between respondent's and respondent's sons' generation is available for only 212 or 23.02 per cent of the 921 respondents. Of these 212 respondents, the sons of a majority of 50.94 per cent are occupationally static, 27.36 per cent are upwardly mobile, and 21.70 per cent are downwardly mobile.

These findings seem to indicate significant differences compared to what we had observed with reference to mobility between respondent's father's generation and respondent's own generation. A majority of our respondents' sons are educationally upwardly mobile, and a majority of them are occupationally static. The percentage of those who are occupationally upwardly mobile is only 27.36. More significantly, while the rate of occupational and educational downward mobility is relatively high between respondent's and respondents' son's generation as compared to the respondent's father's and respondent's generation, it iseems to be relatively marked with reference to occupational status than educational status.

The foregoing analysis seems to generate a few hypotheses.

1. In the first place, presently upward educational mobility smong the Scheduled Castes may not be accompanied by upward occupational mobility. While there is enough scope for educational mobility for Scheduled Castes now, the prospects for occupational mobility seems to be bleak. This is reflected in the relatively high rate of downward mobility in occupational among respondents' sons compared to respondents themselves. Probably education has become weak, if not insignificant, as a generator of upward social mobility through occupational mobility, compared to what it was earlier.

2. In the second place, the increasing trend towards downward mobility, especially in occupation is real and is related to certain factors. This does not, however, preclude the possibility of upward mobility.

3. Finally, the tempo and speed of social mobility among the Scheduled Castes decreases with successive generations, in spite of the continuation of the sponsored efforts in the form

of reservations and other concessions. This may be due to the fact that occupying the lowest levels in the social hierarchy, the earlier generations of Scheduled Castes moved up rather briskly when they were given help and facilities, and presently they have reached a stage from where further upward mobility is difficult if not altogether impossible. In other words, even when mobility is sponsored, it becomes slow and gradual over generations. This seems to be manifested in the differential rates of occupational mobility over generations.

It would have been worthwhile to examine these hypotheses, but unfortunately this is not possible here as comparative information on mobility in education and occupation from respondent's to respondent's son's generation is available only for 154 (16.72%) of the 921 respondents in the sample. It would be hardly possible to generalise from such a small sub-sample, especially so when the hypotheses in question call for a very large sample. Nevertheless, in what follows we shall analyse the data for these 154 respondents and see if any trends or patterns can be delineated, which in turn may help the understanding or reformulation of the hypotheses.

Of the 154 respondents, the sons of 33.12 per cent are upwardly mobile both in educational and occupational statuses, while a greater percentage (44.16%) are educationally upwardly mobile but occupationally static. Significantly enough, as many as 18.18 per cent of the respondents' sons are occupationally downwardly mobile inspite of being educationally upwardly mobile. In all, these trends add up to 95.46 per cent of the sub-sample. None of the other six logically possible trends is found to be significant. Since there is no respondent in the sub-sample who is educationally static the three categories associated with it—educationally static and occupationally upwardly mobile, static or downwardly mobile—are blank. The percentage of respondents' sons manifesting educational and occupational downward mobility, educationally downward but occupationally upward mobility, and educationally downward mobility but occupational staticness are 1.30, 0.65, and 2.59, respectively.

Thus, of the nine logically possible categories as many six are found to be either vacuous or nearly vacuous, and only three stand out pronounced. These three in the descending order are:

1. Educationally upwardly mobile and occupationally static
2. Educationall and occupationally upward, and,
3. Educationally upwardly mobile and occupationally downwardly mobile.

A comparison of these trends with what had been observed with reference to mobility between respondent's father's and respondent's generation yields interesting points. Compared to the pattern of mobility in the earlier generation, in the later generation the number of pronounced trends is less by one. Of the four trends that we had observed earlier only two are found in the later generation, and these are (1) Educationally and occupationally upwardly mobile and (2) Educationally upwardly mobile but occupationally static. But in terms of the relative significance of these trends, it is seen that while in the earlier generation educationally and occupationally upwardly mobile, and educationally upwardly mobile and occupationally static occupied second ann fourth places respectively, in the later generation they occupy second and first places respectively. In the second place, while educational and occupational staticness is the most pronounced trend in the case of respondent's own mobility, educational upward mobility and occupational staticness is found to be the most pronounced trend in the case of respondent's son's mobility. This throws additional light streng thening the hypothesis no. 1. Finally, and more importantly, a trend which had been found to be not of importance with reference to respondent's own mobility, now stands out marked, at least as the last of the only three trends observed with reference to respondent's son's mobility. This not only clarifies the first hypothesis, but also confirms the second and hints at the third.

It is important to note that while 62. 4 per cent of the respondents' sons are educationally upwardly mobile but occupationally static (44.16%) or downwardly mobile (18.18%), the percentage of those who are educationally downwardly mobile but occupationally upwardly mobile (0.65%) or static (2.59%) is as low as 3.24. This only suggests that while upward mobility in education does not by itself guarantee upward

TABLE 3.2

Educational and Occupational Mobility in Respondent's own Generation

Educational Mobility	Occupational Mobility	Upwardly Mobile	Static	Downwardly Mobile	Total
Upwardly Mobile		51 (34.69) 98.08	68 (46.26) 94.44	28 (19.05) 93.33	147 (100.00) 95.45
Static		0	0	0	0
Downwardly Mobile		1 (14.29) 1.92	(57.14) 5.56	2 (28.57) 6.67	7 (100.00) 4.55
Total		52 (33.77)	72 (46.57)	30 (19.48)	154 (100.00)

mobility in occupational status, the latter seems to be almost impossible in the absence of the former. Thus, we may reiterate our earlier observation that upward mobility in educational status is a necessary if not a sufficient condition of upward mobility in occupational status.

A closer examination of Table 3.2 reveals that of the 147 respondents' sons who are educationally upwardly mobile, 34.69 per cent are also occupationally upwardly mobile and 46.26 per cent are occupationally static. The percentage of those who are occupationally downwardly mobile in spite of being educationally upwardly mobile is as high as 19.05. Of the 7 respondents' sons who are educationally downwardly mobile, 1 is occupationally upwardly mobile, 4 are static and only 2 are also occupationally upwardly mobile. On the other hand, of the 52 respondents' sons who are occupationally upwardly mobile, all excepting one (i.e., 98.08%) are also educationally upwardly mobile. The percentage of respondents' sons who are educationally upwardly mobile while remaining occupationally static (N=72) or downwardly mobile (N=30) is almost the same, i.e., 94.44 and 93.33 respectively. These findings throw additional light on the relationship between mobility in education and occupation observed earlier.

An overwhelming majority of 95.45 per cent of the 154 respondents have sons who are educationally upwardly mobile. Comparatively the trend is not found to be significantly varying with referenee to any one of the categories of mobility in occupational status: only a marginal decrease is noticed as we have down from those who are occupationally upwardly mobile (98.08%), to occupationally static (94.44%) and to occupationally downwardly mobile (95.45%). Since there is no case of a respondent's son being educationally static in the sub-sample (N=154), the converse of the above trend is noticeable with reference to educationally downwardly mobile: that is, the percentage of the educationally downwardly mobile in the sub-sample is only 4.55, and their percentage marginally increases as we move down from those who are occupationally upwardly mobile (1.92%), to static (5.56%) and to downwardly mobile (6.67%).

As regards occupation, it is seen that of the 154 respondents in the sub-sample, the sons of 33.77 per cent are upwardly mobile, of 46.75 per cent are static and of 19.48 per cent are downwardly mobile. The same pattern can be found if we take into consideration the educationally upwardly mobile as a separate group, since they constitute an overwhelming majority within the sub-sample. The percentages of respondents' sons in the sub-sample who are educationally upwardly mobile and occupationally upwardly mobile, static, and downwardly mobile are 34.69, 46.26, and 19.05 respectively. Similar reading in the case of those who are educationally downwardly mobile will not be meaningful since they constitute only 4.65 per cent of the sub-sample.

While these findings reiterate in essence the conclusion that we had arrived at with reference to mobility between respondent's father's and respondent's generation, one or two points deserve special mention. In the first place, while the rate of occupational mobility is low compared to that of educational mobility, whatever upward mobility takes place in occupation presumes a similar mobility in educational status. But upward educational mobility does not necessarily facilitate upward mobility in occupation. Thus, education still continues to be a necessary but not a sufficient condition of upward occupational mobility. If anything, the findings only suggest that the role of upward educational mobility as a generator of upward occupational mobility has become weaker between respondent's and respondent's generation compared to the generation between the respondent's fathers and respondents themselves.

In this and the preceding sections we have analysed the trends and patterns in combined mobility in education and occupation among our respondents, at two different levels covering one generation each, namely, respondent's father's to respondent's generation, and respondent's to respondent's son's generation. We shall now attempt a similar analysis covering two generations, namely, from respondent's fathers to respondent's sons.

Respondent's Father's Generation to Respondent's Son's Generation

Of the 921 respondents in the sample information on

mobility in the educational status between respondent's father's and respondent's son's generation is available for 475 or 51.57% respondents. Of these 475 respondents, there has been upward educational mobility over two generation in a majority of 64.64 per cent of cases. The trend is seen to be static in 33.47 per cent, and in the case of a negligible 1.89 per cent the trend is downward mobility.

Information on occupational mobility over the same two generations is available for only 186 or 20.20 per cent of the 921 respondents. In the case of a majority of 52.23 per cent of these 186 respondents, there has been upward mobility in occupation over two generations. The percentages of respondents among whom there has been a static or downward trend are 37.09 and 9.68 respectively.

Thus, educationally and occupationally there has been upward mobility over two generations in the case of a majority of respondents for whom information is available. The rate of educational mobility is higher by over 10 percentage points compared to the rate of occupational mobility, though the respective sub-samples (i.e., 475 and 186 respectively are not of comparable size. While the rate of staticness over two generations is more or less the same educationally (33.47%) and occupationally (37.09%) the rate of downward mobility is significantly more with reference to occupational status (9.68%) compared to the educational status (1.89%). Briefly, there has been a general upward trend in mobility in education and occupation over two generations. While this is expected, especially since mobility is sponsored among the Scheduled Castes, what strikes one is that nearly 10 per cent of the respondents in the sub-sample (N=186) have reported downward mobility in occupation over two generations. Let us see if a closer analysis yields any clues.

Comparative information on mobility in educational and occupationalstatuses over two generations is available for only 184 (19.98%) of the GNP respondents. Of these 184, in the case of nearly a majority (48.91%) there is upward mobility in both education and occupation. Another 17.89 per cent is characterised by staticness both educationally and occupationally. The only other trend that seems to be wroth noting is upward mobility in education combined with stationese in

TABLE 3.3

Educational and Occupational Mobility in Respondent's Brother's to Respondent's Son's Generation

Educational Mobility	Occupational Mobility	Upwardly Mobile	Static	Downwardly Mobile	Total
Upwardly Mobile		90 (63.69) 91.84	37 (27.01) 53.62	10 (7.30) 58.82	137 74.46
Static		8 (17.02) 8.16	32 (68.09) 46.08	7 (14.89) 41.18	47 25.54
Downwardly Mobile		—	—	—	0
Total		98 (53.26)	69 (37.50)	17 (9.24)	184

occupation in the case of 20.11 per cent. The percentage of cases where upward educational mobility is combined with downward mobility in occupation is 5.43. The percentage of cases where there is staticness in education but upward or downward mobility in occupation are 4.35 and 3.80 respectively.

Thus, of the nine logically possible categories, in the pattern of combined Mobility in education and occupation over two generations, as many as six are found to be either vacuous or not of significance, and only three stand out prominently. These three is the descending order are:

1. Educationally and occupationally upwardly mobile.
2. Educationally upwardly mobile and occupationally static, and
3. Educationally and occupationally static.

The fact that the pattern of overall downward mobility is non-existent is by no means fortuitious. As argued earlier, traditionally the Scheduled Castes being both educationally and occupationally the most backward, the question of downward mobility does not at all arise. At the same time, the innumerable measures undertaken by the government over the last three decades, however, unsuccessful they may have been in their overall impact, could not have left the status of Scheduled Castes totally untouched. In the absence of an adequate and representative sample it is not possible to say anything further here.

As regards the impact of educational mobility on occupational mobility over two generations, it is observed that while in 66.30 per cent of the cases there has been upward mobility or staticness in both education and occupation, in the case of 25.54 per cent upward educational mobility is accompanied by occupational staticness (20.11%) or downward mobility (5.43%), and in the case of 8.15 per cent educational staticness is accompanied by occupational upward mobility (4.35%) or downward mobility (3.80%). Thus, in general educational mobility seems to influence occupational mobility. But a closer look at the Table reveals that educational mobility does not necessarily lead to occupational mobility. This is seen from the fact that in nearly 30 per cent of the cases, educational upward mobility or staticness is accompanied by occupational mobility in the opposite direction. Conversely, however, it is seen that only in 4.35 per cent of the cases that upward occupational mobility is accompanied by educational staticness. In brief, we may reiterate our earlier observation that educational mobility is a necessary but not a sufficient factor in occupational mobility.

Analysing the Table in more detail, we find that of the 137 cases where there has been upward mobility in education, in 65.69 per cent there has been upward mobility in occupation also. The percentages of cases where there is occupational staticness and downward mobility are 27.01 and 7.30 respectively. Of the 47 cases where there is educational staticness, in a majority of 68.09 per cent there has been staticness in occupation also. And it is interesting to note that in as many as 17.02 per cent of the cases there has been upward occupational mobility and in 14.89 per cent there has been downward occupational mobility.

Reading the Table columnwise, it is seen that of the 98 cases of upward mobility in occupation in an overwhelming majority of 91.84 per cent there has been upward mobility in education also, and only in 8.16 per cent there has been educational staticness. Of the 69 cases of statieness in occupation, in 46.38 per cent there has been staticness in education and upward mobility in the remaining 53.62 per cent. Finally of the 17 cases of downward mobility in occupation in as many as 10 there is upward mobility in education and in the remaining 7 cases there is downward mobility.

While there has been upward mobility in occupational status in a significant majority of 74.46 per cent of the 184 cases, such a trend seems to be more pronounced among those who are also occupationally upwardly mobile (91.84%), than among those who are occupationally static (53.62%) or occupationally downwardly mobile (58.82%). The tendency toward educational staticness observed among the remaining 25.54 per cent, seems to be least pronounced among those who are occupationally upwardly mobile (8.16) compared to those who are either occupationally static (46.38%) or downwardly mobile (41.18%).

On the ether hand, while there has been upward mobility in occupational status in a majority of 53.26 per cent of the 184 cases, sucn a trend is more proDounced among those who are also educationally upwardly mobile (65.69%) compared to those who are educationally static (17.02%). The tendency towards occupational staticness which is observed in 37.50 per cent of the cases, seems to be more pronounced among those who are also educationally static (68.09%) compared to those who are educationally upwardly mobile (27.01%). And the tendency towards downward mobility in occupational status observed in the remaining 9.24 per cent of the cases seems to be relatively more pronounced among those who are educationally static (14.80%) compared to those who are educationally upwardly mobile (7.30%).

In brief, the findings of this section seem to support the trends observed earlier. Over two generations the rate of occupational mobility is relatively low compared to that of educational mobility. Educational mobility by itself does not guarantee occupational mobility, though the probability of the latter without the former is indeed very low. Thus, upward mobility in education seems to be a necessary but not a sufficient condition for upward mobility in occupational status.

Patterns of Mobility

In the perceding pages of this chapter we have analysed the data on mobility in educational and occupational statuses at three separate levels, namely respondent's father's to respondent's generation, respondent's to respondent's son's generation, and respondent's father's to respondent's son's generations. The main parpose behind this was to identify the main trends in social mobility among the Scheduled Castes and to evolve a typology of mobility patterns among them. We shall now attempt to present the typology of mobility patterns that have emerged out of our analysis. It must be pointed out that this typology is only an exercise in methodology and should be treated as tentative. Substantively, its significance is undermined by the limitations of the sample.

We have analysed two *aspects of mobility*, namely mobility in education and occupation, and we have identified three *direction of mobility*, namely upward mobility, staticness, and downward mobility. Applying the principle of property space we get nine possible patterns of mobility as follows:

1. Educational and occupational upward mobility.
2. Educational upward mobility and occupational staticness.
3. Educational upward mobility and occupational downward mobility.
4. Educational staticness and occupational upward mobility.
5. Educational and occupational staticness.
6. Educational staticness and occupational downward mobility.
7. Educational downward mobility and occupational upward mobility.
8. Educational downward mobility and occupational staticness.
9. Educational and occupational downward mobility.

But our analysis has clarified that not all these patterns are of the same significance. Some of them are pronounced whereas others are either of minimum significance or of no significance at all. The significant patterns in combined mobility in educational and occupational statuses observed over three generations among our Scheduled Caste respondents are as follows.

At the outset it is observed that mobility patterns 1 (Educational and Occupational upward mobility) and 2 (Educational upward mobility and occupational staticness) appear in all the three levels of our analysis and therefore can be considered to be the most general patterns of mobility in our sample of Scheduled Castes. Mobility pattern 5 (Educational and Occupational staticness) is observed at two levels, namely, respondent's father's to respondent's generation, and respondent's father's to respondent's son's generation. Mobility patterns 3 (Educational upward mobility and occupational downward mobility and 4 (Educational staticness and occupational upward mobility) are found at one level each, namely, respondent's to respondent's son's generation and respondent's father's to respondent's generation respectively. Significantly enough,

Generational Level	Pattern of Combined Mobility (In deacending Order of Significance)			
	I	II	III	IV
Respondent's Father's to Respondent's Generation	No. 5 Educational and Occupational Staticness	No. 1 Educational and Occupational Upward Mobility	No. 4 Educational Staticness and Occupational Upward Mobility	No. 2 Educational Upward Mobility and Occupational Staticness
Respondent's to Respondent's Son's Generation	No. 2 Educational Upward Mobility and Occupational Stationess	No. 1 Educational and Occupational Upward Mobility	No. 3 Educational Upward Mobility occupational downward mobility	—
Respondent's Father's to Respondent's Son's Generation	No. 1 Educational and Occupational Upward Mobility	No. 2 Educational Upward Mobility and Occupational staticness	No. 5 Educational and Occupational Staticness	—

mobility patterns 6 to 9 are found to be either absent or insignificant.

It is clear that the predominant trend in our sample is to move up over generations both educationally and occupationally or at least educationally while retaining the occupational status. But it is also noticed that a trend towards retaining both educational and occupational statuses which was especially observed as the most pronounced one in mobility between respondent's father's and respondent's generation, seems to persist over generations (i.e., in mobility between respondent's father's and respondent's son's generation) though only as the last of the three pronounced trends, while being conspicuous by its absence in mobility between respondent's and respondent's son's generations. Finally, the unique pattern of upward educational mobility combined with downward occupational mobility is found, though only as the last of the three pronounced trends, in mobility between respondent's and respondent's son's generation. And the pattern of upward occupational mobility combined with educational staticness is found (as third of the four pronounced trends) in mobility between respondent's father's and respondent's generation. Thus, what we find is that educational mobility is closely related to occupational mobility as a necessary but not as a sufficient condition. In the initial stages of the programme for the uptlifument of the Scheduled Castes educatlonal mobility seems to have generated occupational mobility as well. But with the passage of time. Occupational mobility began to lag behind educational mobility, probably because the expansion of occupational avenues did not keep pace or the not commensurate with the expansion of educational facilities. This actually account for the mobility patterns 2, 3 and 4, found aspecially in mobility between respondent's and respondent's son's generations.

Looking at the direction of mobility we find that downward mobility is very insignificant as a trend. While it logically forms part of five mobility patterns, it has figured only once in our analysis, that is as the third and the last trend in mobility between respondent's and respondent's son's generation. Upward mobility which logically forms part of fiꟴe mobility patterns, seems to be generally prevalent in our analysic peaking in four of them. Obviously, it deed not figure in mobility pattern 7, which is vacuous. Staticness appears in our analysis in three of the five mobility patterns of which it logically forms a part. It does not appear in mobility patterns 6 and 8 which are vacuous or insignificant.

Turate our attentic to the level of mobility analysis we find that at the first level, for respondent's father's to respondent's son's generation, there are four patterns, namely, 5, 1, 4 and 2 in the descending order. Thus, either the trend is to retain both educational and occupational statuses, or move upward on both, or move up in one while retaining the other. At the second level, i.e., respondent's to respondent's son's generation, there are three patterns, namely, 2, 1 and 3 in the descending order. The trend is moving up in educational status while retaining the occupational status, or moving up in both, or moving up in educational status but going down in occupational status. Finally, over two generations, i.e., from respondent's father's to respondent's sons', three patterns are observed, namely, 1, 2 and 4 in the descending order of significance.

4

Youth Sub-Cultures and Social Change

F. RICHARDS

We take seriously the rise especially during the last ten years of a counter-culture based in youth and of mass movements of political opposition also based in youth. We observed that such generational revolts have occurred in other historical times and places and have typically been symptomatic of major social and cultural transformations. Nevertheless, until the last decade, generational revolt has been virtually absent in American society. We wondered whether any major structural changes that could cause a major socio-cultural crisis had occurred. We suggested that fundamental transformations in the political economy associated with dominance of the giant corporation associated with the state and with the rise of advanced technology were having profound disintegrative effects on the culture. These effects were particularly noticeable in the family—especially in connection with raising children—were reflected in a general cultural incoherence, and were producing an increasing number of young people who were experiencing identity crises. Either their character structures (motives, impulses, values, and aspirations) were considerably at variance with the established institutional framework or they were fundamentally dislocated and restless because of the intensifying anomie that they were experiencing.

These structural transformations produced not only culture and identity crises, but also an institutional framework in which youth inevitably became a definite social category. Mass higher education, the conscripted army, and the urban ghetto were social develpments that entailed postponment of adulthood for millions of persons. Simultaneously, these institutions were enclaves within which the discontented young were gathered together, thereby facilitating the development of collective consciousness and action. In themselves, these enclaves were institutions that profoundly reinforced and intensified the grievances, discontents, and alienations of many of those within them. Finally, technology applied to communications provided the structural basis for the interlinking of local enclaves and the emergence of an increasingly homogeneous consciousness among youth throughout the American society and even internationally.

Mass consciousness does not emerge overnight. Neither is it unanimous by any means. If we were to stop our analysis with the arsument as it has so far been presented, we would find it very hard to account for the following facts:

Both the youth counterculture and the new left began as decidedly minority expressions and, initially, were reactions against the values and styles that then prevailed among the young.

Both the counterculture and the movement were originated by a very particular, and rather unrepresentative, sector of the youth population as a whole.

The youth population remains internally differentiated and exhibits a rather wide range of behaviours. Even now, a considerable number of persons do not seem "youth"-ful. The movements in question have themselves changed markedly over the past decade. They have grown numerically; they have become increasingly polarized from the conventional and the established and increasingly hostile to authority. On the other hand, during the early seventies, many of the forms and styles that developed during the sixties seemed themselves to be disintegrating.

Sometimes, however, deviant youths can influence the

majority. Many years ago, Karl Mannheim observed that generational movements have their beginnings in what he called "generational units". When small groups of young people from around a particular set of new perspectives and begin to establish a distinct and visible cultural pattern in opposition to those that are established, they may (or may not) capture the interest of widening circles of individuals in their own age groups. Movements of generational opposition, then, do not arise all at once; instead, small group of peers act as a vanguard to such movements.

I believe that Mannheim's concept of generational units is crucial to understanding the transformation that occurred in American youth culture. Clearly, as I suggested in the Introduction, the youth culture that prevailed in American high schools and colleges prior to the sixties was smoothly integrated with the most conventional values and sentiments held by American adults. Something that happened in the late fifties and early sixties changed this situation; that something, I want to argue, was the emergence of a new generational unit—a sub-culture of youth that looked at first like a deviant group but turned out to be a vanguard.

What did youth culture look like in the fifties? Dimensions of the high school culture that prevailed then included the following: rigid definition of sex role behaviour (boys were expected to be athletic, cleancut and crewcut, antiintellectual and antiacademic, sexually exploitative, and callous; girls were expected to be wellgroomed, to play down their intellectual capabilities, and to be date-conscious and "social", mushily romantic over popular "crooners", and frivolous and marriage-oriented. Teenage activity was organized and supervised by adults through school sports, dances and the like; pop music was created, manufactured, and distributed according to formulas and tastes established by adults. Political interest and activity was "out". Defiance of adult authority existed, but it was expressed largely through overt disdain for academic achievement (though obviously many were covertly conforming in order to get to college) and through experiments with *adult* hedonistic prerogatives—getting drunk, driving fast, smoking, petting. Obviously, overcommitment to this peer culture could be damaging to the achievement of maturity (the story of the aging high school football hero who fails as a man was a cliche movie plot in the fifties). Nevertheless, assimilation into this culture was the obvious way of establishing a conventionally grounded identity and capacity for "normal" social and sexual roles.

Similarly, observers of the college campus scene during the fifties were universal in their reports that the student body was disturbingly "conformist", "complacent", "politically apathetic", and "privatized". Apparently, college students emulated the primary concern of their middle class adult counterparts—concern with their own material security, with the status race, and with bland forms of conventional fun.

To be sure, a large number of boys and girls could not be assimilated by the middle class youth culture. Typically, these were working and lower class youth and members of ethnic and racial minority groups who had been rejected by the school systems and deprived of an opportunity to attain occupational mobility. Such youths adapted to their exclusion by the system and by other youths of their own age by forming "delinquent" sub-cultures—groups that symbolically and behaviourally expressed defiance of school and community authority, carried on self-organized social life in the streets, and, in some cases, engaged in organized truancy, petty theft, vandalism and violence.

There was also a fraction of middle class youth that felt excluded from and repelled by the prevailing youth culture. These were typically young people who were academically motivated and successful, who had internalized middle class norms of citizenship, and who were repelled by delinquency, violence, and aggression. Yet, they were equally (or even more) repelled by the frivolity, antiintellectualism, and social indifference of the middle class peer culture and by its stereotyped sex role definitions and superficial conventionalism. These were boys who were intellectual and aesthetic rather than athletic and aggressive and girls who were "brainy" and assertive and assertive and consciously antagonistic to conventional femininity—young people who were uneasy in the conventional round of dating, disdained careful grooming, and wanted to be serious and individualistic. As a result, their status within the prevailing youth culture tended to be low, and they were likely to suffer from anxiety and self-doubt that such lack of acceptance usually entails.

Where did such apparently "deviant" middle class youth come from? In retrospect, we can see clearly that they represented an important new social type in American culture—they were the offspring of a definite and increasingly established stratum of the American middle class. At the time, however, many perceived themselves to be freaks of nature, mysteriously unable to whole-heartedly embrace what was apparently "normal".

I call such young people "intellectual youth" in part because the identities they sought to establish were intellectual. They were concerned with basic questions of value, with books and the arts, and with critical examination of basic assumptions of culture. They were "intellectual" in the related sense that they identified with that aspect of American and western civilization that was antimaterialistic, and antibourgeoisie—cultural values upheld by many of the artists, writers, poets, and intellectuals of the nineteenth and twentieth centuries.

In earlier eras intellectual youths were likely to be isolated individuals alienated from the mainstream of youth and intensely estranged and lonely in relation to their peers. Such estrangement caused considerable anxiety and unhappiness, but in some fortunate cases strong positive impulses toward introspection, non-conformity, and creativity also resulted. Bookish youths constructed their identities less on the basis of their immediate social relations than on the basis of the literature and art of similarly alienated intellectuals of previous generations.

No doubt this pattern of individuation continues to this day. Toward the end of the fifties, however, a new situation was evident—the emergence of a *critical mass of alienated intellectual youth*. The search for cultural alternatives had become a collective enterprise rather than primarily an individual one. Increasingly, young intellectuals were able to find each other and work out the beginning of a style of being youthful that represented a coherent alternative to the conventional peer cultures from which they had been excluded. By the end of the fifties, their impulses and interests, their tastes and perspectives, and their appearance and demeanor had, for many, ceased to be sources of embarrassment, shame, and worry and had begun to be matters of pride and selfesteem.

If a considerable increase in the number of intellectual youths made possible the emergence of an intellectual sub-culture among them, it is important to understand how and why this increase occurred. Intellectual youths are usually offspring of parents who are engaged in intellectual vocations—doctors, lawyers, teachers, scientists, administrators, and professionals in the social services and communications, for example. This category, which is composed of vocations that require a college education, was one of the labour force sectors that had been most rapidly expanding during the previous three decades. Thus, the increase in the number of intellectual youths during the fifties and sixties is directly traceable to the fact that the proportion of parents of adolescents who had attended college, developed intellectual, aesthetic, and "humanistic" orientations, and been engaged in intellectual and professional occupations had increased.

In, I enumerated a number of unintended consequences of mass higher education. Here, then, is another: mass higher education produces some parents who raise their children to want to be "intellectuals".

Research has found that there is a cluster of values and childraising attitudes and practices that is characteristic of this occupational group (obviously, it is not universal for or exclusive to this group). This cluster of values, interests, attitudes, and practices is particularly characteristic for families in which the *mother* is college educated and career-oriented. It has taken root especially in the largest cities, especially among secularized Jewish and Protestant families.

With respect to *values*, these families emphasized the primary importance of commitment to the world of ideas and the arts rather than to personal material success or religious devotion. One might say that for them, the university, rather than the church or the business concern, has been the primary institutional repository of value and virtue. Furthermore, they tend to be humanitarian in ideological terms—to stress the value of being socially useful in one's work and of taking the role of citizen seriously. With respect to leisure and recreation, these families tend to emphasize pursuits that will promote culture—reading good literature, listening to music, visiting museums, and traveling for cultural enrichment are preferred over spectator sports or escapist recreation. Education is highly valued less for its instrumental value than for its intrinsic merits. Members of this group are politically informed and generally quite liberal, although only a minority are politically active.

Since both parents in these families are highly educated and, often, both are involved in careers or full-time occupations, a relatively high degree of equality between the parents is maintained. Household responsibilities are shared, as are family decisions; these are not families in which the father is the dominant authority or the mother is the controlling figure in day-to-day child care—especially if the mother is working. Typically, family egalitarianism extends to the children as well; the parents espouse support for the autonomy and free expression of their children and often encourage or expect independence and self-expression. Physical punishment is rare, and the parents typically adopt a relaxed attitude in regard to certain traditional middle class areas of rigid parental concern—cleanliness, toilet training, impulsiveness, sexual play, and general obedience, for example. Nevertheless, these parents are *not* permissive with respect to those aspects that are central to their lives; they have high expectations for their children with respect to intellectual achievement, and they expect their offspring to be verbal, interested in books, creative, and talented artistically. These parents are likely to exercise active control over the expression of aggression—actively discouraging hostile and "selfish" behaviour while encouraging co-operative and behaviour. It should be added that ideally, this combination of encouragement of autonomy, control over aggression, and expectation for intellectual achievement is made coherent by the overall value system expressed, and occasionally lived, by the parents.

Perhaps you can see that these families, as I have described them, are less prone than most to some of the frustration, ambivalence, and incoherence that I identified as characteristic of the contemporary middle class family. To a considerable extent, these parents are likely to be *more consistent and principled* than are most parents: this appeared to be true of many families I studied in Chicago and of the families described by Kenneth Keniston in his study of radical youth. Particularly clear was that these parents desired to impart to their offspring a commitment to intellectualism and a critical attitude to prevailing cultural goals—particularly with respect to materialism, conventional morality, status seeking, and mass culture. Clearly, they wanted their children to be academically serious, involved with the arts and books, and oriented toward intellectual careers and social responsibility.

On the other hand, many such parents were likely to express either overtly or covertly some ambivalence about their own lives. They were people who had achieved a considerable degree of material well-being, but were likely to feel some guilt about their own comfort and privatism in a world in which poverty and gross inequality prevailed. They were likely, by the time their kinds were adolescents, to have experienced some disillusionment about the degree to which their vocations were personally rewarding and socially useful or to which society was moving in the political, social, and cultural directions they had hoped for in *their* youth. Although they hoped their children would maintain or enhance their social status through fulfilling and useful occupational attainments, they also tended to stress the necessity of living in accordance with one's values more consistently than they themselves had done.

Thus, by the late fifties, young people who had been infused with critical attitudes toward the culture and endowed with character traits that set them apart from more conventionally raised peers thronged the schools and colleges. Because of their values, interests, and character structures, many of these people felt excluded and repelled by the prevailing youth culture.

These were the youths, then, who formed the nucleus of an *alternative* sub-culture on certain large university campuses during the late fifties—one within which their own values and aspirations could be freely expressed and social acceptance could be achieved.

What attitudes did the intellectual campus subculture express during the late fifties? First, an increasingly overt rejection of the symbols and practices of the prevailing youth culture. Campus non-conformists replaced "good, clean grooming" with casual dress and bearded faces, girls let their hair down and wore little or no makeup, sandals replaced white bucks, and jeans and sweatshirts replaced ivy league attire. Intellectuals preferred modern jazz and folk music to popular, commercial "tin pan alley" music, and many of them took up the guitar and other folk instruments and performed in or frequented the newly sprouting coffee houses in campus neighbourhoods. The young intellectuals sought "intimate" friendships and love relations rather than superficial sociability and the dating ritual. The content of social relationships was defined less by frivolity and gossip than by "serious" intellectual discussions about philosophy, politics, culture, and religion. Friendship, art, ideas, and experience were highly perferred to commercialized entertainment, organized athletics and spectator sports, school spirit, and other conventional uses of leisure time.

Above all, the intellectual sub-culture expressed a romantic identification with the life styles of bohemian artists and with rather sanitized versions of folk culture, especially American Negro culture. A powerful influence by the end of the fifties were the beat generation poets and writers whose stance of bohemian opposition to American culture was vividly publicized. Most participants at the time probably did not conceive of being bohemian as a possible vocation; instead many hoped that academic careers would give them the personal freedom and intellectual stimulation necessary to avoid the "rat race". Undoubtedly, many were attracted to the "hipster" apotheosized by Norman Mailer: a man who could reap the material benefits of a conventional career while cultivating a *Psychological* disaffiliation from it, exploiting organized society while living psychically apart from it. Thus, initially, the mood of campus intellectuals was one of alienation from prevailing culture, especially the culture of their peers. On the other hand, it shared with that culture a rejection of collective action and public protest, although a minority of participants maintained an interest in the tiny radical and socialist sects and clubs that continued to survive on a number of the big campuses.

Thus, the emergent intellectual sub-culture expressed, explicitly and implicitly, alienation from middle class conformity and conventionality; superficial social relations and role playing; conventional definitions of "success" based on money, consumership, and careerism; and the trival, commercial, and inauthentic character of pop culture. For its adherents, creativity, individuality, personal authenticity, intellectual seriousness, and cultivated cultural tastes and preferences were the highest personal virtues. And it expressed aspirations for the attainment of a genuinely individual identity and for the discovery of ways of being adult that would enable such identities to fully realize their potentialities.

Even in its earliest beginnings, participation in the emergent sub-culture was not restricted to youth who had been explicitly socialized with these sentiments—although we are arguing that such youth were the primary element in its creation. Nevertheless, it is crucial to recognize that in addition tot he sons and daughters of the "intelligentsia", substantial numbers of other upper middle class young people were finding the conventional youth culture inadequate for resolving problems of identity.

Of particular relevance in this regard is Kenneth Keniston's depiction of "uncommitted" youth. In the course of conducting a study at Harvard University during the late fifties, Keniston discovered a small group of undergraduates who were highly estranged from their peers and had profoundly rejected American culture. As he describes them, these students had not been reared in the coherent, liberal, humanist style that we have attributed to "intellectual" families. Instead, Keniston's family type was composed of the following elements: a father who was substantially inadequate as a model for his son either because of actual physical absence, psychological distance, or personal inadequacy; a mother who was considerably ambitious, talented, or artistic but who was unlike the typical intellectual mother in that she was trying to satisfy her extremely frustrated ambitions through her son's achievements. This combination of parents, according to Keniston, caused a situation in which the son identified wsth the mother, adopting many of her interests and aspirations, and was likely to have been protected, indulged, and psychologically seduced by the mother. Moreover, neither parent was likely to possess or communicate to their children any coherent value system or personal direction. Such young men, Keniston argues, had major problems in achieving independence and profound difficulties in relating or conforming to conventional definitions of masculine sex roles. In short and in an extreme form, Keniston's subjects represent one outcome of the confused middle class family described. Very likely, some young men of this type found the emergent intellectual youth culture attractive because it offered avenues of expression and recognition that were denied by the conventional youth culture and the school system.

As we have described them, intellectual and "uncommitted" youth shared a sense of revulsion with and exclusion from the collective life of their peers. They shared impulses and interests that made them diverge from standardized sex role definitions. Both types were considerably uneasy about entering the occupational world for which school was preparing them. Both sought interpersonal depth, experiential richness, and moral seriousness—dimensions they found absent in the social life of their peers and in conventional adult society as well. Both sought new bases for identity that would permit these impulses and aspirations to be realized.

The fundamental difference between the two types rests on the fact that the "intellectuals" had some coherent value system provided by their parents to sustain and orient them while in the pure case, the "uncommitted" were more confused and adrift and, therefore, more passive and present-oriented.

On the surface, formation of a sub-culture of alienated, intellectual youth may be interpreted as an inevitable and functional development. Given the growth of a highly educated segment of the labour force, dissatisfaction of a large number of youths who had been born into this stratum with the conventional youth culture was inevitable. Since peer cultures appear to be an essential ground for identity formation in advanced industrial society, it was to be expected that youths from this stratum, once they had become sufficiently numerous to do so, would create a differentiated subculture more in accord with their motivational and character structures. From the perspective of functional analysis, one could argue that such differentiation enables such youth to develop more easily the identity structure and interpersonal competences appropriate to intellectual and professionalized careers—to grow up in the relatively highly individuated fashion necessary for certain elite roles in established society. This analysis would predict, then, that young people would be relatively stably stratified, with a variety of youth sub-cultures co-existing and, in a sense, channeling youth into the various strata of pre-existing adult society. Indeed, one would expect youth cultures to be *alternatives* to overt rebellion, as long as they are adequately tolerated and legitimized by adult authorities. The energy of alienated intellectual youth, once institutionalized in a distinctive sub-culture, would serve the functional requirements of the going system.

But the sub-culture of young intellectuals did not remain deviant. Nor did its members become less rebellious as they found means to social acceptance. On the contrary, this apparently deviant sub-culture came to influence and attract the apparently conventional majority of the young. Moreover, over the course of the subsequent decade the initially mild cultural criticism articulated by young intellectuals became increasingly political, radical, and rebellious.

How did the intellectual youth sub-culture *diffuse* beyond the ranks of its initial participants? In a society with very little precedent for radical political movements among its youth, how did a mass movement with revolutionary overtones come into being? These are the problems I want to look at next.

DIFFUSION OF THE "INTELLECTUAL" YOUTH CULTURE

As I have suggested, youth culture appears to be a functional requisite of advanced industrial society as a medium for identity formation and preparation for adulthood. That the prevailing youth culture of postwar America could not encompass the needs of certain types of high status youth was not particularly surprising, nor was it unusual that these youths should band together to form a counterculture that provided the basis for a more individuated, intellectual, and critical identity. Particularly surprising is the fact that this counterculture did not remain (as "deviant" sub-cultures usually do) a restricted enclave for the marginal few, but became the dominant sub-culture on many campuses and in many regions of the country and a significant force in all locations where youth were aggregated.

In interpreting processes of diffussion, it is very important to strive for some precision in specifying the manner in which various discrete cultural elements diffuse. Clearly the "alienated" youth culture did not constitute a single, seamless entity, and in our discussion thus far no doubt we have been guilty of treating "it" as a thing. Instead, we are talking about a cluster of interrelated but separable elements: art forms, fashions, jargon, behaviour patterns, values, and norms. We are also talking about social circles, friendship groups, and acquaintance networks. Thus, "participation" in a sub-culture is a convenient but oversimplified way of talking about a very diverse number of ways in which persons may orient to the cultural and social syndrome we are describing. They may accept some cultural elements, while being ignorant of, indifferent to, or repelled by others. The meaning of various cultural symbols may be quite different for the various individuals and groups that adopt them. Some people may feel positive toward, or sympathetic with, the cultural complex without taking part in its practices or its social circles. The degree of personal self-conscious commitment to the culture will vary widely.

With these considerations in mind, let us look at some of the major elements of the new youth culture that began to exert a steadily widening appeal to youth of diverse classes, background, and character structure during the sixties.

New Music

The role of music as a medium of cultural and sub-cultural expression and as a primary means for defining identity is discussed very little in sociological literature. The issue is especially fascinating in the United States because while some ethnic and other sub-cultures have developed their own indigenous musical forms, a popular music and entertainment industry both disseminates and homogenizes ethnic music continuously.

Since the jazz era of the twenties, while youths have devoted much of their energy, interest, and income to the consumption of pop music. In addition to whatever intrinsic enjoyment may be derived from listening and dancing to it, popular music plays a very important social function as well. The live performance of pop music in dance halls and concerts has, for many years, been the occasion for large, intensely emotional, and uninhibited gatherings of youth. Therefore, it has served as a major stimulus to, and reinforcement of, a sense of common consciousness. Because there are always adults who express revulsion at the explicit sexuality and apparent irrationality that seems to characterize these events, for decades, such occasions have served as mild expressions of defiance of adult authority. Moreover, status in teenage groups often depends on the ability of its members to display their appreciation of currently popular music conspicuously—by attending live performances, collecting records, displaying the right tastes, dancing well, and so on. For a long time, pop music has been an important ingredient in lovemaking, courtship, and other emotional experiences. As the same music is broadcast across the country (and to a great extent around the world), it becomes a common frame of reference—a basis for communication and mutual recognition. Moreover, since adults are likely to find the current forms repulsive or unintelligible, pop music is an important means for defining the distinctiveness of one's generation.

I think that one of the most important sources of alienation of intellectual youth from their more conventional peers during the fifties was the quality of the music that was popular among teenagers. It seemed to be entirely a product of tired formulas developed out of Tin Pan Alley. It was always a source of astonishment to me that kids in my age group could tolerate—let alone buy—records made by people like Eddie Fisher, Patti, Page, and Joni James. In reaction, many young "intellectuals" became "high brows" and cultivated their tastes in classical music. But by the late fifties, a few intellectual, alienated youths invented a kind of popular music that turned out to be a major historical breakthrough. Out of the intellectual sub-culture emerged creative musicians and songwriters who sensed that it was possible to have a music that was both connected to pop and made serious artistic claims, was musically advanced and poetically sophisticated, and expressed the sentiments and experiences of the alienated and intellectual sub-culture.

These young poets and minstrels were heavily influenced by several ethnic musical traditions that were becoming commercialized during the fifties—black rhythm and blues, southern bluegrass and rockabilly, urban concert, and coffeehouse folk music. What was ingenious about these young performers was that they found ways to fuse these traditions: they remolded them to fit the needs and tastes of middle class white intellectual young people, added to this mix efforts at avant-garde poetry and composition, and made an enormously successful popular art form in commercial terms.

The new performers began in essentially two different ways. Some, like Bob Dylan and Joan Baez, got their start by appealing directly to the intellectual sub-culture on campuses and in city coffeehouses; they began as performers for a special audience and were not regarded as pop stars. Others, especially the British groups, aimed more directly for mass commercial appeal to mainstream teenage audiences.

But I find it fascinating that *both* the folk and the rock performers who became superstars by the mid-sixties tended to have both higher status and more advanced education than any previous generation of pop stars. Most had attended college, or had parents who did, and almost all began their careers by playing for audiences much like themselves; that is young people with intellectual, educated tastes. This social background was shared by virtually all the white American superstars and musical innovators of the sixties: Bob Dylan, Joan Baez, Jefferson Airplane, the Byrds, the Beach Boys, Janis Joplin, the Doors, James Taylor, and so on. The British groups were more likely to have working class origins, but they had risen out of that background to start art school or college (Mick Jagger attended the London School of Economics).

The contemporary white pop star, then, has markedly different roots from those of his predecessors. Prior to the sixties, pop music, like other aspects of the popular entertainment and sports industries, was an avenue for expression and status for working class and minority youth. It is still possible for lower status youth to gain fame and fortune through pop singing—but only because there remain some distinctive pop music "sub-cultures"—soul music and country western. Nevertheless, by the mid-sixties, the new music that originated among intellectual youth had become the dominant popular music for white youth of many strata and in many countries.

Not only did the new music dominate the "top forty" lists during the sixties, but the concerts and open-air festivals devoted to its performance attracted crowds of historic proportions by the late sixties. In addition, the record albums and concerts of performers judged too "controversial" or "uncommercial" for standard AM radio play or television appearances were tremendously successful. Moreover, millions of young people in the United States and Europe followed the personal lives of rock "superstars" such as John Lennon, Mick Jagger, Bob Dylan, and Janis Joplin with intense fascination and concern.

Thus, no detailed data or argument is needed to demonstrate the extensive and intensive popularity of the new music and its performers. For many youths, music became the decisive feature of their lives—the major focus of uncommitted time, money, and energy.

It is also clear that the music, in both its form and its content, was an expression of alienation, group consciousness, and revolt. The form and manner of presentation and the environments of live preformance were not only explicity designed to be an ecstatic *release* from the regulations, routines, and repressions of everyday life, but were intended by the performers to stand as a definite *criticism* and assault upon them. In addition, many performers—often self-consciously—publicy adopted life styles that were unconventional or oppositional. Many represented or advocated mind-expanding drugs, mysticism (and a rejection of Western religion), communal living, sexual freedom, and non-violence, as well as a variety of more specific social and political causes. Finally, song lyrics, often in very explicit terms, expressed all forms of cultural opposition, social criticism, generational consciousness, and the quest for new cultural identity. Indeed, the fact that serious philosophical, political, and cultural issues were addressed in popular song lyrics and in styles heavily influenced by the literary avant-gardes of the past hundred years was one of the most crucial ways in which the new music was new.

Obviously, however, the difference between the meaning intended by an artist or performer and the meaning given his work by various audiences is substantial. Popularity of the new music does not necessarily signify popularity of the counter-cultural themes and sentiments that motivated its creators. Indeed, at least one systematic study of the question indicates that many teenagers did not hear the lyries of popular songs or, if they did, did not attribute general political or cultural meanings to them.

An alternative explanation of the new music's popularity would emphasize both the elaborate machinery of exploitation, publicity, "payola", and other forms of manipulation employed by the entertainment media and the extreme vulnerability of youth to fads and crazes. In its pure form, such an explanation would propose that content of the new musical forms was irrelevant to its success. Rather, the primitive rhythms and simple melodic structure of this music and the personal lives of its performers were appealing because they permitted forms of vicarious unconventionality, release, and revolt that actually reinforce established convention, routines, and norms. Furthermore, the taste of the young is largely manipulated by a combination of public relations, incessant repetition, and the social pressures of an adolescent peer culture.

However, such considerations do not adequately account for the specific content and qualities of the new music and its associated environments and life styles. For example, it is clear in retrospect that the emergence of a highly educated mass audience created a basis for the development of intellectually and aesthetically sophisticated and serious new forms of popular art. In this respect, the new popular music is an aspect of the same process that resulted in the rising popularity of film as a serious art form and the appearance of formerly avant-garde and underground art forms and themes in mass-circulation magazines. In short, one aspect of the cultural change of the past decade has been the emergence of a fused intellectual and popular culture that appeals most directly to the very large educated audience created by mass higher education. Previous barriers between intellectual and popular culture have crumbled substantially not, as some intellectual reformers would have hoped, by inculcation of the masses with high culture or, as intellectual elitists have always feared, by the destruction of serious culture, but by the creation of new art forms and media that synthesize aspects of both high and low culture. Although many teenagers failed to perceive the "newness" of the new music and responded to it as they had to the old, it is obvious that many thousands of youth shared the sensibilities of the young poets and minstrels who composed this music and grasped their meanings and purposes.

We need to know much more than we now do about the bases for the appeal of the new music and the reasons for its profound impact. For example, in addition to the fact that it was more intellectually and artistically serious, new music was intensely expressive of alienation and opposition. To what extent can the widespread acceptance of the new music be attributed to the values that it was designed to express? To which segments of the young were these values and the associated life style immediately appealing? We know almost nothing systematic about such questions as these. All one can say with confidence is that emergence of the new music *popularized* the idea of cultural opposition and generally made available to youth materials for the construction of unconventional identities that had previously been the property of small groups of those we have been calling "intellectual" youth. Whether this fact accounts for the appeal of the new music in any significant degree is still largely a matter of speculation.

Finally, a point to which we shall return. Irrespective of the determinants for the initial diffusion of the new music, it is clear that by the end of the sixties, it plus its associated cultural traits had become almost universally defined—by youth, adults, and the media—as a form of opposition and revolt. If interest in it earlier in the decade had a quite ambiguous significance, this is much less true as this essay is being written.

Hair and the New Fashions

Perhaps even more dramatic than the thansformation of musical preferences among youth has been the transformation of fashion. As I have said before, the socially preferred appearance and attire of high school and college males during the mid-fifties were typified by the crew cut and crew neck, slightly scuffed white buck shoes, ivy league cut, and charcoal gray suits. Girls waved their hair and wore shirtwaists, loose sweaters, and skirts or bermuda shorts. In short, the preferred dress accentuated sobriety, cleanliness, and conventionality.

In the emergent intellectual sub-culture, appearance tended to follow the classic bohemian pattern: males generally appeared neglectful of their attire, wore work clothes, and some grew beards; girls let their hair grow long and wore handcrafted clothing and jewelry and little or no makeup. In general, the emphasis was on the natural and the comfortable.

A more explicit and general revolt against conventional middle class dress was given great impetus by various pop music performers. The Beatles, whose hair was uncommonly long for the time, sparked widespread imitation. By the late sixties, long hair had become characteristic of elite college males and a significant number of high school youths defied school dress regulations in order to sport long sideburns and hair. To complement these changing hair styles, young people adopted a riotous array of unconventional costume-like clothing that bore traces of Indian, cowboy, military, and working class cultures and was overlaid with the brilliant and surrealistic colour associated with psychedelic experience. If any generalization about appearance can be made, it was that distinctions in appearance between the sexes were greatly blurred. As boys adopted the long hair, necklaces, headbands, and bright colours that were traditionally feminine, girls bought their clothing in the men's departments and abandoned their makeup.

The underlying meanings of such changing dress fashions are even harder to specify than are the social and psychological roots of the new music.

As hair and dress fashions became more and more widely adopted, it became obvious that many adults were shocked and disturbed by them—again for reasons that are not entirely clear. Many adults and youths felt that the male "costume" was used to express defiance of conventional expectations about the male role. Such costumes represented a direct assault on some of the most basic and problematic assumptions about identity in American culture. In addition, acceptance of such garb as suitable implied a lack of elementary discipline and an aristocratic or feminine attentiveness to personal beauty inappropriate in a culture one is expected to be busy with serious work. In short, the new youth fashions, whatever they might have meant to those who adopted them, quickly became labeled as a direct challenge to deeply held cultural values with respect to the sex role, work, sensuality, and efficient use of time and money. Moreover, since the prevailing fashions were associated in the media with illicit, immoral, and degenerate behaviour, it was not surprising that many would quickly assume that individuals who dressed in this fashion were likely to engage in such behaviour. Thus, the fully dressed "hippie" youth became a target of verbal insult, physical abuse, and discrimination in many communities. Also, he was likely to experience forms of harassment from law enforcement agencies. In short, to the extent that young people adopted new fashions—even though they may have done so without any significant initial alteration of their commitment to conventional values—they were likely to experience troubles and punishments that resembled those that were experienced by blacks and other racial minorities in urban ghettoes daily.

Drugs

The increasingly common use of marijuana and psychedelic and mood-manipulating drugs on college campuses and among youth in general needs no documentation. Prior to this decade, the illicit use of drugs was commonplace among ghetto youth and minimal among middle class whites (although fairly prevalent in bohemain circles). Bohemain youth dropout enclaves in the Bay Area and in Manhattan constituted important locales for the spread of psychedelic drugs among white youth. By 1966, rock music groups had emerged from these bohemain drug cultures on both coasts. Not only did they perform, but they also sponsored large outdoor love-ins and indoor light shows that had the total effect of simulating and enchancing the psychedelic experience. These events and explicitly "turned on" music helped popularize the use of marijuana and more potent psychedelic drugs.

As a result of media promotion and underground publicity, by 1967 the Haight-Ashbury district of San Francisco had become—both actually and symbolically—a haven for drug-oriented youth who wanted to live in a manner that was becoming wellknown as a total way of life. For a brief period, the Haight symbolized the idea of the "hippie" culture—a way of life in which love, freedom, mysticism, music, youth, and beauty were coupled with mind-expanding and emotionally liberating drugs, communal living, and a "do your own thing" ethic. Thousands of youths flocked to San Francisco to absorb the new culture, then returned to their campuses and towns to spread the myth of Haight-Ashbury. Tens of thousands more shared in their experience from afar and used the myth as a way of legitimizing drug use. Although the Haight myth collapsed, incorporation of marijuana and drugs by the general youth culture was the net result.

The number of young people who regularly use various types of drugs is impossible to estimate and the number who only experiment with drugs is even higher, but the number of those who regard the use of marijuana and related illegal drugs as legitimate probably constitutes a majority. To a very great extent, the widespread use of marijuana was inevitable once it became commonplace on campuses and in other locales where youth interact intensively. The typically innocuous or euphoric effects of marijuana, its enhancement of social experience, the reduction of anxiety, and the apparent lack of ill effects among friends and acquaintances who use it guaranteed its widespread acceptance. A deeply rebellious or alienated disposition was no more a factor in the use of grass by large numbers of young people than it had been in the acceptance of new music and hair styles. Grass became a symbol of defiance and revolt almost entirely because its possession and use are illegal. As a result, all users or holders have had some contact with the police or other authorities—either directly or indirectly. For many youths, the illegality of a drug that is either innocuous or, at worst, no more deleterious in its effects than is alcohol, tobacco, or barbiturates is a clear sign of the irrationality and hypocrisy of established authority. There is little evidence that drug use itself is "caused" by more general sentiments of an oppositional or antiauthoritarian character.

Obviously, I have been cautious about arguing that the *spread* of new music, fashion, and drug use was due primarily to the rebellious impulses of those who adopted these new cultural elements. These elements *originated* very largely in the sub-culture of alienated intellectual students that began to emerge during the late fifties. For this sub-culture, I would argue, these elements *were* associated with a general antipathy to central aspects of conventional culture and functional to provide new bases for identity formation and collective life for such youth. To a great extent, the rapid diffusion of these cultural elements can be accounted for by the factors discussed.

First, the new cultural elements emerged at just that point in time when the proportion of youths who were being segregated and herded together in schools, military bases, and urban ghettoes was extremely high. This fact alone helps us understand the reasons that new practices do spread so rapidly. When a substantial number of people who share common problems are thrown together for prolonged periods, ground for the rapid spread of virtually any activity which appears relevant to their common problems is fertile.

Second, the mass media serve a somewhat similar function—a kind of substitute for face-to-face interaction—on a national and international scale. Practices and perspectives which might have diffused very slowly in the past are now broadcast throughout the world and youths who are geographically isolated from centers of the avant-grade are immediately made aware of anything that is new, interesting, pleasurable, or potentially popular.

Most likely, the first youths on any campus or in any community to respond to the new cultural elements were those who confronted most sharply the problems of identity we have attributed to the intellectual and the alienated. The new styles of appearance enabled such young people to make themselves visible to each other and thereby unite to form a local version of the nationally emerging sub-culture. In many locales, such youth were regarded as deviant, not only by adults, but by those their own age as well. Nevertheless, one important function of the new music and certain kinds of media publicity was to dissolve many of the tensions among peers. Even those who initially did not share the profound cultural alienation of the hippies were likely to share a liking for the Beatles, some respect for their collective visibility, and a derise at least to experiment with marijuana.

Thus, one explanation for the spread of elements of the new youth culture during the sixties ignores the intentional symbolic content of these elements and accounts for their diffusion on the basis of commonplace processes of social influence; group pressure, and contagion. To accept this account in its purest form would lead to the view that virtually any cultural practice widely broadcast and celebrated by the media or repeatedly defined as "popular" or "in" or "the coming thing" by disc jockeys and magazine articles would be widely adopted by young people. The problem with this view is it fails to account for the specific content of that which is celebrated (for example, why have the media felt it necessary to celebrate *alienated* cultural styles and expressions?). If youthful tastes are so easily manipulated, why haven't more conventional "straight" styles, forms, and practices become popularized?

A somewhat more sophisticated account would assume that youth generally are likely to be attracted by particularly hedonistic activities and that they find vicarious experiences of defiance of convention and authority particularly appealing as forms of emotional release and relief from boredom. Indeed, such impulses are not restricted to youth, but are experienced most intensely by white middle class American youth whose daily lives are characterized by regulation, competitive pressure, sexual deprivation, and dependency. It is not surprising that under these conditions, counter-experiences, particularly those that are vicarious, are intensely attractive and are part of the normal process of identity formation and stabilization. From this viewpoint, youth culture, whether it is conventional or counter-conventional, need pose no threat to established values; indeed, providing youth some opportunity to be released from convention *as youth* may actually strengthen the hold of established cultural perspectives in the long run.

It may be that for many youth who attend rock festivals, wear their sideburns long, and try pot once in a while, the new youth culture is no more significant than any fad or craze is. Nevertheless, even fads may have major implications for social and cultural change. Furthermore, explaining the new culture as only a fad or craze fails to account for either the emotional intensity of its members, the values they live by and represent, or the intense conflict this culture has generated in American society.

It is plausible that the cultural elements we have been discussing achieved their popularity for reasons that are deeper and more historically specific than are those we have emphasized. Perhaps the intellectual and alienated youths of the fifties were more prophetic than they realized at the time. If their revolt began primarily in opposition to the prevailing youth culture, it entailed explicit criticism and rejection of the general culture—particularly the Protestant Ethic. If this value syndrome *is* losing its vitality under the impact of affluence, bureaucratization, and advanced technology, the problems of identity experienced by intellectual and uncommitted youth are being experienced in varying degrees by many other young people. The culture expressed by small and relatively isolated groups of youth attracted the interest of mainstream youth because all youths shared problems of self-definition, vocation, and sexual identity.

On the surface, Dylan, long hair, and pot many have satisfied the hedonistic impulses and needs of conventional as well as new youth. They awakened consciousness of the contradictions in a culture in which thrift is a virtue made obsolete by abundance; competitive individualism is inappropriate because the social system maximizes interdependence, co-ordination, and rational planning; male dominance and aggressiveness and female passivity and dependence cannot coexist with a family and educational system that rests on a considerable degree of sexual equality and in which women are given the central socializing roles.

Relatively few young people may have been able to verbalize contradictions such as these—and our culture embodies many others as well—but by the 1960s the confusions and discontinuities they produced were an integral part of the very character structure and emotional life of millions of American youth.

Moreover, other aspects of the cultural crisis affected large numbers of youth. For instance, many-observers have discussed the rapidity of social change as a source of dislocation and "alienation". Since rapid change is inherent in our political economy and social system, they argue, parents and other adults are inscapably inadequate as models of future adult roles for youth. Margaret Mead goes so far as to claim that the pear group is the prime socializing agency in advanced technological society. Furthermore, she argues, we have reached the point where youth constitutes the most viable model of cultural adaptation. In such a "prefigurative" culture, young people are the guides of their elders rather than the reverse.

The result of erosion of traditional values and the rapidity of social change is a situation in which many institutions operate at cross-purposes or are out of phase with each other and considerable conflict within institutions is readily observable. Of all segments of the population youth, who are attempting to establish a stable identity and personal direction, are most severely affected by cultural incoherence, decay, and transformation.

Although it is hard to demonstrate empirically, it is very plausible, then, to argue that the emergence and spread of an "alienated" youth culture in the sixties was not simply a functional adaptation by "the system" or some ordinary expression of youthful faddishness and exuberance, but rather an expression and a catalyst for profound cultural disintegration and transformation. If intellectual and "uncommitted" youth were the innovative agents of this cultural change, they were agents because they were least able to accept or be accepted by conventional peer society and, therefore, most vulnerable to cultural strain and most ready for cultural change. If out argument is correct, the problem of identity for youth in our society is not at all marginal or peripheral. It is the direct result of central social and cultural changes that impinge on youth of all strata and character types.

THE EMERGENCE OF STUDENT RADICAL ACTIVISM

The United States has not been as hospitable to left-wing anticapitalist political and social movements as some industrial societies have been. Populist and socialist movements have had a major impact on national and local politics and social reform during some periods, but invariably, the political system and economic growth have had the capacity to absorb and integrate such movements before they could establish permanent roots in the working class or other sectors. As a result, Americans have been relatively a political: generally, they supported the political system and typically, they have not linked their personal troubles to the need for major social and political change.

Against this background, it is not at all surprising that the emergent cultural alienation among youth during the fifties should reflect the political indifference that was then general in the society as a whole. Political privatism of the young intellectuals in the fifties was further heightened and reinforced by a mood of conservatism and political pessimism that prevailed among previously politicized adult intellectuals and academics. One source of this mood was the disillusioning effect of Stalinism on the American left, which had become a political factor during the Depression of the thirties. Another source was the conviction that, whatever flaws American culture might possess, the society was relatively humane when placed in the context of fascist and Stalinist barbarism. This mood also stemmed from the wide public attack during the fifties on liberals and intellectuals, as conservative politicians used anticommunist crusades as a means for undermining the mood of social reform that had developed during the Depression and war years. Finally, postwar prosperity led many intellectuals to feel that the basic ideological issues of industrial society had dissolved, and that the very grounds for political conflict and mobilization in the United States no longer existed.

During the late fifties, every observer of the American campus was likely to comment on the surprising political indifference of American students. Most went on to predict that this apathy was likely to continue, because the society offered a wide array of economic opportunities and because these youths had been reared in a society of general affluence that they expected to attain if not to surpass. It seemed natural that young people, however discontented they might feel with certain aspects of the quality of American life, would not risk their highly promising futures by undertaking political dissent or protest.

In retrospect, a major factor in generating student political disaffiliation probably was the absence of uncorrupted models of effective political action. The Communist Party and its associated political structure, which had mobilized many students during the thirties and forties, had been entirely discredited by such events as the Khrushchev revelations about the Stalin era and the invasion of Hungary. Liberal political organizations and the labour movement, which had also won the support of considerable numbers of students in earlier generations, now seemed bureaucratic and largely quiescent. The faculty and other intellectuals were either highly cautious or cynical about political activism of any sort. Everyday electoral politics appeared either to be devoid of moral content or seriously corrupted. The critical mood that prevailed in the emerging campus intellectual sub-culture could not be stably contained in a posture of social withdrawal, especially since many intellectual youth, as we have pointed out, had been raised to have a sense of social responsibility. Nevertheless, there were no means of political expression that were both effective and morally valid.

Then, on February 2, 1960, four Negro students in Greensboro, North Carolina "sat-in" at a segregated lunch counter. Almost immediately, the sit-in movement spread throughout the South, as hundreds of black students found a way of directly undermining segregation in public facilities. Within a short time, a black student movement took form in the South. In uneasy alliance with the minister-based non-violent movement led by Martin Luther King, the black students created a broad, many-pronged movement against legal segregation and for full citizenship for southern Negroes.

Almost immediately, a response to southern sit-ins was heard on a number of northern campuses. White students picketed local branches of five-and-ten-cent stores that practiced segregation in the South. Support groups for the Student Non-violent Co-ordinating Committee sprouted on many campuses, and white students began to trek South to participate in freedom rides, voter registration campaigns, and other supportive activities.

It is not entirely clear why sit-ins "triggered" white young radicalism. Evidence suggests that those who responded to this movement were members of the campus intellectual sub-culture. Why did the sit-ins have such an impact on young white "intellectuals"?

First, the sit-ins were a very dramatic demonstration of the major failure of America's democratic claims—failure to guarantee the constitutional rights and elementary conditions of citizenship of southern Negroes. This failure and the profound injustices that were its results were a crystallization not only of the more abstract discontents that intellectual youths felt about the moral hypocrisies of the society but about its political stagnation as well. Also they highlighted the *privileged*-position of white students dramatically: since many student intellectuals had been reared with considerable guilt about their status and disdained material success, such a demonstration was particularly compelling for them.

Second, the sit-ins occurred in the context of international events in which students played an effective role in shaping history. Recently, students had overthrown military dictatorships in Turkey and South Korea through militant street demonstrations; they had blocked the visit of President Eisenhower to Japan, and they had played a central role in the victorious Cuban revolution.

The sit-ins and the black student movement seemed to be part of a general historical process in which students, *acting in their role as students,* han become effective agents of social change. Instead of waiting, for leadership from other elements in the society to promote social reform, students themselves could actually have historical effects.

Third, the sit-ins and the southern movement as a whole involved the use of profoundly moral means to attain profoundly moral ends. Indeed, rarely has there been a social movement in which means and ends were so intimately connected. The civil rights movement seemed free of the brutality, manipulation, and callousness that political action had been assumed to require during the fifties.

Forms of pacifist direct action that SNCC, King, and other civil rights leaders advocated and practiced were seen by white intellectual students as ways of living one's values and simultaneously changing the world. They seemed to be genuine breakthroughs beyond the classic dilemma of *moral purity v. practical action.* Moreover, one could be for civil rights without being concerned with the generalized political ideology and thereby avoid all the sour dilemmas of cold war politics.

Fourth, the five-and-dime picketing brought student intellectuals together around a political issues and generated social interaction over political and social problems. Once such groups became aware of their capacity for collective action, it was quite unlikely that they would dissipate. The concept of the student as an agent of social change, modeled on the actions of Latin American and Asian student movements, took root very quickly.

It is useful to consider the American student movement as having passed through roughly three major phases. Each phase was quite distinct from the previous one in many respects; each new phase was the result largely of the interaction between the movement and the political authority structure. In each phase, the movement grew in size and scope, become more radical ideologically, and more militant tactically.

I now review these phases schematically. This is not the place for a detailed or fully rounded history of the American student movement. Rather my analysis is designed to see how its development was associated with historical events and processes to which students reacted.

Phase I: Pacifism, Protest, and Reform, 1960-64

As I have suggested, during the first years of the sixties, increasing numbers of white students became involved in the civil rights movement. The most dramatic forms of commitment were displayed by the hundreds who "went South" to join the struggle directly as actionists and organizers. Hundreds of other students worked in northern ghettoes in tutorial programmes and direct action campaigns against job and housing discrimination. Throughout these years, the appeal of the civil rights cause was based not only on the just aims of the movement, but on the perception of the black actionists as saintly heroes who received harsh brutality but returned love, and who were viewed as the conscience of the nation.

In these years, non-violent direct action and passive resistance were seen as radical weapons in a struggle for social reform. On the one hand, they appeared as tactically appropriate means for a physically weak minority to force society to fulfill its professed ideals. On the other hand, pacifist action projected a vision of society in which the threat and use of force could be replaced by exchange and co-operation as the basis for social relations. Finally, passive resistance and civil disobedience were appealing because they could be employed effectively by small groups and by individuals and because they enabled the activist to act effectively without having to wait for collective decisions to sanction his actions.

Direct-action tactics applied by small groups of pacifists to issues other than civil rights paralleled the non-violent civil rights movement. In particular, a movement opposed to her arms race, nuclear testing, civil defense and other manifestations of the cold war was gaining widespread support. This loosely organized movement in which students from "intellectual" campuses such as Harvard, Swarthmore, Michigan, and Brandeis played an active role relied largely on mass marches, vigils, and other forms of legal protest. Some civil disobedience occurred—for example radical pacifists attempted to board Polaris submarines and to sail small boats into nuclear testing areas while New York college students defied civil authority by refusing to take part in civil defense shelter drills. In 1962, hundreds of students became invoved in congressional campaigns of "peace" candidates—the most dramatic being the third party senatorial campaign of Harvard Professor H. Stuart Hughes in Massachusetts.

During these years, small groups of campus intellectuals intensively debated the viability of student political activism as a basis for a general "new politics" in the United States. Within a year after the southern sit-ins had begun, numerous little magazines and campus political discussion groups had sprouted at major universities and colleges. Several interrelated themes were topics of all these discussions: the need for intellectuals to become politically engaged, the inadequacy of classical political ideologies and categories for guiding political action, and the need for new theory or ideology to provide a general social analysis and critique and the basis for a new political programme.

By 1962, interest in developing a general political thrust among students had led to formation of the Students for a Democratic Society that announced its hope for what it called a "new left" (a term that its founders had borrowed from a comparable British group of radicals who had broken with both communist and traditional labour politics) and issued a manifesto containing many of the elements for constructing a new radicalism.

In its beginnings, the new left neither envisioned a mass student movement nor imagined that students, by themselves, would be primary agents of social change. Instead it hoped for an alliance for social reform that would combine elements of the labour movement, liberal political reformers, the civil rights movement, liberal churches and students and intellectuals—a movement that would use both direct action and the electoral process to build a political base for achieving racial equality, eliminating domestic poverty, ending the arms race and the cold war, and building a more democratically organized social order. These early student activists defined their on-campus role as educating their fellow students to the need for political engagement and support of civil rights and other off-campus reform movements. For them, the most virtuous role for the student activist was seen as getting off the campus and becoming involved directly in "real" social problems.

The early new left's optimism about the possibilities for societal reform was reinforced by its perception of the Kennedy administration. Admiration of John Kennedy as president was a factor less important than was the belief that his administration would be necessarily responsive to the pressure for reform being applied by Negroes, labour, and the universities (obviously, the administration's political base depended heavily on these constituencies). Essentially, the early young radicals believed in the necessity and efficacy of grassroots pressure in impelling established institutions and the government to move in progressive directions.

Research on the social origins of the early student activists strongly supports our view that, overwhelmingly, they were sons and daughters of "intellectual" and liberal parents who saw the activity of their offspring as fulfilling, rather than rebelling against, their families' tradition of social concern. Typically, they shared with their parents a reverence of the university; like their parents, they found organized religion an inadequate source of values, and perhaps even more than their parents, they identified the university as the sole established institution in the society that could facilitate the search for new values and meanings and help define a morally coherent and humanistic way of life. Far from wishing to destroy the university, radical students were among the most committed to its fulfillment as a central institution in their lives. Many expected eventually to end up as university faculty or as intellectuals associated with the academic community; they hoped it would become a place hospitable to the grassroots movements for change with which they also identified.

Activist students sustained many sharp disillusionments during the Kennedy years. The Cuban invasion, the missile crisis, and other incidents of great international tension. These events seemed to confirm the view—enunciated several years before by the maverick sociologist C. Wright Mills—that enormous power, including the power to destroy humanity, was vested in the hands of a tiny group of men who were substantially irresponsible, and that this situation was intolerable. A further source of disillusionment was the federal government's posture in relation to the civil rights movement in the South. The Justice Department often was extremely cautious or negligent about protecting the persons and rights of civil rights workers and about enforcing elementary constitutional rights in the deep South. Moreover, the Kennedy forces refused to mount a frontal attack to challenge the power of southern segregationists within the Democratic Party and in Congress.

Such disillusionments were balanced by certain positive trends. By the summer of 1963, the United States and the Soviet Union were moving toward a detente symbolized by the nuclear test ban agreement, and the undertone of President Kennedy's speeches represented a marked departure from traditional cold war rhetoric. At the same time, a reform coalition for civil rights and domestic equality—symbolized by the massive march on Washington, in August 1963—seemed to be emerging. At the time of Kennedy's assassination in November, 1963, his death did not appear to affect this general situation.

In Lyndon Johnson's first year as president, many of the legislative demands of the civil rights movement were enacted, and a general war on poverty was announced. A period of domestic reform seemed definitely in process. Furthermore, a relaxation of the threat of nuclear war was evident.

During 1963 and 1964, thousands of students became actively involved in the reform effort. Thousands attempted to relate to northern urban ghettoes, to Appalachia, and to the campaign in the South to build black political strength. Thousands volunteered for the Peace Corps. At the time, many of these voluenteers hopefully defined the Corps as a possible replacement of military conscription and intervention overseas. Such volunteer commitments were sponsored by institutions such as government agencies and private foundations. Involvements that were more politically focused and activist were mobilized by SNCC, SDS, and other radical and civil rights groups.

In 1964, these efforts culminated in the Mississippi Summer Project, which attracted at least 1,000 northern white students for fulltime voter registration and related activity in some of the most oppressed counties in the United States. At the beginning of the summer, three volunteers were murdered by a racist gang; still, student volunteers worked throughout the summer, and many stayed on for a longer period.

Creation of an integrated alternative to the segregated Mississippi Democratic party was one aspect of strategy involved in the Mississippi campaign. It was hoped that the Freedom Democrats could win recognition as the official Mississippi delegation to the Democratic convention. Mainly, the campaign ended in bitter disillusionment. Students were shocked by their first-hand experience with southern justice and rural poverty. Black activists were disturbed by the white students' tendency to dominate and patronize. Ultimately, many participants concluded that the cause of black self-determination was one that blacks must control and from which whites must be excluded as coequal participants.

Both black and white civil rights activities were deeply embittered by failure of the Democratic Convention in Atlantic City in August, 1964 to recognize the effort for which they had risked so much; they were particularly embittered by liberal

Democrats who had taken the lead in urging them to compromise their political goals in the interest of Democratic Party unity.

For many members of the growing student and black movements, this Democratic Convention represented a profound turning point. Four years of effort to galvanize established liberal and moderate political efforts for fundamental reform within the framework of the formal political system and to form a national coalition of labour, blacks and liberals had not produced the desired effects. Goals of southern civil rights had been legislated on paper, but the realization of these goals, in terms of full citizenship for the black population, seemed as far off as it ever had been.

By summer 1964, black protest had moved to the urban North and violent insurrection had overshadowed non-violent direct action. Early new leftists had realized that the only alternative to taking to the streets was a broadly based political movement that would directly challenge the entrenched power of racist, commercial, militarist, and reactionary interests that effectively blocked the socio-economic changes necessary for racial equality. Labour and liberal leadership had the capacity to mobilize such a movement, but by 1964 this possibility seemed far less likely than it had when the decade opened.

Parenthetically. it is interesting to note that the "new politics" advocated by the new left in the early sixties was not seriously undertaken until the 1968 presidential primaries, when a few liberal politicians embodied this concept. Significantly, thousands of youths enthusiastically participated in the McCarthy and Kennedy campaigns.

Had the new politics been mobilized four years earlier, patterns of youth behaviour might well have taken a fundamentally different path. Instead, as the summer of '64 ended, the most actively engaged student activists felt a deepening sense of frustration with and isolation from established institutions.

Moreover, as the southern struggle for desegregation and civil rights culminated, the black movement entered a new phase. Its youthful wing oriented increasingly toward black urban ghetto youth and away from integration, non-violence and simple visions of brotherhood and the beloved community.

Black militants had become disillusioned not only with the political system, but with white students as necessary collaborators. Their message to the white new left: don't keep organizing us, make your own struggle for social change among your own people. Thus, by the end of 1964 many of the initial assumptions and modes of action of the emerging white student movement had been substantially undermined by the pressure of external events.

Phase II: Confrontation, Radicalization, and Resistance, 1964—68

The 1964—65 academic year began under dramatic circumstances. As the Berkeley campus of the University of California, thousands of students engaged in rallies, sit-ins and other demonstrations to protest administration maneuvering to prevent the use of a strip of university-owned sidewalk by the political groups for the purpose of recruiting participants for off-campus political action.

The Free Speech Movement was the first large-scale mass movement of students to use direct action to change the policies of university administrators. It represented a successful effort to utilize the tactics and spirit of the civil rights movement in relation to university issues. The FSM culminated in a mass seizure of the administration building at Berkeley by a mass of students, establishment of a "free university" in the building that lasted for many hours, clearance of the building by the state highway patrol at the governor's order, ond arrest of approximately 800 students. These events were followed by a university-wide strike and a vote by the Faculty Senate to meet the basic demands of the FSM.

Berkeley had a profoundly transforming effect on the students movement for several reasons. First, it demonstrated that although committed activists might comprise only a small fraction of the student body on a day-to-day basis, most students can be persuaded to join actions that they define as being in their interest. Furthermore, it was clear that at Berkeley the sub-culture that provided the immediate constituency of the movement had grown substantially in a relatively short time.

Second, the public impact of Berkeley suggested that the campus was not irrelevant to major social conflict, as most new leftists had assumed, but might well be a major arena of struggle. Berkeley dramatized the fact that the university had itself been transformed during the fifties and was now intimately and fundamentally connected to the major centers of power and political initiative in the larger society: It was an important element in the defense establishment, its educational function was decisive in providing the manpower to operate the corporate and governmental organizational structure; its policies regarding admissions, personnel, curriculum, and research had substantial effects on change related to blacks and other ethnic minorities; and its internal life and administrative structure symbolized the general social consequences of bureaucratization just as the gap between its rhetorically proclaimed ideals and its actual practice typified the chasm between the ideal and the real that prevailed in the society as a whole. Such a representation was particularly painful to intellectual, socially concerned students, who, as we have seen, had hoped that the university would symbolize an *alternative* to the prevailing culture and social order, rather than merely reflect and submit to dominant values, trends and interests.

The Berkeley FSM and the enormous amount of discussion and analysis that it generated dramatized for the new left the possibility that one did not have to go South or into the ghetto to confront the basic problems of society. Indeed, as black activists had argued, it might be more authentic to fight one's own battles on one's own turf. Not incidentally, such a changed perspective was reinforced by the startling observation that such a tactic could be more effective in gaining student participation than off-campus actions had been. For less politicized students. Berkeley served to raise fundamental questions about the nature of university education. As we have seen, in addition to the committed activists, a rather broad group of students confronted basic problems of value and identity. Perhaps to many of them it had been obvious that university education was quite inadequate in helping them cope with such issues, but that something might be done to change the situation had not been.

After Berkeley, "university reform" activities swept through

American campuses. Some of these were sparked by the organized new left, but most were not. In the period immediately following the confrontation at Berkeley, such activity did not take the form primarily of overt protest; instead, "free universities" and other experimental educational activity became widespread, student political parties were formed and petitions circulated, and rallies and picket lines became commonplace as students pressed for a greater voice in university governance and sought an end to restrictive regulations on social life and political activity.

Meanwhile, in early 1965, the Johnson administration initiated the systematic bombing of North Vietnam and sent American combat troops into South Vietnam in force. The Tonkin Gulf bombings and congressional resolutions of August 1964 had confirmed intimations that the war would be escalated, and on many major campuses, concern and debate about Vietnam increased—a concern that had been sparked considerably by several leading academic figures. Almost immediately after escalation became a fact, faculty and student groups on a large number of campuses initiated teach-ins that were prolonged, intense discussions and debates about Vietnam and were aimed at stimulating a national process of debate over administration war policy. SDS called for a national student march on Washington in April, 1965, and much to the surprise of the organizers, some 25,000 students participated—by far, the largest national student protest activity in the United States since the 1930s. In a short time, a "university perspective" of the war had developed. This prospective—based partially on the intensive analyses of Vietnam and foreign policy specialists and partially on careful reading of major newspaper reports on Vietnam—incorporated the following convictions: the war was fundamentally a civil war in which the United States had neither the moral right nor the practical capacity to successfully intervene; United States intervention was illegal under international agreements and the United States Constitution; United States military activity and bombing involved an immoral devastation of civilians; the United States was siding with a brutal military regime that had no popular base against an insurgent nationalist movement that did and that such a stance was both impractical and immoral; and United States interests were not involved in Vietnam and even if they were, the most hardheaded analysis would show that any gains for United States interests would be offset by the damage to our international position that prolonged involvement would entail. Not only did the administration and its spokesmen rarely deal with the substance of these analyses, but often, administration claims and arguments were falsified by journalistic reports and subsequent events.

Instead of responding to rising protest in a positive fashion, the administration steadily escalated its involvement in the war. Increasingly, both students and distinguished professors questioned the rationality, veracity, and democratic responsiveness of the administration. Mass public rallies steadily increased in size, and on campus, bitterness with the administration grew. Increasingly, the new left argued that the war was not an "error" of policy, but a built-in consequence of the imperialist-militarist organization of American society. Increasingly, such arguments were received attentively by less politicized university people. Meanwhile, the American domestic crisis was dramatized and intensified by an accelerating number of ghetto riots and by an increasingly militant rhetoric and organizational thrust in the black community. The war and the military priority were identified more and more on campus as major barriers to urgently needed domestic social reform.

For increasing numbers of students, especially the activists, these events were having a radicalizing effect. In this context, radicalization meant, above all, a shift in the definition of the political situation away from the view that popular protest and pressure could lead toward positive change and toward the view that the dominant elites were not open to democratic pressure, that they exercized authority illegitimately, and that trust could not be placed in conventional political processes. In this situation, changes in tactics were felt to be urgent. Domestic costs of waging war had to be raised—particularly the costs of mobilizing young men to fight the war. Furthermore, the illegitimate character of the was justified and necessitated forms of civil disobedience that would force the authorities to choose between violent repression of dissent or accommodation to it. Such confrontation could also expose to uncommitted people the underlying brutality of the society's managers.

A major precipitant of such radicalization occurred in the Spring of 1966, when Selective Service Director Lewis Hershey announced that student deferments from the draft would henceforth be based on the academic standing of students. This decision (which, ironically, was never implemented) occurred in the context of startling revelations about the involvement of universities in government-sponsored covert intelligence operations in Vietnam and elsewhere and in research on germ warfare and other weapons as well as in dramatic exposes about the penetration of the CIA into domestic student and academic organizations and activities.

For student radicals, university complicity with militarism offered the opportunity to combine student power and antiwar entergies and of implementing a strategy of resistance to the war within the institutions of society. On campus, occupation of administration buildings on many campuses served to urge universities to refuse to comply with draft board demands for student class rankings. Almost overnight, the draft became a major issue on campus. Students quickly became conscious of the use of Selective Service as an instrument for channeling youth educationally and vocationally. They perceived conscription as a primary source of competitive pressure among youth and as a mechanism for caste-like stratification of the youth population. The idea of resistance to the draft spread rapidly; by Spring, 1967, hundreds of draft cards had been burned or turned back to draft boards and the number of young men who publicly refused to serve was rising. Public opinion polls indicated that the majority of graduating seniors were contemplating either evading the draft or refusing to recognize its legitimacy; thousands of youths sought to emigrate to Canada rather than face the draft.

Meanwhile, campus confrontations concerning university relations to military institutions became commonplace. Students worked to block military and defense industry recruitment on campus and disrupted university functions in protest over war-related research.

In October, 1967, nearly 100,000 youthful demonstrators converged on the Pentagon. The rising spirit of resistance to the war was symbolized by these demonstrators who sat down illegally on the Pentagon steps and were met with a night of mass arrests and occasionally brutal beatings. Simultaneously, in Oakland, California thousands of students spent a week disrupting the functioning of the Induction Center. Their actions were highlighted by overt resistance to the police, mobile street tactics, and barricades. The temper of the campuses had become so bitter that few administration officials could peacefully address college audiences; the president could not appear in public without almost certain exposure to hostile demonstrations.

Since the advent of Vietnam protests, the organized student left had grown enormously. The SDS, which had barely 20 functioning chapters in 1963, was represented on at least 350 campuses by 1968 and claimed a participating membership in the tens of thousands.

A *Fortune Magazine* survey conducted in late 1968 suggested that about 10 per cent of the total American student body identified with the new left. On each major campus, hundreds of students were ready to be mobilized for mass actions and thousands more typically empathized with their positions, although they avoided or opposed disruptive demonstrations and direct confrontations.

Underlying the intensifying radicalization and militance were continuing escalation of the war and the growing conviction that disruption was the only method of effecting a change in policy or, at least, of galvanizing moderate political forces into opposition to the war. Radicalization was reinforced by instances of arbitrary and brutal police activity against demonstrations. Moreover, as increasing numbers of youth adopted the styles and orientations of the youth culture and used drugs, they were met with police harassment and public abuse. By 1966, the protest-folk music and hard rock styles had fused, and the sounds and lyrics that were most widely popular contained increasingly heavy undertones of alienation and hostility. Many a political youths were attracted by the new music and by drugs. As their identification with the youth culture increased, so did their identification with one or another from of cultural alienation or political opposition.

Leading spokesmen and gurus of the youth culture continued to derogate political protest and emphasize the superiority of "dropping out" and "doing your own thing"; many a political youth undoubtedly agreed. Thus, a certain tension within the youth culture persisted between "politicoes" and "hippies", although the radicalization of the latter and the hair of the former were evidently growing.

By the spring of 1968, the situation seemed likely to change. The antiwar candidacy of Eugene McCarthy and the emergence of Bobby Kennedy in direct oppostion to Johnson led to the latter's withdrawal from the presidential race and an outpour of student involvement in the primary races. McCarthy's "children crusade" was composed of many adherents of the new left, but primarily it was not an alternative to the streets—as the candidate liked to fancy. Rather, it represented involvement in politics of tens of thousands of students who had not been activists before.

But hopes for a "new politics" within the American mainstream were soon dashed by the assassination of its two most charismatic proponents—Martin Luther King, Jr. and Robert Kennedy—and the evident strength of Richard Nixon and Hubert Humphrey within the regular party machinery. The primary results provided evidence that public opinion favoured an end to the Vietnam war, but the political system seemed organized to prevent the reflection of such popular opinion in presidential nominees and party platforms.

Meanwhile, a revolt of black students and SDS at Columbia University resuled in the prolonged seizure of several university buildings and a rhetorical militance unprecedented on American campuses. The Columbia militants proclaimed revolutionary objectives (rather than university reform or student power) as their real intentions. They were met by a particularly brutal police response, the ferocity of which stunned the attentive academic community across the country. The Columbia events were followed shortly in time by the French general strike that was catalyzed by Columbia-like building seizures at the Sorbonne and other universities and fierce street-fighting in the Latin Quarter. The fact that a student uprising could set off a general strike and threaten the De Gaulle regime reinforced the already developing revolutionary consciousness of many new left activists in the United States.

Once again a Democratic Party presidential convention marked a major turning point for the new radicalism of the sixties. The slim possibility that the convention might recognize the antiwar movement in its platform and candidacies provided hope for more moderate youth. Others thought that the candidates might be swayed by massive street demonstrations. More radical activists agreed on the desirability of mass demonstrations, but mainly as a way of dramatizing the undemocratic character of the political system. By the time of the Convention, fears of a "bloodbath" kept thousands away from Chicago; the relatively small number who came were met by an extremely brutal and repressive police response that was fully and internationally telecast.

As 1968 drew to a close, it was clear that discontent and radicalization permeated both the campus and the black ghettoes. The opportunities the year had presented to channel this discontent back into the political system had been lost. As youthful rebelliousness increased, so did hostility toward it. Radicalism among white youth was still predominantly the expression of those with intellectual origins and aspirations, but the events of the previous eight years had demonstrated that this segment of youth was far more extensive than anyone had previously thought and far more capable of having an impact on wider circles of young people than new left ideologues had, for the most part, imagined. That impact was, in large measure, a consequence of the general cultural crisis of American society, but its profound *radicalization* was attributable to the incapacity of established liberal and moderate forces to promote effective social reform. The failure of reform had several interrelated consequences.

First, and most important, it was central to the delegitimation of the political system and of established authority generally. To accept a political system—especially when its outcomes run counter to the interests of one's group—requires that it convincingly demonstrate its openness and potential responsiveness to personal grievances, demands and aspirations. This is especially pressing at a time of crisis, when many individuals feel that their very lives are endangered by a continuation of existing policies. That reform-minded politicians and administrators repeatedly called upon youth to "work within the system" was not helpful to maintaining its overall legitimacy when efforts to do so were met with total rejection in a context of urgency and many moderate leaders seemed unready to take the necessary political risks to improve the chances for positive change. All of this was symbolized very clearly by the Democratic convention of 1968.

A second consequence of the failure of reform is that it sharpened generational conflict. A historically validated generalization is that generational revolt is most likely to occur when *adult* political reform movement and activity is weak. Generational conflict expressed through collective action is neither inevitable nor the result of repressed Oedipal impulses. The history of the new left in the United States, and student movements elsewhere, suggests that *hostility toward the older generation becomes fully manifest when substantial segments of the adult generation do not use available opportunities to oppose the existing regime and to promote social reform. When adult reform movements are vigorously active, youth are more likely to join them than to seek independent means of political expression.*

Phase III: Beyond Student Protest

Trends in youth consciousness evident in 1968—increasing politicization and radicalization—continued and the student movement underwent further transformations during 1969 and 1970.

First, the organization and militance of black youth crystallized in two ways. On many campuses, the increasing number of black youths at major universities resulted in the formation of militant and disciplined Black Student Unions, which used the threat of disruption and the guilt of white faculty and administrators to win concessions with respect to cultural recognition for blacks within university curricula, a measure of black student control over relevant university resources, and positive changes in university admissions and hiring policies to increase black participation. Meanwhile, in the urban ghettoes, the Black Panther Party spread its influence among school and street youth in the direction of "armed self-defense" against police occupation and explicitly revolutionary organization within the black community.

The new left, from its inception, had followed the leadership of the black youth movements; in this instance, the impact of the BSU and the Panther Party was to reinforce and intensify the developing revolutionary mood among organized student radicals.

But it was far easier to express a revolutionary mood through rhetoric, posters, and other symbolic means than it was to work out its concrete political meaning. In this period, SDS broke into extremely hostile factions as it tried to cope with the following ironic situation: its constituency among youth appeared very large and growing, but many SDS ideologues mistrusted the "revolutionary commitment" of youth; on the other hand, it was clear that revolutionary spirit was restricted to youth and no basic social transformation could occur without the support or acceptance of the majority of Americans. Out of this dilemma arose factions that differed sharply over the relevance of the youth revolt to "revolution", over the relevance of the industrial working class, and over other fundamental issues of strategy and tactics. The outcome of this internal conflict in the new left was the demise of SDS as a national organization. By summer of 1970, no national organization had the capacity to speak for white radicals or to mobilize radical activism.

Meanwhile, mass confrontations on the campus were becoming increasingly costly for participants as a result of severe police attacks, court sentences, and suspensions and expulsions from the schools.

During the 1969—70 school year, despite the dissolution of the organized new left and despite the increased costs of protests, the scope and intensity of student and youth protest reached its peak. Student protest tended to shift from the campus to the surrounding youth "ghettoes", and street fighting, "trashing", and burning became visibly more prevalent than non-violent civil disobedience was. An underground composed of small guerilla-like bands emerged, claiming responsibility for a growing wave of bombings of military installations, corporate headquarters, banks, and ROTC buildings. Police and national guard occupations and terrorization of campuses and youth ghettoes became increasingly common.

Dissatisfaction during the 1970 school year culminated in the Cambodian invasion, an event that sparked an unprecedented nationwide strike of students. The strike was spurred by the killing of students in Ohio and Mississippi by national guardsmen and police. The national strike revealed the extent of student opposition to the war and disaffection with the political system as hundreds of schools were closed for several days and hundreds of thousands of previously inactive students took part in an enormous variety of strike-related activity, jointed by thousands of faculty members and in some cases even by the staffs of school administrations. Most of this activivy was essentially non-violent and non-confrontational—it involved an enormous amount of lobbying, canvassing and other efforts to reach out beyond the campus to the presumably anti-student public. But confrontation and violence did occur on a substantial proportion of campuses during the weeks of striking—including campuses that had previously experienced little or no overt unrest.

By the end of the school year, several things were evident. The campus shift to the left on war—and on other issues as well—was massive. At the same time, there seemed to be a rising tide of public hostility to students, hippies, and protesters—a hostility assiduously exploited by the Administration and by local politicians. Finally, it appeared that students, acting as students, could have an effect on national policy: for instance, it was widely believed that the Cambodian invasion was limited by the intensity of the youthful reaction to it—but this effect was modest considering the emotion, energy, and organization that had given rise to the national strike.

By the summer of 1970, many believed that the universities and the government were on a collision course and that growing civil strife was in the offing. Many expected that the new school year would bring an escalation of the campus crisis, the closing of universities, more youth rioting, and deaths. As the congressional election campaign heated up, certain politicians used the "students" and "law and order" as prime issues, and columnists widely predicted conservative electoral triumphs because of adult backlash. Prior to the elections, it seemed that the public was about to give a mandate to escalated repression of dissent, of universities, and of youth.

In fact, however, such a mandate was not forthcoming from the electorate. Many "law and order" candidates were defeated; Congress remained firmly in Democratic control; and

Democrats swept gubernatorial contests in many states. In California, Governor Ronald Reagan, who had based much of his political thrust for several years on a hardline policy toward students and the university, was returned to office with a significantly reduced margin of victory and despite weak opposition. At the same time, the Democrats took control of the California legislature. In short, the 1970 elections suggested that a politics of repression did not have sufficient appeal to the electorate to offset public concern with more personally urgent economic issues or to fundamentally disrupt conventional voting patterns.

Meanwhile, a new mood seemed to be emerging on the campus and among youth generally. As the Fall semester of 1970 opened, the sense of imminent revolution seemed to be receding. Among young radicals, there was increasing criticism of bombing and other guerilla activity and an increasing tendency to seek forms of political action that would bridge the isolation of the Movement from other sectors of the population. As opinion polls showed growing public opposition to the war and growing popular anxiety over the economy, many Movement adherents argued that violent tactics were self-defeating. They contended that radicalized youth had more in common with discontented adults than had previously been thought, but that these potential allies were alienated by campus confrontation and terrorism. Even the Weathermen—the undergrounds SDS faction that had been claiming credit for many major bombings—confessed to having over-emphasized the military dimension of the struggle and called for a new strategy that would emphasize organizing and educating uncommitted people.

These changes in the perspectives of organized radicals were comparable to changes in the more general campus mood. Many concerned students had come to feel that both "peaceful protest" and "revolution now" strategies were either futile or counter-productive. As a result, there was a noticeable withdrawal of many from active political participation, a decline in dramatic protest activity, and a shift away from action to introspection, self-expression and privatism.

Many interpreted the decline of student militance as a result of repression—that is, the strict enforcement of legal penalties against civil disobedience, an increase in the use of force against demonstrators, and an increase in the covert surveillance of the campus by police agencies. But it would be too simple to assert that students were fearfully retreating in the face of overwhelming force.

The force was undoubtedly there, and there is no question that radical activists felt increasingly threatened, restricted, and spied upon and that many left-oriented students increasingly wondered whether expressions of overt dissidence were worth the possible personal consequences, but countertendencies were also evident. For example, as I have suggested, hard-line politicians were not winning the expected popular support. There was little evidence of a building public consensus in favour of a harsh crackdown; in fact, the concern of the "silent majority" was far more evidently directed against the war and unemployment than it was against the protesters.

Furthermore, government efforts at repression were less than uniformly effective. Public exposure of undercover surveillance activity by the army and the FBI led to widespread opposition to such government practices. In several crucial trials of Black Panthers and other militants, juries refused to return convictions. A rising tide of vocal criticism of the Justice Department, the FBI, and the police was emanating from Congress, the media, and other centers of established opinion. In the summer of 1970, after Cambodia, Kent State, Jackson State, and so forth, virtually all observers assumed that the youth and the state were on a frightening collision course and that the adult majority was lining up behind the state. A year later, it appeared that the collision had temporarily been averted. Presumably, the threat of social disaster had resulted in reconsideration on all sides.

Young activists began an intense process of reassessment of strategy and tactics. The wides mass of disaffected youth remained deeply mistrustful of established authority and the political system, but many continued to hope for an answer from within the system.

As I write this, it appears that several new developments are likely to be decisive in shaping the future of radicalism and youth politics in America. Among these are: the rise of youth "ghettoes"; the emergence of organized resistance in the military; the sharp constriction of employment opportunities for college-educated youth; the 18 year old vote; a renewed interest among radicals in both electoral politics and non-violent direct action; the Women's Liberation Movement; and signs of renewed militance among workers. I will consider some probable consequences of these developments.

Before we try to look into the future however, it seems necessary that some of the implications of the history of student protest I have just tried to sketch be considered. So, by way of summary and interpretation here are some general propositions about the rise of student radicalism in the sixties that seem to be derivable from the historical sketch I have drawn:

1. Political radicalism among American youth was rooted in the rise of a new social stratum—the mass intellegentsia whose social position, shared values, and personal aspirations made them unusually ready for political activism and social reformism. Thus, an overwhelming number of the first white youths to become activated in the sixties had been born into this stratum and raised to be socially concerned.

2. Students born into older social strata were activated early in the sixties to the extent that (a) they aspired to become members of the Intelligentsia; (b) they shared problems of identity similar to those of "intellectual" youth. Many more students had these characteristics than most researchers had realized.

3. Grouping of large masses of youth in large universities was a critical structural condition for mass politicization and radicalism. This situation freed youth to devote time and energy to social issues. It created an excellent opportunity for intense interaction over such issues and for the development of a broad collective consciousness concerning such issues. Furthermore, the universities served as political microcosms within which political conflict could be conducted on scale small enough so that individuals and small groups could feel that they were having effects. Furthermore, the increasing centrality of the universities to the functioning of the society as a

whole meant that such local conflicts had a wide social and historical impact.

4. Thus, in retrospect, rise of a student movement and emergence of internal conflict within the university seem to have been an inevitable consequence of the creation of a system of a mass higher education. The student movement, in its early phase, did not enunciate revolutionary aims, and it was decidedly an expression of a minority of the student body. It is therefore plausible that both the student movement and the "intellectual" youth culture *could* have been incorporated as "functional" components of the ongoing system and served as sources of creative tension to facilitate the progressive modernization of education, politics and mass culture, while restricted in membership to a minority and managed to prevent extreme polarization. Instead, however, an initially reformist movement became avowedly revolutionary; an initially "deviant" sub-culture became the dominant one on the campus.

5. These transformations of the student movement are a consequence of what may be the single most important development of the sixties in the United States--the decline in the legitimacy of the established political system. An authority structure is legitimate to the extent that those living under it perceive those in authority as deserving of their positions, as rightfully fulfilling their duties, as giving orders that are proper and obligatory, and as capable of being influenced by the use of established procedures. In the United States, the fundamental ground of such legitimacy is the perception that those who govern authentically express the will of the majority, that they protect the rights of minorities, and that their policies will be designed to provide for the progressive improvement of the well-being of the people as a whole.

SOME REASONS FOR DECLINING LEGITIMACY

The delegitimation of national authority is a process that

began among black youth as a consequence of their struggle for constitutionally guaranteed civil rights and for fulfillment of endlessly reiterated promises of economic equality. Despite a continuous stream of pledges, the government repeatedly failed to provide full protection of rights and to implement an effective programme of economic improvement for blacks and other poor people. The emergence of black nationalist and revolutionary ideology in the black community is an advanced symptom of the delegitimation of the established political order in the black community.

White activists in the early sixties experienced much of the same disillusionment with governmental authority as a result of their active involvement in the civil rights and antipoverty struggles. The sharpest disillusionment that both black and white activists experienced, however, was failure of the established coalition of liberal and labour organizations to actively press for fundamental change in governmental policy with respect to civil rights, slums, and unemployment.

The Democratic Convention of 1964 may be taken as a critical watershed; had liberal Democrats actively pressed for the incorporation of the civil rights movement into the party at that time, relations of trust might well have been maintained, and both the black movement and the new left may well have continued to operate (albeit uneasily) within the framework of the established two-party system and regular politics. Instead, that Convention confirmed the growing estrangement of young activists from conventional politics. Out of that period emerged black militance and separatism on the one hand and the independent, confrontational radical student movement on the other.

Obviously, the Vietnam war was the second and even deeper disillusionment. Not only did the war reinforce already brewing mistrust and cleavage between young activists and the "old" liberalism, but created a situation in which *all* forms of non-violent pressure on authority appeared largely futile. *Both* the conventional politics of lobbying, canvassing and voting and the unconventional politics of protest and non-violent civil disobedience failed to reverse the war policies *even when it became clear that withdrawal from Vietnam had the support of the majority of the electorate.* Moreover, the war had other major delegitimating features: the inequitable and coercive draft, the evident "credibility gap", the fact that it had not been declared a war by Congress, the atrocities and barbarities that flowed from the war strategy, and so forth. Probably no single policy in American history has had as disillusioning an impact on American youth as has the decision to prosecute the war.

But the war and the racial crisis—and the implication of the established political structure in the continuation of both—do not exhaust the conditions that helped the delegitimation process. For example, a crisis in "public happiness" was becoming acute (that is, the apparent incapacity of local and national political institutions to effectively deal with such problems as the deterioration of urban life pollution of the natural environment, and the decline in the quality of public services). This problem was critically heightened by the fact that the deterioration of public happiness was occurring in the context of a steadily expanding national economy, rising taxes, and public budgets (that is, material resources for dealing with the crisis seemed abundant). Delegitimation was reinforced by the seeming inability of *any* established leadership group to offer a credible way out.

Finally, delegitimation of authority was accelerated because most leaders in government and other positions were failling to articulate the need for a new cultural framework; they seemed to be primarily responsive to those constituencies most attached to the very traditions that numbers of youth found obsolete. Indeed, political leaders within the system who *did* seem to side with the "new" tended to lose their effectiveness (McCarthy, Hickel, and Lindsay, for instance) and some were killed because they did. As I write this, the "establishment" appears to be experiencing a widening and deepending rift on a variety of issues, yet few observers are predicting that political forces espousing change have much chance of winning effective power in the near future. Both the traditionalism and the divisions of governmental and institutional authority promote delegitimation, especially when those who most profoundly mistrust the present distribution of power can see little chance of improving their effective representation.

One of the critical lessons of the past decade, in my view, is that when significant sectors of the youth are losing trust in established authority, much depends on the actions of established agencies of reform. In the United States, such established agencies have included the labour movement, liberal organizations, and segments of the religious and academic community. These are groups that have the potential of mobilizing significant numbers of adults and substantial amounts of money. To the extent that they can engage in effective mobilization around a credible programme of reform, yotths are likely to participate in such an effort and generational conflict and delegitimation of authority will not be evident. The default of these reformist forces has been an important aspect of the past decade. These forces either tended to resist the demands of youth and Blacks and continued to support established foreign and domestic policies or gave verbal support to change but failed to mobilize a semblance of effective power to bacg up their rhetoric. Even now when for the first time, a significant section of established liberalism is undertaking rather fundamental criticism of certain policies, there is little evidence of effective mobilization in behalf of a programme of change. Simultaneously, many liberal spokesmen call on youth to "return to the system" but offer few grounds for so doing.

As the process of mistrust of authority deepens, those who are actively involved in seeking change feel an increasing need to resort to tactics of extreme pressure. To the extent that they perceive authority as illegitimate, they come to feel morally bound to defy it and morally free from the traditional boundaries of the low. As its legitimacy is overtly challenged, the authority structure increasingly resorts to naked force to suppress such challenges, and as a rule, such resort to force further delegitimates those who use it. Although government is defined as that body which has a monopoly on the means of legitimate violence, the increasing *use* of such violence by the government to suppress internal opposition is a clear sign that its legitimacy is eroding.

As the cycle of popular protest and official violence proceeds, protest leaders begin the serious contemplation of "revolution"—that is, they come to define their mission less as a matter of putting pressure on those in power than as one of overthrowing them. In the atmosphere of crisis, delegitimation of authority, protest, and violence, the revolutionists find a widening circle of receptivity. This, indeed, was the situation in the United States by 1970.

Nevertheless, revolutionary rhetoric and action may well be premature or historically out of place. Just as those in power may exaggerate reliability and support of the underlying population, so revolutionists may misjudge the meaning of delegitimation. Despite deep distrust and skepticism of established authority, most people—even those who are quite alienated—retain some hope that peaceful reform is possible and that all-out warfare between the state and its active opposition can be avoided. Indeed, revolutionary rhetoric and guerilla action can have the paradoxical effect of both intensifying mass desire for change *and* heightening mass fears of total breakdown, chaos, and repression. It is clear that throughout the sixties and despite their increasing sympathy for radical change, both black groups and student groups were highly responsive to leaders (Kennedy, McCarthy, and Ralph Nader, for instance) who seemed to promise change through system reform. As long as the process of delegitimation is not total, people retain a residue of hope; as long as this is true, virtually everyone (including many revolutionaries) will resist total commitment to revolutionary solutions.

However, I think that the decline of student protest since Kent State is not attributable primarily to students' hope for progressive reform as an alternative to revolution (although I think this remains a *wish*, if not a hope, for many students). More fundamental, in my view, has been the realization that students, acting as students, can have only limited success in realizing their goals and aspirations with respect to social change. Despite their increased numbers, students represent a small and special minority of the total population; they have few levers on power; and above all, they are isolated.

The isolation of students creates a profound paradox. As we have seen, the segregation of students is the very factory that made the collective consciousness and mass mobilization of youth possible. Furthermore, because universities are key social institutions, campus conflicts have had major historical impact. But the history of student movements everywhere suggests that a point is reached in their development when their isolation and parochialism becomes self-defeating. As students came to define their goals in terms of fundamental reform or revolution, their need to ally themselves with other groups favouring change becomes critical. Nevertheless, such alliances are made problematical by the very characteristics of student life that provide collective strength in the first place—their physical isolation, their privileged freedom from the responsibilities and burdens of adult life, and their speech, dress, tastes, and idealistic impatience.

Second, the student challenge to the university can become self-defeating. In its first phase, that challenge opens up the possibility for basic reform of education, gives students valuable experience in political action, and has profoundly educative effects for many who participate. Campus confrontations, however, are largely unintelligible to many in the outside world who cannot understand the seeming ingratitude of "these pampered kids" for the privileged sanctuaries with which they have been provided. Meanwhile, the authorities learn how to cope with campus disruption, and the limited freedoms on the campus that have facilitated the growth of the movement are called into question. Ultimately, the very existence of the universities seems jeopardized to many faculty and students. Student activists come to see that the political value of campus confrontation is limited or that fundamental university reform cannot occur before general social reform is achieved. Youths who continue to *need* the university (and there are many more who do than will admit it) become increasingly cautious, while others give it up in disgust and drop out.

Third, the student movement is an ambiguous framework for the establishment of personal identity. On the one hand, participation in student protest activity can be enormously liberating and crystallizing. The movement "changes one's life" by freeing many students from the anxieties of individual status-seeking and careerism, by offering alternative to materialism, by providing opportunities for deeply fraternal and communal relations with others, and by fostering deep commitments to the pursuit of social justice. Few activists, as far as I can tell, return to conventionality after they have been involved with the movement; most find that the movement's values have become deeply internalized as their own. But a student movement, as such, offers very little guidance in determining *concretely* what one should do with one's life after "graduation". There is a timeless quality about the movement; it embodies an assumption that one always will be a student or an ex-student—leading the freelance, experimental, not-tied-down existence of youth. Such timelessness fits well with apocalyptic visions of the future: since nuclear war, fascism, or revolution are imminent (as many activists come to feel they are), one cannot plan one's future anyway. Nevertheless, if a part of you cannot accept the reality of the apocalypse, then the problems of the future become acute. One cannot go "back" to societally programmed identities, but the movement offers little to help the process of going forward.

Thus, *the logic of student movements is that they must transcend themselves if the collective consciousness they express is to survive and realize itself.* Youth must find a way to connect its interests with those of other groups that potentially or actually are in motion for radical change. The students' privileged sanctuary in the university must somehow be transcended. A radicalism relevant to those who are not youth must be created.

I think that if the era of intense campus conflict has come to a pause, this is so because socially concerned students sense the need for such a transcendence but have not yet found the means to achieve it. The organized new left disintegrated into warring factions over precisely the question of how to transcend the limits of student radicalism. Furthermore, it does appear that many new left ideologues have felt disoriented or discredited as a result of their overemphasis of "revolutionary" rhetoric and action and their misjudgment of the imminence of social breakdown.

In short, the era of *campus* confrontation and *student* revolutionism has ended not because it failed, but because it reached the limit of its possibilities. In a real sense, the new left and the student movement succeeded in ways that were hardly imagined by those who founded it. The two social inventions of intellectual youth—the youth counterculture and the student new left—have been crucial in the transformation of the consciousness of an entire generation. By creating new modes of being young, these inventions helped to undermine an already obsolete cultural framework and an already stagnating political order. But, we ought to ask, having performed work of necessary destruction, has the youth revolt created any potentialities for positive transformation?

REFERENCES

The concept of identity has been developed by Erik Erikson. See, *Identity: Youth and Crisis* (New York: Norton, 1968). The functions of youth cultures are elaborated in a classic essay by Talcott Parsons, "Age and Sex in the Social Structure of the United States", *American Sociological Review* 7 (1942): 604—614. Mannheim's analysis of generation appears in, "The Problem of Generations", *Essays on the Sociology of Knowledge* (New York: Oxford, 1962).

Some standard works on middle and working class youth cultures prior to 1960 are: James Coleman, *The Adolescent Society* (Glencoe: Free Press, 1961); Albert Cohen, *Delinquent Boys* (Glencoe: Free Press, 1955); James Coleman, "The Adolescent Sub-culture and Academic Achievement", *American Journal of Sociology* 65 (1960): 337—347; Kenneth Keniston, "Social Change and Youth in America", *Daedalus* (Winter 1962): 145—171; August Hollingshead, *Elmtown's Youth* (New York: Wiley, 1949); Rose Goldsen *et al.*, *What College Students Think* (Princeton, N.J.: Van Nostrand, 1960); and R. Nevitt Sanford (ed.), *The American College* (New York: Wiley, 1962).

The rise of a new bohemianism during the fifties among intellectual youth is documented in Theodore Newcomb *et al.*, *Presistence and Change* (New York: Wiley, 1967); Burton Clark and Martin Trow, "Determinants of college student sub-culture", Mimeographed (Berkeley, Calif.: Center for the Study of Higher Education, University of California, Berkeley, 1960). The links between the youth culture of the sixties and the "beat" movement of the late fifties are explored in Bruce Cook, *The Beat Generation* (New York: Scribners, 1971). Norman Mailer's definition of the "hip" during the fifties appears in "The White Negro", *Dissent* 4 (Summer 1957): 276-293.

The American tradition of youthful intellectual radical bohemianism is explored in the following: Martin Sklar, "On the Proletarian Revolution and the End of Political-Economic Society", *Radical America* 3 (May—June 1969): 1—41; Richard Flacks, "The Revolt of the Young Intelligentsia", in Rod Aya and Norman Miller, *The New American Revolution* (New York: Free Press, 1971). See, also, David Matza, "Subterranean Traditions of Youth" *The Annals* 338, (November 1961): 102—118.

For a discussion of family origins of radical and alienated students, see

Richard Flacks, "The Liberated Generation", *Journal of Social Issues* 23 (1967): 52—75; Kenneth Keniston, *The Uncommitted* (New York: Houghton Mifflin, 1965); Kenneth Keniston, *Young Radicals* (New York: Harcourt, Brace and World, 1968).

Some insight into the origins and development of the sixties rock can be obtained from: Nick Cohn, *Rock from the Beginning* (New York: Pocket Books, 1970); Jerry Hopkins, *The Rock Story* (New York: Signet, 1970); and Paul Williams, *Outlaw Blues* (New York: Pocket Books, 1970).

On the history of the new left and the student movement of the sixties see: James J. O'Brien, *A History of the New Left, 1960-68* (Boston: New England Free Press, n.d.); Massimo Teodori, *The New Left: A Documentary History* (Indianapolis: Bobbs-Merrill, 1969). The section concerning the history of student protest during the sixties is based in part on earlier work of mine incorporated into Jerome Skolnick, *The Politics of Protest* (New York: Ballantine Books, 1969), pp. 87—109.

The spread of student protest is reported and discussed in *The Report of the President's Commission on Campus Unrest* (Washington, D.C.: U.S. Government Printing Office, 1970). This report is a reasonably good summary of social science thinking on the causes and extent of student protest and contains a very good bibliography on the subject. Some other recent material of importance on the history, development, and comparative analysis of student protest may be found in: Philip Altbach and Robert S. Laufer (eds.), "Students Protest", *The Annals* 395 (May 1971) whole issue.

5

Class and Race in Cross-Cultural Perspective*

In new York, some people taxi home at night from Madison Avenue offices to Sutton Place; others leave a factory left in Brooklyn and subway home to East Harlem. In Detroit there is Grosse Point, with environs, and there is Hamtramck, without environs; in a thousand small towns the people live on either side of the railroad track. In Moscow, high party members ride cautiously in Black cars to well-policed suburbs; other people walk home from factories to cramped apartments. And in the shadow of swank Washington, D.C. apartment houses, there are the dark alley dwellings.

With these words, C. Wright Mills introduced his 1951 essay on "The Sociology of Stratification", and he went on to say, "in any society of which we know some people seem to get most of (the valued things and experiences), some least, others being in between". (Mills 1963:305). Only two years earlier, Robert Lynd began a review of Richard Centers' book. *The Psychology of Classes* 1949), with the comment that "class stratification is the most awkward fact in our American society. It renders democracy impossible, but without it

* The original version of this paper was delivered as the "Howard Lowry Memorial Lecture of Anthropology".

capitalism is impossible", and continued, "as a power relation, it never relaxes its grip save as a superior power forces it to do so. It is not surprising that liberal democracy tries to dodge the fact of class; that our schools and colleges ignore it in their curricula; that business propaganda tells us it is not relevant to our society, and that the social sciences tiptoe evasively around the problem' (Lynd 1949:17).

The situation has been corrected to some degree in the intervening 25 years with innumerable sociological works on class, many of them turning critically to the insights of Karl Marx and Max Weber for inspiration and to their authors' own research for data. Now, almost every college and university has a course on social stratification in its sociological curriculum. A few anthropologists, such as Morton Fried (1960), Lloyd Fallers (1973), and the contributors to collections of essays edited by Andre Beteille (1969a), and by Leonard Plotnicov and Arnold Tuden (1970), have contributed to our understanding of social inequality by looking at such phenomena historically and comparatively, by which I mean cross-culturally. Nevertheless, there remains little reason to modify Paul Bohannan's assessment of 1963, that "probably no range of social phenomena (unless it be the economy) has been so badly observed cross-culturally as that of the institution of inequality" (Bohannan 1963:166). Because of the direction events have taken in the world since World War II, with the end of colonialism, the emergence of the Third World as a potent international force unwilling to submit any longer to second-class membership in the community of nations or as second-class individuals in world society, and with associated events in this country where our internal colonies has emerged as powerful, proud and articulate political and social forces unwilling to be oppressed any longer—because of these events, I believe, scholarly attention has turned toward the analysis of even more rigid and humanly destructive kinds of social stratification than that of class; systems based on parentage and heritage, variously described as race, caste and ethnic stratification.

Let me illustrate such stratification by quoting again, this time from a study carried out in 1933-35 by two couples, one Black, one White, in America's deep south. Allison Davis and the Gardners reported:

The fundamental division in the social organization of Old City and Old Country is that between the Negroes and the 'white folks'. This social cleavage is such that all privileges and opportunities, as well as duties and obligations, are unequally distributed between the two groups. The whites receive by far the larger portion of all economic and social rewards, while the Negroes have an undue share of the more onerous duties. Both Negroes and whites recognize the fact that the white group is super-ordinate in power and prestige, and they exemplify this awareness in both their behaviour and thought. Furthermore, each of the groups is endogamous; that is marriage between them is absolutely forbidden, and any—children of extralegal sex relations are automatically relegated to the sub-ordinate Negro group. Each individual is born into the Negro or white group and must remain in it for life. He may neither earn nor wed his way out.

To [the whites], the Negro is a lower form of organism, biologically more primitive, mentally inferior, and emotionally undeveloped.

Not only is the . . . system believed by the whites to be based on inherent differences between the two groups, but it also carries sacred sanctions in their society. To them, it is the "will of God" (Davis, *et al.*, 1965: 15-16).

Although that was written 40 years ago, it still holds true in much of the rural South, and other versions of it have been manifest in Boston, for example, as we know from reading the papers, and almost everywhere else in this country. That is what I mean by racial stratification. In his powerful book, *Crisis in Black and White*, in 1964, Charles Silberman emphasiged the contrast between a class system and a system of racial startification, noting that many of the characteristics of the Black experience in America are basic ingredients of any lower-class community. "But there is a special quality to the despair of the Negro slum that distinguishes it from any other. For the youngster growing up in Harlem or any other Negro slum, the gates of life clang shut at a terrifyingly early age. For one thing, the children become aware almost from infancy of the opprobrium Americans attach to colour. They feel it in their parents' voices as they are warned to behave when they stray beyond the ghetto's wall. They become aware of it as they begin to watch television, or go to the movies, or read the mass-circulation magazines; beauty, success, and status all wear a white skin" (Silberman 1964:49). They wear a white skin because power wears a white skin.

These descriptions characterize two forms of institutionalized inequality in American society, class and race stratification. This distinction is central to what I wish to say in this essay, for I want to formulate a way of describing and analyzing those modes of institutionalized inequality that are termed class, ethnicity, race and caste. My aim is to facilitate cross-cultural comparison of the social structures they describe, the belief system in which they are imbedded, their dynamics, and the consequences they generate in the lives and experiences of those who live them.

Fallers (1973:161) has observed that social inequality is both a *structural* phenomenon, in the sense of institutionalized social differentiation (according to such criteria as age, sex, kinship, occupation, ethnicity, etc.) and a *moral* phenomenon in the sense of evaluation of those differentiated components. Both of these dimensions of inequality are crucial for analysis and understanding, and they will be attended to closely in that which follows. I would add, however, that in addition to being structured and evaluated, it is equally important that systems of social inequality are *behavioural* and *existential* phenomena. That is, the fact of institutionalized inequality, and its form, have an important effect on what people do—the behavioural choices they make—in their social, political, economic and religious relationships, and they have direct and fateful consequences in the life-experience of those who comprise such social systems. All four of these dimensions must be attended to if we are to understand our subject.

Accordingly, I have been interested not only in the social structural similarities and differences in various systems of inequality, and in their consequences in social functioning, and not simply in comparing criteria of evaluation and modes of selection and allocation of rewards, but equally in understanding the nature and consequences of the differential behaviour and experience which such inequality engenders. I am interested in the effect which social structures bring about in liberating or suppressing the human spirit as well as in their material understandings. To this end, as an anthropologist, I have engaged in comparative research in the United States (Berreman 1960) and in both rural and urban India (Berreman 1972a; 1972b), and have studied the literature on other societies notably Japan, Swat (in northwest Pakistan), Rwanda and Burundi. I have brought this research together in a preliminary way in two comparative essays (Berreman 1972c; 1973), which in turn are based on several more specific articles of my own (e.g., Berreman 1965; 1966; 1967; 1968; 1971a; cf. 1976), and the writings of others including notably works on Japan by DeVos and Wagatsuma (1966), on Ruanda by Maquet (1961), on Swat by Barth (1960), on India by Srinivas (1962; 1966), Beteille (1965; 1969b), Gould (1971), and others, and innumerable writings on the United States, including those by Dollard (1937), Mills (1951; 1956) Sennett and Cobb (1972), and Warner and his associates (Warner and Lunt 1942; Warner, Meeker and Eells 1949).

My intention in this essay is not to describe the ethnographic facts of inequality in these societies—these can be ascertained from the sources cited above or in thumbnail sketches contained in my essay, "Caste in the Modern World" (Berreman 19/3). Rather, my intention is to draw on those facts in order to suggest a systematic way of describing and analyzing comparatively systems of institutionalized inequality with special reference to complex societies. Therefore, I will apply the insights to which these data and this analytical framework have led me, to some commonly accepted proportions about social inequality.

I have thought this inquiry worthwhile because I think social inequality—the gain of some at the expense of others—is the most pervasive and pernicious injustice in the world today, manifesting itself in poverty and oppression, hunger and fear, frustration and resentment, leading to untold suffering and to portentous conflict among individuals, groups and nations. A first step toward eliminating the inequities inherent in social inequality is to understand it. This essay is an effort in that direction. There will not be space in it to well substantiate what I have to say. Doubtless my discussion will raise more questions than it will answer, and it may engender more doubts than convictions. But I am convinced that the questions and doubts are ones worth raising, and that in any case it may be of some general interest and practical import to convey what I have concluded as a result of looking in depth at a variety of systems of inequality.

A Typology

My comparative study has led me to attempt a systematic way of looking at systems for organizing, legitimizing and enforcing inequality. I have devised a texonomy beginning with the general concepts which define social inequality, and moving deductively to specific varieties, proceeding from the most individualistic to the most group-oriented of systems, from the most flexible and permeable to the most rigid. In this essay I will focus on one part of that taxonomy; the part called 'stratification', and associated with complex, state-organized societies based on agriculture and/or industry. I leave to a future paper the task of extending my discussion of social inequality to smaller, more homogeneous societies. I trust that it will be clear that what follows is not intended to describe a developmental sequence nor a value hierarchy. Rather, it is an attempt at a set of logically possible and empirically demonstrable types of social organization, hence an instance of an oft-proclaimed species: an heuristic device.

Inequality, Differentiation and Dominance

The most general condition to which I address myself, of course, is the occurrence of human inequality—an issue that has been a focus of scholarly and political attention from at least the time of the classical Greeks to the present. This concept follows almost inevitably from the fact of human differentiation, and in fact is often described as an inherent feature thereof. Differentiation refers to non-identity, i.e., to heterogeneity, and may be based on features which occur naturally, socially, or both. Natural differences include those of sex, age, size, strength, stamina, quickness, etc., while social differences include acquired capabilities and talents, roles associated with sex, age, occupation, kinship, etc., and identities associated with culture, religion, language and the like.

Particular differences may or may not be socially recognized or acted upon in any given society. particular manifestations of social inequality are shaped by the kinds of differences recognized and the manner, circumstances and extent of their recognition. Inequality thus implies socially *evaluated* differentiation. That evaluation, in turn, implies consequences for those to whom are attributed the evaluated features. Inequality can therefore refer to the unequal distribution among people within a society of almost anything in the biosocial realm to which social significance is attached: of natural and social attributes and their consequences, including opportunities, experiences, access to goods, services and privileges, public- and self-esteem, power to control people's activities and destinies (including one's own). In short, it can refer to the recognition of differential attributes and to resultant differential allocation of any valued things, opportunities, and experiences including life itself.

Fallers (1973:27) has emphasized that social inequality is inherent, although not necessarily always acted upon, "in socio-cultural differentiation in all its dimensions: sex, age, descent, occupation, religion, race, ethnicity, and even—on a wider scale—nation". Thus, it is not simply an objective phenomenon; it has to be understood in cultural context—in terms of the meanings attributed and the experiences engendered among people in the particular societies in which it occurs. To be socially significant, that is, any type or instance of inequality must be both perceived and acted upon. In order for this to occur it must be socially recognized as significant, and it must be incorporated into an organized system of social valuation.

Just as many aspects of human differentiation are evaluated, resulting in inequality, so they are often acted upon interpersonally in ways such that one or more persons prevail over others—succeed in achieving their interests at the expense of the interests of others. When this occurs, we speak of a relationship of dominance and sub-ordination. The dominance may be situational, role-specific, temporary, or generalized and lasting. The manner and circumstances in which it is asserted and in which it is conceded vary widely, as do the social entities who assert and concede it. An individual's dominance with respect to another may be asserted in politics and relinquished in ritual, for example; it may be asserted in the kin group but relinquished in the marketplace, it may be acted upon whenever the two interact, or only on particular occasions or in particular places or before particular audiences. The social uses of dominance, in other words, are diverse.

Differentiation, inequality and dominance—human differences, evaluated and acted upon—are the constituents whose systematic, culturally mediated interrelationship is termed "institutionalized inequality". It should not be overlooked, however, that in many societies (mainly those of small scale), social inequality is limited primarily to the expression of these features in face-to-face relationships. Fallers (1973:4) has noted the importance (and frequent scholarly neglect), even in complex societies, of such mutually negotiated dominance relationships and hierarchies conceived of "in dyadic, patron-client, master-servant terms", as contrasted to the more widely remarked systems of group dominance or categorical dominance, which are the principal subject of this paper. Only differences of sex and age, and a few kin relationships, are virtually universal as criteria for inequality and as bases for dominance.

Rank

The term 'rank' refers basically to inequality and dominance which are patterned and legitimized—hence institutionalized—according to a normative system (a system of values) recognized and acted upon, although not necessarily endorsed, throughout the society, and enforced by those in positions to do so, namely the powerful. Rank tends to be generalized rather than situationally or temporally specific or role-specific. Bohannan (1963:164) comments that "rank can be seen as a summary of human modes of dominance".

If dominance is so institutionalized in society that individuals who exhibit particular socially defined and valued attributes are also the ones who consistently arrogate to themselves, or are accorded power, privilege and esteem (and in most societies such is the case), then social ranking can be said to exist. That is, if dominance relationships are clustered into differentially evaluated and rewarded (hence hierarchically ordered) statuses, then we can (speak of a system of ranks.

There is considerable variety in the nature, bases and extent of social ranking, and in whether and to what degree it applies to individuals, to social categories, or to corporate groups. Weber (1946; 1968) immortalized three dimensions of social rank: 'class' (market situation or economic interest), 'status' (style of life and community of values), and 'power' (ability to influence communal action), and in some of his writings he cited a fourth, ethnicity (consciousness of common heritage). Runciman (1968) has argued that social inequality consists of precisely the three dimensions most often cited by Weber: class, status and power; that each is entirely distinct and that there are no others.

Bohannan (1963:1f4-184) has described four distinct and recurrent bases for ranking in society: ranking of roles (which he calls 'status'), of groups (caste'), of social categories ('estate'), and of cultural traits or attributes ('class'). These distinctions will appear later in my discussion. Fried (1960) has emphasized the distinction between ranking on the basis of one's place in the network of kin or one's specialist role e.g., priest) in society, on the one hand, and ranking on the basis of shared social identity, on the other. The former he terms 'rank', and he finds it to be expressed, legitimized and perpetuated through generosity and redistribution of goods, and to occur in non-state (stateless) societies with little occupational specilization or differential access to productive means. The latter he terms 'stratification', and he finds it to be expressed, legitimized and perpetuated through accumulation and exploitation, and to occur in state-organized societies whose very organization is directed to the preservation of the order of stratification, and which are occupationally specialized with sharply differentiated access to productive means.

Stratification

In general, 'social stratification' refers to social ranking organized or institutionalized into a system wherein all members of society are ranked relative to one another as members of categories, defined according to share characteristics regarded in the society as relevant and important. In such systems, people who share the significant characteristics share, at least roughly, or potentially, the same rank, so that they constitute social layers, hence application of the term 'strata'. That they are ranked means, of course, that some get more and some get less of what society and the environment have to offer, and those who get more tend to accumulate it at the expenses of those who get less. Stratification is characteristic of state societies, which in turn are based on agriculture, often (and latterly) combined with industrialism, and with complex divisions of labour and differential access to and control over means of production and political power.

My interest in this paper is primarily in three kinds of stratification: class, ethnic and caste (or race) stratification. These will be discussed in turn.

Social Class

Social class refers to categories of people—social strata—ranked according to socially significant attributes and behaviours which have been acquired by, or bestowed upon, them. These attributes include notably their economic status (bluntly put, their income and wealth or lack thereof, and their access to the means to produce it), their power (the ability to control people's lives, including their own), the privileges they enjoy (education, security, leisure, luxury, and other valved things and experiences), their ability to escape unwanted experiences and obligations—in short, their life-chances, as Weber called them, and their life-style. That these characteristics are acquired or bestowed means that, at least in theory, they are achievable. Once they have been acquired and recognized, the appropriate class status is accorded the individual. Thus, in a class system, people are ranked on the basis of characteristics which are *extrinsic* to the individual—on the basis of features which are attached to, or associated with, individuals, but which are separable from them. Social mobility may be unlikely; it may be difficult to acquire or shed class characteristics, but it is possible and the means to mobility are socially prescribed.

Because movement up or down the social scale is possible and does occur, and because individuals differ in the degree of their access to, and manifestation of, life-styles, a class system approximates a continuum. The classes may be distinguished both by public opinion and by sociological analysis, but in fact people range along a continuous hierarchy of power, privilege, esteem and life-style without absolute discontinuities. Another source of ambiguity in the class identity of individuals is the fact that there are multiple criteria for rank (e.g., wealth, occupation, life-style) which are not entirely mutually consistent. Some individuals rank higher according to some criteria than according to others. Nevertheless, there is a tendency in class societies for consistency among criteria of rank, and for lumping of people into strata of roughly equivalent rank, with all individuals assigned or assignable to one position in the class hierarchy at any given time. The basis for that assignment is entirely extrinsic to those assigned.

Ethnic Stratification

When social entities ranked in the manner just described for class systems also comprise discrete cultural entities whose members are cognizant of a common culture or heritage, and are regarded by themselves and others as being culturally distinct, we may refer to 'ethnic stratification'. This is essentially class with the addition of the ethnic component, i.e., a distinct cultural identity shared within the ranked entity as both necessary and sufficient for inclusion within it. (Of course, if the ethnic groups are not ranked relative to one another, we have an instance of ethnic pluralism rather than ethnic stratification—something that is more often advocated than achieved.) In ethnic stratification the ranked qualities are *intrinsic* to the culture or heritage of those who are so identified and ranked. If one exhibits the culture or claims (or is assigned) the heritage, then one is ranked accordingly regardless of other characteristics. But in such systems the ranked qualities are *extrinsic* to individuals, because cultures are learned and can be unlearned or relinquished; heritages are claimed and acted upon, and they can be repudiated or ignored. Thus, ethnic stratification combines intrinsic and extrinsic criteria: intrinsic to the culture, extrinsic to the individual. So long as the individual is regarded as exhibiting the heritage (in language, religion, dress, diet habits, customs, occupation, etc.), he or she is a member of the ethnic group and ranked accordingly; as soon as the heritage is no longer evident or claimed, the ethnicity and consequent rank is lost. There are thus sharp discontinuities in the hierarchy, and the criterion for ranking is unitary. Ambiguity occurs only as individuals or groups start to become 'assimilated'.

Ethnic stratification has occurred in the ranking within American society, for example, of English, German, Irish, Italian, and Polish immigrants and their immediate descendents, at different times in the history of the United States. Because it is the culture and heritage of these groups which determines the individual's social identity and because it is that identity which determines his or her social rank in a system of ethnic stratification, when the individual or group adopts the life-style of the dominant group, the rank of the ethnic group ceases to be relevant. Then assimilation occurs and individuals or families move into the system of class ranking that usually prevails in the society at large.

Relative interactional isolation of the group—that is, more frequent and intense interaction among its members as contrasted to that between its members and aliens—is characteristic of ethnic stratification, as it is to a lesser degree of class stratification, and to a greater degree of caste and race stratification (see below). Such differential association is the mechanism through which the cultural distinctiveness of the groups is perpetuated (or even generated).

Ethnic stratification has been a stumbling-block in realization of 'the American dream' of free competition under conditions of equal opportunity in a putatively open class system, but it has not been an insuperable one. When its distinctive features has been unrecognized or denied, this has led to confusion about the nature of the class system. A far more frequent and misleading confusion has arisen, however, from lack of understanding of another quite distinct kind of stratification, that of race or caste. The latter type, to which I now turn, has frequently been confused with ethnic stratification, or with class stratification or both. Its characteristics merit close attention.

Caste/Race Stratification

When membership in discrete, culturally distinct groups, i.e., ethnic groups, is defined not by culture and heritage but entirely, exclusively and unalterably by birth, that is, by parentage, then we are speaking of a caste system or a system of racial stratification. I use the two terms interchangeably, or jointly, because I think they are significantly similar in both structure and consequences, even though the first is generally associated with the Hindu manifestation of the phenomenon in South Asia, and the second is generally associated with the so-called 'colour-bar' which grew out of European colonialism and is found in many places today, notably the United States (cf. Berreman 1960; 1966; 1968; 1972c; 1973). To be sure, there are culturally specific differences between these two manifestations—as there are between any two systems, and as there are regionally and culturally wiihin each of them—but it is the effective similarities which are of interest here.

In such systems, all people defined as having significantly similar parentage—common ancestry—share membership in the caste or race, and that group is ranked relative to all other groups as superior or inferior. That is, to its members is attributed a distinctive, ranked degree of *intrinsic* worth (e.g., purity, honour, genetic capability)—intrinsic because inborn and unalterable; ranked because to those of common birth is accorded a shared and distinctive degree of access to the rewards available in the society. Social mobility is prohibited; the ranks are discontinuous, the groups discrete, the basis for ranking (birth) is absolute. Because the criterion of rank is intrinsic, there is no means to alter one's rank or its consequences, and in this crucial respect, systems of caste/race stratification differ fundamentally from those of class and ethnic stratification. The difference is not only one of social structure, but carries with it profound implications for the experience and psychology of those within such systems (cf. Berreman 1966).

Contrasts

Four statements deriving from the above discussion will

serve to emphasize significant differences among these three types of stratification: class, ethnic and caste/race stratification:

1. *Class* systems assign one's status according to one's attributes and behaviours, whereas *caste/race* systems assign one's attributes and behaviours according to one's status. The members of castes and race groups are ranked according to assumptions about the *intrinsic* worth of individuals and groups inherent in themselves as a result of their birth; classes and their members are ranked according to *extrinsic worth,* attributed to things associated with persons, acquired by or assigned to them, but not part of them.

2. Systems of *ethnic stratification* rank people by their culture—by assumptions regarding the worth of learned, shared and transmitted features attributed to the heritage which they claim, display or are assigned. Because cultural attributes are a product of early socialization and constant reinforcement, ethnic identity is more rigid than class identity; because they are learned, rather than innate, it is less rigid than caste/race. The ranking of ethnic grougs is thus made on the basis of features *intrinsic* to the culture, but *extrinsic* to the individual, hence midway between class and caste/race in social rigidity.

3. In class systems, the means to social mobility are *prescribed*; in caste/race systems, the means to social mobility are *proscribed.* In ethnically stratified systems, social mobility requires surrendering one culture (hence one identity) for another.

4. In sum: in class, *attributes* are ranked; in ethnic stratification, *cultures* are ranked; in caste and race, *birth-defined categories of people* are ranked (cf. Bohannan 1963: 164-184).

It is essential to bear in mind in this discussion that "race" as used here is defined as the social significance attached to ancestry, and has nothing whatsoever to do with genetics. In a caste/race system it does not matter what your genes are any more than it matters what your behaviour is. What matters is your ancestry; the socially ranked group you are consigned to as a result of that ancestry. Both the cause and the effect of racism, therefore, are social. Only the rationale is genetic and of course, it is false genetics at that.

The Typology Summarized

Although within societies the differential distribution of attributes, opportunities and rewards takes many forms, these forms can be usefully classified in a rather simple scheme:

1. Individual differentiation and inequality—the facts of heterogeneity or non-identity and of unequal occurrence of attributes within a population—exist a natural conditions in human society. The ways in which they are organized and evaluated are culturally diverse.
2. Inequality, when expressed interpersonally as differential power, is dominance.
3. Dominance, when patterned and institutionalized into differentially valued and rewarded statuses, is social rank.
4. Social stratification is social rank organized and applied so that a society is made up of ranked categories of people, each category defined by significant shared characteristics among its members, and differentially powerful, rewarded and esteemed.
5. Stratification wherein ranking is on the basis of *extrinsic* attributes is class stratification. Extrinsic attributes are those acquired by or assigned to individuals, e.g., income, occupation, education, life-style.
6. Stratification on the basis of distinctive cultural heritage is ethnic stratification. Such ranking is assigned on the basis of criteria *intrinsic* to the culture which people carry, but *extrensic* to the individuals who carry it.
7. Stratification on the basis of birth or ancestry—i.e., ascribed entirely on the basis of characteristics *intrinsic*

to those ranked—is caste or race stratification. The terms 'caste' and 'race' may be used interchangeably for purposes of cross-cultural comparison.

Sexual Inequality

Clearly, in most societies, females and males are assigned at birth differential intrinsic worth, and their life changes are determined thereby. This dichotomy is rationalized, as are all caste/race relationships, in terms of biological differences (even where none at all exist, cf. Berreman 1972: 392-393). Kate Millett (1971: 19) has referred to this as the "view or sex as a caste structure ratified by nature", and notes that "many people who are very hip to the implications of the racial caste system . . . don't seem to be able to see the sexual caste system and if the question is raised they respond with: 'that's the way it's supposed to be. There are biological differences. Or with other statements which recall a white segregationist confronted with integration". As if on cue, anthropologist Lionel Tiger, defending his book, *The Imperical Animal* (Tiger and Fox 1972; the title refers, needless to say, to the human male), responded to an interviewer's suggestion that its explanation for woman's roles was sexist, with a vehement denial: "These are the facts, don't accuse [me] of making up the species" (Hawthorne 1971).

I would say that men and women constitue categories analagous in many ways to castes or races, with many of the same features, but with important distinctive features as well. Like caste and race, sex identity is intrinsic, it is birth-ascribed and it is evaluated, but unlike caste and race, it is not based on parentage, for the parentage of both sexes may be the same. Each sex has a distinct heritage and culture, to be sure, but because of the nature of the family and of sociallization in the family, the cultures of the sexes are not as separate nor are they of the same order of distinctiveness as cultures of castes, races and ethnic groups in societies ranked on those bases. Because they occupy complementary familial roles, the differential association between the sexes is not of the same order as that of other groupings ranked on the basis of intrinsic characteristics. The group distinctiveness and coherence of the two sexes is consequently both less and different than that of ethnic groups, castes and races.

Tiger was quoted, in the interview cited above, as having said also: "Because this is a racist country, people relate sexism to racism. But these two reactions are actually different because while there are no important differences between races, there are very important differences between the sexes". And I agree. Who would deny or deplore sexual differences? But the sociological and humanistic question with reference to sex is the same as that for race or caste: do the differences require or justify differential opportunities, privileges, responsibilities and rewards, or put negatively, do they require or justify domination and exploitation? If racism and casteism are indistinguishable in the annals of man's inhumanity to man, as I believe they are, then sexism is closely allied to tem as man's inhumanity to woman.

Age and Inequality

Age, like sex, carries elements of ascription, for it too is ineluctable, and it too is a basis for differential access to opportunities and rewards—to what Jules Henry (1973: 22) has called the "success mechanisms" of a society. Henry says, "in all cultures the nature of attachment of an individual to the social system varies through time and is usually related to the economic and symbolic contributions made by him [or her] to the culture", and age is an important factor determining the nature of that attachment.

As with stratification by sex, age lacks the element of common and distinct origin and heritage force in caste/race and ethnic stratification. Unlike any of the other bases for rank and reward, an individual who survives will experience all of the ranked positions in a lifetime. He or she will not, however, control entry to, and departure from, these positions and their consequences any more than sex, caste or race can be controlled. Thus, age stratification has a number of the features of these other kinds of ascribed stratification based on intrinsic characteristics, and it entails a number of the same consequences in the experience and response of individuals; consequences associated with ineluctable assignment to fixed degrees of access to opportunities and rewards in society.

Generalizations and Contentions: A Critique

Bearing in mind the typology of institutionalized inequality defined and characterized above, I turn now to consider some recurrent assertions and prevalent assumptions about stratification. Put more directly, I want to draw on my cross-cultural research to set straight what I regard as misleading, naive, sometimes ethnocentric and even self-serving generalizations, by making some counter-generalizations (which I am sure will be equally criticized by others). I will address eight such generalizations, contentions and assumptions.

(*1*) *Institutionalized inequality is a functional requirement and a functional advantage in society* (cf. Davis and Moore 1945). *It assures that the most capable people will perform the most important tasks in society. What is needed for smooth social functioning—in the nation or the world—is not to change the system in any fundamental way, but to accept this fact gracefully—to adopt what has been termed 'a certain civility' toward those both more and less advantaged than one's self* (Kraft 1972; cf. Moynihan 1972; 1975). This is by now a familiar (and to many a comforting) argument, which bears cross-cultural examination.

It would surely be nice for the powerful and privileged if others would gracefully accept the system of stratification, but it adds insult to injury to ask people to be gentle victims and docile scapegoats for the privilege and power of others, and in-fact they never are.

Stratification, which is what Davis and Moore meant by institutionalized inequality, far from assuring that the most able will do the most important jobs in society, assures that whole categories of people will be *prevented* from performing those jobs regardless of their abilities. Institutionalized inequality also assures that people—whole categories of people—will be available to do the dirty work—the undesirable, unrewarding and dangerous jobs—for others, again regardless of their abilities. Thus, while it does not assure that the best will do the most rewarding jobs, it does assure that *someone* will have no option but to do the least rewarding jobs.

Stratification is an artifact of the ownership of land and other means of production, of the occupationalization of work (cf. Gould 1971), and of the elimination of kin-based social organization (cf. Fried 1960). It is a learned way of doing things—a way many peoples have done without. It is nothing more nor less than a cultural trait; not an inherent feature of humanity. If indeed it was a necessary adjunct of agriculture or industrialization, it nevertheless had to be invented and learned along with those productive systems themselves. It may now be necessary to eliminate it because it is the source of potentially devastating conflict which we already see in our city streets, in our international political posture, in the internal politics of innumerable nations, and in the rapidly decaying international economic system. What worked for—perhaps was even necessary to—the emergence of modern agriculture and industry many prove destructive of the post-colonial world.

(2) *Caste systems, such as that of India, differ from systems based on race, such as that in the United States, in that the former are based on a religious or moral consensus—agreement as to the criteria of rank and the legitimacy of the hierarchy—whereas in race systems there is disagreement on precisely these issues* (cf. O.C. Cox 1945; Berreman 1960; 1973; Cox and Berreman 1961).

Ten years ago this was a hotly debated issue. Now, there are few who would deny that caste ranking in India is, like race ranking in America, based largely on power rather than consensus. For exceptions to *this* consensus see Dumont [1966], who has worked in India, and Pitt-Rivers [1971], who has not. For assessments of Dumont's work, see the papers in Madan, *et al.*, [1971], which are primarily critical of his viewpoint, and those in Richards and Nicholas, *et al.*, [1976], which are primarily supportive of his analysis). The crucial consensus in such systems is not on the legitimacy of the hierarchy or of anyone's place within it, but on who has the political, economic and physical power to enforce their will, when and how it is likely to be used, and with what results. When this consensus breaks down—when the possibility of altering the system or the specific hierarchy emerge—then groups are either accorded the rewards they demand, or else their resentment and longing is expressed in overt action which most often leads to conflict. The way this has been discovered is really very simple: anthropologists and others learned to know oppressed peoples, such as untouchables in India, and observed and talked with them. In other cases such people spoke for themselves. It was found that the oppressed universally cherish hopes or harbour plans to alter their condition. This is also revealed by the study of history and of contemporary events, wherein one discovers how recurrent are efforts at upward mobility and emancipation in even the most rigidly oppressive societies. Seymour Martin Lipset and Reinhard Bendix have made relevant comments in two different places: "The fact that there is constant striving for upward mobility in the most status-ridden society in the world [India], adds considerable weight to the hypothesis derived from Veblin, according to which a system of stratification is a fundamental source of mobility motivation in and of itself. Apparently, there are imperatives which prompt men to resist and reject an inferior status and these imperatives presist regardless of the way in which any given society has legitimized inequality" (1960: 63). "A society is characterized not only by the facts of social stratification, but also by a system of power-relations between conflicting social groups. Hence, the fact that a dominant social group possesses most of the power in a society may be a more important reason for the apparent stability of that society than the fact that people accept privileges and burdens which are theirs by virtue of their social and economic position" (Bendix and Lipset 1953:13).

If one wonders about this, one can read of the rapid expansion in the past years of the Dalit Panthers, a militant low-caste group in western India; on can follow the fortunes of revolutionary movements in eastern and southern India as they appeal to the oppressed in those areas; one can study the history of religious conversion in India for the past 2500 years, almost almost always with a strong element of anti-caste motivation—motivation which is found also in the political reform movements of the past 100 years there. Or, one can follow the thoughts, actions, and decisions in the lives of untouchables in rural or urban India, as I did those in the village of Sirkanda—to see how often they manipulate tneir interactions with others to escape the most painful consequences of inherited oppression, how often they move away from daily contact with their oppressors, how often they opt to give up conventional rewards of family and meagre security in order to escape traditional caste roles—even at the cost of being deemed insane, in the case of one man I knew (Berreman 1971a). Such behaviour demostrated how excruciating is "the burden of screaming bloodstained pain", as one untouchable poet described untouchability (Randheer 1973; cf. *Times Weekly*, 1973; Malik 1974).

In other societies one can look to the history of Black emancipation, nationalism and militance in the United States, and among Chicanos, Native Americans and Asians, too many of whom have been martyred for their courage and determination. The same has been documented for the Burakumin of Japan (Totten and Wagatsuma 1966; Wagatsuma 1966), and in the rebellions of the Hutu of Rwanda and Burundi (cf. Berreman 1973: 4-5). Wherever there is caste or racism, there is suffering and there is conflict because these are systems which assure privilege to some at the expense of others, and people do not acquiesce easily to that situation. When they do, it is not because they agree to its legitimacy or inevitability, but because they know the uses of power. Caste, like race, is everywhere charocterized by conformity rather than consensus, by conflict rather than tranquility, by enforcement rather than endorsement, by resentment rather than contentment. It generates resistance and revolt rather than support and loyalty.

(3) Systems of birth-ascribed ranking must have a physical, i.e., racial basis, otherwise everyone who wanted to would 'pass'. Accordingly, systems of stratification without a basis in physical distinctiveness are fundamentally different from those with such a basis.

In fact, what is required for such a system is not physical distinctiveness, but any means of categorizing people by birth that is believed to work, or can be enforced to work. This, we learn from the instances of Japan and India, can be social or cultural as well as physical. Language, occupation, culture, genealogy, ghettoization all serve to identify people as well as does colour, so long as they are enforced.

All such systems seem to include a biological and often a supernatural rationale or justification, sometimes ingenious but more often mundane or even ludicrous. Here, Japan's Burakumin come to mind, traditionally alleged to have a dog's bone in their bodies, to have less than the usual number of fingers and vertebrate, and to have a distinctive digestive tract—this despite the fact that physically these people are totally indistinguishable from other Japanese. The biological differences are used to explain and justify the inevitability, importance and legitimacy of the social separation and ranking which defines caste and race, even when it is imaginary. Just as societies frequently dramatize the social differences among kin groups (e.g., sibs, clans, phratries) by giving to them totemic names and attributing to them characteristics of animals or plants, thereby identifying the social differences with biological species differences (cf. Levi-Strauss 1963), so also societies with birth-ascribed status hierarchies dramatize and legitimize *these* crucial social differences by attributing to them innate biological, hence "racial", differences. As a result, the concept of miscegenation arises, based on the ideology of innate difference.

The pseudo-scientific racism of Arthur Jensen and Ernest Shockley is of this order in our scientifically oriented society (cf. Jensen 1969). They claim a relationship between race and intelligence which is genetic, inevitable and therefore a charter for differential opportunity in society. The fallacy in Jensen's case is simply that he has selected for investigation two socially defined groupings in American society (Whites and Blacks) whose genetic differences he takes for granted but does not investigate, groups which are commonly regarded as innately different in social worth and which as a result are accorded widely and crucially divergent opportunities and life experiences. Upon finding that they perform differentially in the context of school and test performance, he attributes that fact to undemonstrated and univestigated biological differences. Thus, socially defined populations perform differently on socially defined tasks with socially acquired skills, and that is attributed by Jensen to biology! I am reminded of E.A. Ross' (1914:3) succinct assessment of over fifty years ago, that "race' is the cheap explanation tyros offer for any collective trait that they are too stupid or too lazy to trace to its origin in the physical environment, the social environment or historical conditions". Stratification by sex and by age is often similarly justified, even by critics of racism, as being biologically necessary.

(4) *Our society is a melting pot of peoples where any determined and able person may overcome any social disadvantage to achieve the rewards society has to offer. If only Blacks, American Indians, Chicanos and others in the United States (or Untouchables in India, or Burakumin in Japan, or Hutu in Rwanda) would act like the rest of us, we would accept and assimilate them.*

A long and frustrating history of attempts to act on this injunction has demonstrated its falsity. Birth-ascribed ranking whether we call it race or caste, means just that: in those respects in which race or caste are relevant, one is ranked by intrinsic criteria—birth or parentage—*not* by behaviour, attributes or accomplishments. To check on this, ask a Black physician, an Untouchable lawyer, or a Burakumin school teacher where they can eat, play, worship, live; whom they can date and marry; how they are treated when they apply to join social clubs or show up at social events planned for the dominant groups in their societies. They are admitted, if at all, not because of their appropriate behaviour, or their accomplishments, but because it is more troublesome or costly or embarrassing to deny them than to admit them. That is, they are admitted when power has been implemented by them, or in their behalf—as a result of the acquisition of economic power (new jobs, unionization), political power (the vote, representatives in governing bodies, favourable legislation), powerful allies, new opportunities (through education, employment, compensatory discrimination), etc., (cf. Berreman 1967; 1966).

(5) An extension of the above is the idea which Glazer and Moynihan (1963) have championed (among others), that *Blacks, American Indians, Chicanos and Asians face the same problems in America as the "White ethnics" faced—the Irish, German, Polish, Italian and other European immigrants and their progeny. If those groups have made it, why can't the others?*

Those who ask this question, which they doubtless regard as rhetorical, have failed to discern the essential fact that racism or casteism—which means birth-ascription—is the basis for the social positions and opportunities of Blacks, American Indians and other victims of racism, and thal it is different in crucial respects from class and ethnic stratification. Racism or casteism bestows a unique social, political and economic stigma which is not bestowed by class, culture or national origin—unique because it is intrinsic—unalterable. Second generation White Europeans can meet all of the criteria for acceptance into the American White caste/race, because they are regarded as being different only in ways extrinsic to individuals—in attributes which are learned and alterable, i.e., cultural attributes such as speech, dress, manners, occupation and income.

A fifteenth generation American Black or a fifteen-hundredth generation American Indian cannot achieve the degree or kind of acceptance available to a second generation White ethnic, because *there* differences are regarded as innate, immutable and uniquely importent. They may be encouraged to "act like White people" on the promise of assimilation, but it is a cruel life, for as they invariably find out, it is not how you act or what you have which makes assimilation possible, but how you were born. That is what racism and casteism are all about.

(6) Another extension of the misperception of the nature and power of racism/casteism is the contention—often from quite a different political quarter—that *race and caste are reducible to social class; they are expressions of economic differences both in their origins and in their consequences: racism is essentially an economic problem.*

Those who make this assertion are correct in seeing the economic implications of the ranking system despite the smokescreen of biological and religious rationale, but they are wrong in seeing nothing else. Race and caste *are* bases for differential access to income, goods and services; occupations, ownership and power. They are thus class phenomena, in Marxian terms. But they are a very special kind of class phenomenon, as we have seen, because for the individual birth status is the determining factor—the independent variable—and class status is the consequence—the dependent variable: status is not a result of income or relationship to the means of production; rather, income and relationship to the means of production result from birth-ascribed status. Industrial society, and especially its Capitalist manifestation, surely exploits the poor and the vulnerable at the expenses of the rich and powerful. But if race and caste were reducible to economics, why should Blacks in the United States and Untouchables in India so consistently be the vulnerable and the poor? The answer is that a *function* of racial and caste stratification is to guarantee a vulnerable category—a labour pool in society—to do the work others wish to avoid, and for their benefit.

It is racism which makes Blacks and those in like situations consistently vulnerable. They are exploited because they are vulnerable; they are vulnerable because they are powerless and poor; they are poor because they are discriminated against; they are discriminated aganist because they are Black; and they are Black not because of their colour (many are not black at all), but because of societal definition of their parentage, and the degree of intrinsic worth ascribed to their ancestry. They are thus available, according to racial stratification, regardless of personal characteristics to compete for whatever scraps society may throw them, and to serve as scapegoats for the failures of everyone else.

A caste/race system enjoins a peculiar hopelessness on the members of groups deprived of economic, political and social advantages, and a peculiar arrogance among members of the privileged groups, including those individuals who derive rather minimal material rewards from their cherished elite status—they can feel secure in their birthascribed public esteem and advantage even in the absence of other attributes which might seem to justify it. This is the classic claim of the "poor White trash" so familiar in the literature on the South. One consequence is to prevent people of different races and castes from joining forces for their common advantage, by identifying them as being at odds with one another socially on the basis of their birth, even though they would seem to be at one in terms of economic and political interests. Poor Whites have rarely joined forces with Blacks in the United States, nor have poor Brahmins and Sweepers in India.

On the other hand, class stratification also involves its own denial of dignity. As Sennett and Cobb (1972) have so tellingly argued, if caste and race stratification sets rigid, demoralizing and resented limlts upon what one may experience and possess in life, class stratification exacts a different toll: "The working people of Boston have been denied the *presumption*, rather than the *possibility*, of societal respect, denied some way of moving through daily life without being defensive and on guard, some way of being open with other people without being hurt. The humbling to today is as oppressive as that of the *ancien regime* but of a different kind: it is at once less brutal and more insidious" (Sennett and Cobb 1972:248). The reason is that under the "flawed humanism" of the class system, every individual is held accountable for his or her station in life as a result of the theory that it is a station achieved in free and individual competition with others. "The lesson of this historic flaw is that once respect is made the reward for human ability, no matter if the ability is seen potentially in all [I would say *especially* if it is seen potentially in all], the stage is set for all the dangers of individualism: loneliness for those who are called the possessors, a feeling of guilt for those who do not come off as well" (Sennett and Cobb 1972:256).

I do not mean to imply in this discussion that caste, race, enthnicity and class are mutually exclusive. Despised races, low castes, ethnic minorities, colonized people, all comprise economically and occupationally exploited classes whose members are politically and socially oppressed; exalted races, high castes, privileged ethnic groups, and colonizers comprise privileged, power-wielding, elite classes who live off the labour of others. In this respect, class differences pervade and reinforce systems of birth-ascribed stratification such as the American raeial one. Also, it is not unusual to find significant class differences within a race, caste, or etunic group, or within a colonized or colonial group. But my point is that it is not possible to analyze birth-ascribed stratification solely in terms of class, for no amount of class mobility—upward or downward—will exempt a person from the crucial implications of his or her birth in such systems.

(7) This brings me to the contention or expectation by Karl Marx, and even more so by many of those who cite him, that *common, class position will generate class consciousness among people, followed by mobilization for concerted action in their*

shared interest. That is, the workers of the world will unite. This has rarely happened. What *has* happened is that ethnic, caste and race groups have united for their group interests—in this country the slave revolts, the Ku Klux Klan, the Garvey movoment, the White Citizens' Councils, the Nation of Islam, the Black Panthers, Red Power and the American Indian Movement, etc. Elsewhere it has been the Hutu rebellions of Rwanda and Burundi, in India the Untouchables' Republican Party and the Dalit Panters, in Japan the Burakumin Emancipation organizations. Repeatedly, ethnic, national, regional, religious and linguistic entities have mobilized for their common good, as they defied it (cf. Geertz 1963; Isaacs 1975). It seems that what Marx expected to happen on the basis of class has more often happened on the basis of socially defined caste, race or ethnic group—that is, on the basis of shared culture rather than simply shared economic position; on the basis of shared identity rather than simply on the basis of shared relationship to the means of production.

The reason, I think, is not far to seek. Class is an analytical category, for the most part, not a self-conscious one. It is, as some anthropologists would say these days, an *etic* phenomenon—discernible by the trained observer but unrecognized by, and not significant to, the observed (the actors). The "hidden injuries of class", so well described by Sennett and Cobb, are exactly that—hidden. Their source (the shared experience of class position and class exploitation) is hidden from those who suffer them. But their effects are all too apparent: frustration, disappointment, guilt, inadequacy, insecurity, isolation, and alienation among working people (cf. Sennett and Cobb 1972; Terkel 1974). It generally takes monumental effort to educate people—to raise their consciousness—to the point that they will recognize and act upon the common cause they may be thought to have with others, based on like economic and political position; in short, to accurately identify the source of their injuries, the fact that they are shared, and that they might be rectified collectively where they cannot be individually. This is especially difficult in a complex society with many dimensions of inequality—a society such as our own.

Ethnic, caste and race categories, on the other hand, are by definition groups of people who are aware of of their common identity and interests. The source of *their* injuries are not hidden; they are only too readily apparent. People in these categories see the world as made up of groups competing with their own, acting in self-interest. They are forced into such awareness by the actions and expectations others, and they enjoin it upon themselves. They are repeatedly told that their group identity, their race, their cultural heritage and natural endowments, their karma, are the causes of their experiences and opportunities. Their group membership is what some anthropologists would call an *emic* phenomenon as contrasted to an etic one—recognized by an significant to the people who manifest it.

Thus, although living and working in an industrial society is no doubt alienating, as Marx observed, alienation is evidently not enough to ensure class consciousness and class mobilization. The motivation may be there, but the mechanism—the vehicle—is not. Being a member of an exploited or threatened cultural *group* in such a society is not only alienating, but group consciousness is present, and the potential for mobilization for action is consequently high; both the motive and the are mechanism at hand.

I must comment in this context that while materialist explanations of social rank carry much explanatory power and display important insights, they cannot suffice. The role of ideas is equally important. Material deprivation is devastating, but so is the denial of justice, human dignity and fulfilment. To understand inequality and its implications, therefore, we surely need Marx and his materialism, but we need W.I. Thomas as well, and his famous dictvm that "if man define situations as real, they are real in their consequences" (Thomas and Thomas 1928:572; cf. Volkart 1951:14). If people *think* they are privileged or oppressed—if they *feel* fulfilled or thwarted—if they are *regarded* as superior or inferior—they often act accordingly, especially if they believe that their actions may be successful in achieving their ends. If people *think* their interests are at odds with one another, they often act as though they were, and they do so regardless of how we might analyze the situation. That is what racism is, what ethnic competition is, and what these primordial attachments do to people.

(8) Finally, I want to attend simultaneously to two responses anthropologists have made to the study of poverty, oppression, class and caste. The first is to seemingly "blame the victim" (to paraphrase the title of a recent book by William Ryan 1971)—to look to the cultures of poor people and and/or their personalities and the way they raise their children, for the cause of their poverty. This is a point of view often attributed to Oscar Lewis (1966) and his well-known concept, "the culture of poverty". I do not think Lewis meant by the phrase what many others who have adopted it have meant and what many of his critics have assumed Lewis meant, namely that *poor people share a way of life which perpetuates and aggravates their poverty through apathetic and improvident acceptance of it, and through addiction to modes of coping which preclude escape from their poverty*. This interpretation, I think, is based on misreading or not reading Lewis. Lewis was well and explicitly aware of the material, social and political causes of poverty, and was interested in how poor people make the best of their bad situation. Be that as it may, many others *have* adhered to the kind of view that has become associated with Lewis' phrase, "culture of poverty". I would maintain that apathy, acceptance, and perpetuation are not characteristic responses to the deprivation which defines poverty, or to the systematic subjection to the will of others which defines oppression. They are therefore not the characteristics responses to class, ethnic or caste/race discrimination and deprivation.

Critics of the culture of poverty, such as Charles and Bettylon Valentine (Valentine and Valentine 1975), on the other hand, have sometimes come perilously close to implying that *poverty and oppression are rewarding, even enjoyable*. This it the second response to studies of poverty and oppression to which I wish to respond. I think it is as erroneous and misleading as the assumptions attributed to the culture of poverty.

What the cross-cultural evidence seems to me to show is that people experience their poverty and oppression as painful, frustrating, and unjust. The fact that they demonstrate remarkable ingenuity in creating stimulating environments against formidable odds, as the Valentiness have shown to be the case, must not be allowed to obscure the fact or experience of poverty and oppression, or the nature of people's responses to them. These conditions are psychically and physically costly to those who suffer them, as they are socially and economically costly to the societies which harbour them. They are associated regularly with malnurition, disease, high infant mortality, short lifespan, suicide, hypertension, alcoholism, drug abuse, violence and crime, both within the group and outside of it, applied both by and to the oppressed who are inevitably vulnerable to others and to dominant institutions, and who are deprived of most of society's rewards and protections. In short, people are damaged by poverty and powerlessness, and they know it and they don't like it.

The common response to this condition is not apathy or improvidence, it is not carefree enjoyment or creativity, but it is resentment, resistance, avoidance and escape. Such resistance is likely to be closely attuned to the realities of the situation, including notably the distribution of power and rewards. It may take the form of individual escape from oppression (ranging from suicide or alcoholism to emigration), artful manipulation of the situation, thoughtful use of whatever legitimate or illegitimate means of amelioration are available (cf. Berreman 1971 a). Part of any culture of poverty and of any culture of oppression is insightful knowledge of the elite and the powerful. In general, people know well those who dominate them, whereas those who dominate know little of those they dominate. Powerless people know their oppressors: their social organization, their ways of doing things, their beliefs, values, vanities and vulnerabilities. The reverse is not the case. Those of lower status have both the opportunity to know their superiors (because they perform services for them), and the need to know them, because in the absence of power they must manipulate their superiors by subtle means if they are to achieve any of their ends. The superiors, on the other hand, need know only the extent of their own power and how to apply it in order to command the services of others. Subtle knowledge of those to whom it is applied is irrelevant. This was amply demonstrated in my study of urban ethnic relations in India, where the disparity in mutual knowledge between the high and the low, the powerful and powerless was striking (Berreman 1972b).

Another recurrent kind of response of oppressed people is

that of organized overt challenge or revolt when the opportunity seems to present itself (see Berreman 1972c, for relevant citations). The apparent universality of such responses is portentous for societies which are rigidly stratified, particularly when that stratification is ethnically or racially based. It is a source of anxiety for those who profit by such stratification, and of hope for those who suffer from it.

The history of all socially stratified societies is one of upward mobility-striving, of conflict and occasional revolt intensified in proportion to the magnitude of the disparities and the rigidity of the systems. The *success* of such efforts is inhibited to the degree that power is concentrated in the hands of the privileged, and it is enhanced whenever that concentration of power is diminished, or when the cost of enduring comes to be defined as greater than the risk of resisting or escaping. That these facts are not generally acknowledged is largely because such systems occur in the context of overwhelming power, and resistance is therefore squelched so quickly—or suppressed so throughly or so subtly—as to go unremarked. Also, of course, it is the elites who are threatened by resistance and who fear even to admit that it occurs, and it primarily they who write the histories and control the media where it might be acknowledged.

Even where escape and resistance are unattempted, deprived and oppressed people consistently harbour plans or cherish hopes to effect them. I have never heard of a low caste in India which did not claim higher status than that accorded it by others, and whose members did not engage in at least sporadic attempts to have that status recognized—often at great cost to their own security and immediate tranquility. To them it has seemed worth the cost and the risk, even in that rigid and virtually hopeless situation. In my first publication on India, a brief account of responses to untouchability in village India, compared to those to racism in America. I concluded: "a comparison of the realities of caste attitudes and interaction in India and the United States suggests that no group of people is content to be low in a caste hierarchy—to live a life of inherited deprivation and subjection—regardless of the rationalizations offered them by their superiors or contructed by themselves" (Berreman 1960:127; of 1971b). Nothing I have learned since has led me to alter that conclusion.

Conclusion

As I look at America, and outward to the rest of the world, it appears to me that relations among caste/race groups, ethnic groups and classes are becoming starkly simplified—that the lines are being more clearly drawn between those who have and those who have not; between rich and poor; between powerful and powerless; between Black and White; between high caste and low; between "developed" nations and "developing" ones. The subtleties and complexties seem to be diminishing, and with them the niceties are being dropped. Naked power is being resorted to more unabashedly as the conflict becomes more evident, the contenders more clearly identified, the means less camouflaged, the rules less constraining, *noblesse oblige* less practiced, the use of force more blatant, the stakes greater, the rewards and injuries more stark. Therefore, I think, the incidence, the likelihood and the impact of overt conflict between unequals is increasing both within and between societies and nations.

Poverty and affluence, power and privilege, class, ethnicity, caste and race, seem to me to be the conditions, principles and entities which confront one another in a world of increasing competition for scarce goods and privileges. The confrontation is likely to be costly and painful, but among those presently poor and oppressed, that cost and pain are regarded as less than the cost and pain of enduring the *status quo.* To the privileged, on the other hand, the cost and pain are often regarded as less than would be the case if the *status quo* were to be relinquished. We, or our children, shall see. But I hope that the privileged will give in gracefully. It would be wise of them to do so, for they are the real minority, and time as well as justice is against them. Whatever the outcome, the attempt to diminish inequality—to share more equitably the world's goods and privileges and power—is sure to come and it is bound to be uncompromising. The grace, humility, civility and restraint required in America today are not to be employed in the tolerance of "inevitable, even beneficial" inequality which exemplars of "the new conservative creed" have suggested (Kraft 1972), but instead in the elimination of inequality, even when it means giving up conspicuous advantages. This must be done whether these advantages rest ultimately on extrinsic factors such as education, occupation, income and life-style, that is, on class; on the intrinsic features which define caste and race; or on the combination of the two which is the basis for ethnicity. There is no way that institutions of inequality can be reformed to our common advantage; the only solution is their dissolution. Abram Kardiner and Lionel Ovesey (1962: 387) said it long ago: "*There is only one way that the products of oppression can be dissolved, and that is to stop the oppression*". This is confirmed by the research cited in this paper, as it is by an assessment of political and economic relations between the Third World nations—the recent colonies—and the heretofore dominant nations, and of relations between elites and dominant groups in those nations and their internal minorities. With an increasing parity in the technological capability for acting out those tensions in overt and fateful conflict, the only hope for avoiding catastrophe lies in restructuring society within and between nations, and redistributing rewards and opportunities so as to end or drastically reduce inequality. Present trends suggest a worldwide polarization in access to power, privilege and resource—the gap between the "haves" and the "have nots" increases with a diminishing willingness among the poor to continue to suffer deprivation, and among the wealthy to ameliorate it. The disparities must be ended, and inevitably will be, by conflict if not by accommodation. It would be to the advantage of everyone that it be done graciously, quickly and well, lest it occur brutally, perhaps by holocaust.*

To those who fear eliminating of inequality on the grounds

* The original lecture presentation of this paper was reported with this concluding paragraph: ' "I see the time coming when the 'haves' will-I hope—give up their power gracefully, because it's in their best interest and the best humanitarian interest to do so. 'He admitted, however, it's 'unlikely to happen' " (Reidel 1975:1). The reported internal contradiction was perhaps truer (if not more accurate) than I at first thought or than the reporter realized. I believe that relinquishing power and privilege within and between nations and groups is necessary for survival, but I think it is unlikelv to come about because people who have those advantages are probably too selfish and fearful to relinquish them, and too short-sighted to realize the urgent necessity of so doing in their own self-interest.

that it will be traumatic, costly, painful and dangerous, I would say that it will be less so than the futile attempt to maintain the *status quo.* Some societies have discovered this, generally to their sorrow. Now we too must understand and act upon it. At this point, social justice and self-interest have finally met on common ground.

REFERENCES

Barnett, Steve, Lina Fruzzetti and Akos Ostor 1976 "Hierarchy Purified: Notes on Dumont and His Critics". *Journal of Asian Studies* 35: 627-650.

Barth, Fredrick 1960 "The System of Social Stratification in Swat North Pakistan". In *Aspects of Caste in South India, Ceylon and Northwest Pakistan,* edited by E. Leach, Cambridge: Cambridge University Press, pp. 113-146.

Bendix, Reinhard and Seymour, Martin Lipset (eds.) 1953 *Class, Status and Power.* Glencoe, Illinois: The Fress Press.

Berreman, Gerald D. 1960 "Caste in India and the United States", *American Journal of Sociology* 66: 120-127.

1965 "The Study of Caste Ranking in India". *Southwestern Journal of Anthropology* 21: 115-129.

1966 "Caste in Cross-Cultural Perspective". In *Japan's Invisible Race: Caste in Culture and Personality,* edited by G. DeVos and H. Wagatsuma Berkeley: University of California Press pp. 275-324.

1967 "Caste as Social Process". *Southwestern Journal of Anthropology* 23: 351-370.

1968 "Caste: The Concept." In *The International Encyelopedia of the Social Sciences,* edited by David Sills, New York: Macmillan Company and The Free Press, Vol. II, pp. 333-339.

1971a "Self, Situation and Escape from Stigmatized Ethnic Identity". In *1971 Yearbook of the Ethnographic Museum, University of Oslo,* Oslo, Norway: Universitetsforlaget, pp. 11-25. Also published stimultaneousy, with permission in *Man and Society,* Silver Jubilee Number of *The Eastern Anthropologist,* edited by K.S. Mathur and S.C. Varma, Lucknow: Ethnographic and Folk Culture Society, U.P. 1972: 95-108.

1971b "The Brahmannical Views of Caste". *Contribution to Indian Sociology* N.S., No. 5: 18-25.

1972a *Hindus of the Himalayas: Ethnography and Change.* Berkeley: University of California Press (1st edition, 1963).

1972b "Social Categories and Social Interaction in Urban India". *American Anthropologist* 74: 567-586.

1972c "Race. Caste and Other Invidious Distinctions in Social

Stratification". *Race*. (Special Issue: *Race and Stratification*, edited by W.G. Runciman) 23, 385-414.

1973 *Caste in the Modern World*. Morristown, N.J.: General Learning Press (A module).

1976 "Social Mobility and Change in India's Caste Society". In *Responses to Change: Society, Culture and Personality*, edited by G. DeVos, New York: D. Van Nostrand Company, pp. 294-322.

Beteille, Andre 1965 *Caste, Class and Power*. Berkeley: University of California Press.

1969a *Social Inequality: A Reader*, Middlesex: Penguin Books.

1969b *Castes Old and New*. Bombay: Asia Publishing House.

Bohannan, Paul 1963 *Social Anthropology*. New York: Holt, Rinehart and Winston.

Centers, Robert 1949 *The Psychology of Social Classes*. Princeton: Princeton Uuiversity Press.

Cox, Oliver C. 1945 "Race and Caste: A Distinction" *American Journal of Sociology* 50: 360-368.

Cox, Oliver C. and Gerald D. Berreman 1961 "Berreman's "Caste in India and the United States' ", (an exchange of letters), *American Journal of Sociology* 66: 510-512.

Davis, Allison, B.B. Gardner and M.R. Gardner 1965 *Deep South: A Social Anthropological Study of Caste and Class*. Chicago: University of Chicago Press, (2nd edition, abridged).

Davis, Kingsley and Wilberl E. Moore 1945 "Some Principles of Stratification". *American Sociological Review* 10: 242-249.

DeVos, George and Hiroshi Wagatsuma 1966. *Japan's Invisible Race: Caste in Culture and Personality*. Berkeley: University of California Press.

Dollard, John 1957 *Caste and Class in a Southern Town*. Garden City, N,Y.: Doubleday and Co.

Dumont, Louis 1966 *Homo Hierarchieus: The Caste System and its Implications*. London: Weidenfield and Nicolson.

Fallers, Lloyd A. 1973 *Inequality: Social Stratification Reconsidered*. Chicago: The University of Chicago Press.

Fried, Morton H. 1960 "On the Evolution of Social Stratification and the State". In *Culture in History: Essays in Honour of Paul Radin*, edited by Stanley Diamond, New York: Columbia University Press, pp. 713-731.

Geertz, Clifford 1963 "The Integrative Revolution: Primordial Sentiments and Civil Politics in the New States". In *Old Societies and New States*, edited by C. Geertz, Glencoe, Illinois: The Free Press of Glencoe, pp. 105-157.

Glazer, Nathan and Daniel P. Moynihan 1963 *Beyond the Melting Pot*. Cambridge: The Massachusetts Institute of Technology Press.

Gould, Harold A. 1971 *Caste and Class: A Comparative View*. Reading, Mass: Addison-Wesley Modular Publications (A module).

Hawthorne, Fran 1971 "Female Roles Examined by Rutgers Professors". *Daily California* (University of California, Berkeley), October 6, 1971, p. 5.

Henry, Jules, 1973 "Personality and Ageing—With Special Reference to Hospitals for the Aged Poor". In *On Sham, Vulnerability and Others Forms of Self-Destraction*, edited by Jules Henry, New York: Aintage Books, pp. 16-39.

Isaacs, Harold R. 1975 *Idols of the Tribe: Group Identity and Political Change*. New York: Harper and Row, Publishers.

Jensen, Arthur R. 1969 "How Much Can We Boost I.Q. and Scholastic Achievement?" *Harvard Educational Review* 39: 1-123, (See also the "Discussion" of this article, in the following issue of the same journal).

Kardiner, Abram and Lionel Ovesey 1962. *The Mark of Oppression*. Cleveland: World Publishing Company.

Kraft, Joseph 1972 "A Portentous Sign," *International Herald Tribune* (New York), (November 6, 1972), p. 6. (Also appears in *The Washington Post*).

Levi-Strauss, Claude 1963 "The Bear and rhe Barber." *Journal of the Royal Antropological Institute* 93: 1-11.

Lewis, Oscar 1966 "The Culture of Poverty", *Scientific American*, Vol. 215, No. 4 (October, 1966), pp. 1925.

Lipset, Seymour Martin and Reinhard Bendix 1960 *Social Mobility in Industrial Society*. Berkeley: University of California Press.

Lynd, Robert S. 1949 "Tiptoeing Around Class", *New Republic*: July 25, 1949, pp. 17-18.

Madan, T.N.E. Leach, G.D. Berreman, C., von Furer-Haimendorf, R.S. Khare, V. Das, J.S. Uberoi, J.C. Heesterman, D. Kantowsky, M. Singer, and L., Dumont 1971 "On the Nature of Caste in India: A Review Symposium on Louis Dumont's *Homo Hierarchicus*", *Contributions to Indian Sociology* 5: 1-81 (New Series).

Mahar, J. Michael (ed.) 1972 *The Untouchables in Contemporary India*. Tucson: University of Arizona Press.

Malik, Harji 1974 "India's 'Untouchables' Step Up Protests". *The Christian Science Monitor*, April 24, 1974, p. 3.

Maquet, Jacques J. 1961 *The Premise of Inequality in Ruanda*. London: Oxford University Press.

Millet, Kate 1971 *Sexual Politics*. New York: Avon Books.

Mills, C. Wright 1956 *The Power Elite*. London: Oxford University Press.

1963 "The Sociology of Stratification". In *Power, Politics and People: The Collected Essays of C. Wright Mills*, edited by I.L. Horowitz, New York: Ballentine Books, pp. 305-323 (first published 1951).

Moynihan, Daniel P. 1972 "Equalizing Education—In Whose Benefit?" *The Public Interest* 29: 69-89.

1975 "The United States in Opposition". *Commentary* March, 1975), pp: 31-44.

Pitt-Rivers, Julian 1971 "On the Word Caste". In *The Translation of Culiure. Essays to E.E. Evans-Pritchard,* London: Tavistock, pp. 231-256.

Plotnicov, Leonard and Arthur Tuden (eds). 1970 *Essays in Comparative Social Stratification.* Pittsburgh: University of Pittsburgh Press.

Randheer, Umakant 1973 "Heirs". Translated by Gauri Deshpande, in "Special 8-Page Issue on Dalit Literature", *Times Weekly (Times of India),* November 17, 1973, p. 8.

Richards, J.F., R.W. Nicholas P. Kolenda, J.D.M. Derrett J.M. Massom, S. Barnett, L. Fruzzetti, A. Ostor, and M. Francillon 1976 "Symposium: The Contributions of Louis Dumont". *Journal of Asian Studies* 35: 579-650.

Riedel, June 1975 "Berkeley Professor is Lowry Memorial Speaker", *Wooster Daily Record* (Wooster, Ohio) May 1, 1975, p. 1.

Ross, E.A. 1974 *Sacial Psychology,* New York: Macmillan Company.

Runciman, W.G. 1968 "Class, Status and Power?" In *Social Stratification,* edited by J.A. Jackson, London: Cambridge University Press, pp. 25-61.

Ryan, William 1971 *Blaming the Victim.* New York: Random House.

Sennett, Richard and Jonathan Cobb 1972 *The Hidden Injuries of Class.* New York: Random House.

Silberman, Charles 1964 *Crisis in Black and White.* New York: Random House.

Srinivas, M.N. 1962 *Caste in Modern India and Other Essays.* Bombay: Asia Publishing House.

1966 *Social Change in Modern India.* Berkeley: University of California Press.

Torkel, Studs 1974 *Working.* New York: Random House.

Thomas, William I: and Dorothy Swaine Thomas 1928 *The Child in America.* New York: Alfred A. Knopf.

Tiger, Lionel and Robin Fox 1972 *The Imperial Animal.* New York: Deil Publishing Company.

Times Weekly 1973 "Special 8-Page Issue on Dalit Literature". *Times Weekly,* (Times of India), November 25, 1973.

Totten, George O and Hiroshi Wagatsuma 1966 'Emancipation: Growth and Transformation of a Political Movement". In *Japan's Invisible Race,* edited by G. DeVos and H. Wagatsuma, Berkeley: University of California Press.

Valentine, Charles, A. and Bettylou Valentine 1975 "Brain Damage and the Intellectual Defense of Inequality',, *Current Anthropology* 16: 117-150.

Volkart, Edmund (ed.) 1951 *Social Behaviour and Personality: Contributions of W. I. Thomas lo Theory and Social Research.* New York: Social Science Research Council.

Wagatsuma, Hiroshi 1966 "Postwar Political Militancc". In *Japan's Invisible Race*, Berkely: University of California Press, pp. 68-87.

Warner, W. Lloyd and Paul S. Lunt 1942 *The Status System of Modern Community*. (Yankee City Series, Volume 2), New Haven: Yale University Press.

Warner, W. Lloyd, M. Meeker and K. Eells 1949 *Social Class in America: A Manual for Procedure for the Measurement of Social Status*. Chicago: Science Research Associates.

Weber, Max 1946 *From Max Weber: Essays in Sociology*. Edited by H. Gerth and C.W. Mills, New York: Oxford University Press.

1968 *Max Weber: Economy and Society, An Outline of Interpretive Sociology*. Edited by G. Roth and C. Wittich, New York: Bedminster Press, Volume 1.

6

Social Inequality in Malaysia

A.N. JUDITH

The question of social inequality has been approached from many angles in different ages and environments, from the Bible and the Koran to Marx and modern sociology. The concept of inequality presupposes two distinct but complementary elements: social cleavage in one dimension, and social clustering or unity in another. Both require exploration simultaneously.

Two of the most frequently used concepts in anthropology dealing with social cleavages are stratification, and more recently pluralism, with their various related sub-concepts of class, status, rank and ethnic group. In combination, these two concepts have become particularly important in recent anthropological work on inequality in the new nations, the complexity of whose social structures and organisation is such that considerable conceptual virtuosity is required to provide a suitable analytical framework. This is even more true if we attempt, as anthropologists customarily do, to take cognisance of the popular or indigenous models of social inequalities held by people about their own society (the "folk taxonomy" or "emics") in addition to applying more objective criteria of analysis.

In the following pages both the "objective" and "subjective" approaches to social inequality in the context of Malaysia will be mounted. The first is necessary as a baseline from which general theoretical statements and comparisons with other areas can be made. To be successful, it requires drawing upon knowledge of Malaysian society at its broadest, as well as the more traditional local level of social relationship. The interest of the second lies to a great extent in the degree to which it contrasts or tallies with the first, and it too, to be meaningful, must take account of the entire body of social and cultural traditions which shape the outlook of the people whose views we are examining. This includes their awareness of even external peoples and situations as well as past events, all of which constitute part of their social experience (cf. Arensberg 1961).

Debates on the topic of pluralism and stratification are numerous and intricate, and as yet unresolved to the satisfaction of all concerned. The range of views is from those who see the two phenomena as mutually independent theoretically, although in some cases empirically overlapping or co-including, to those who feel that pluralism is but a special form of stratification.

Stratification

Most studies of stratification in anthropology have been conducted within the context of the new African nations (e.g., Schwab 1961; Lloyd 1966; Tuden and Plotnicov 1970 and Tuden 1970), although Evers' contributions on Southeast Asia cannot be ignored. From the standpoint of the outside observer i.e. the anthropologist, there is some agreement that an elite stratum is clearly emerging in most countries, but that a complete system of classes. (Tuden 1970:19) has yet to develop. Presumably the reasoning behind such assertions is similar to that argued by Morris (1967), who maintains that in a true system of stratification all members of society must be assignable to one stratum or another; can belong to only one at a time; that each stratum must be rankable in relation to all other strata; and that intrastrata interaction must be greater than that occurring across stratum lines. In many new countries where members of even the same nuclear familiy would clearly cut across stratum boundaries, the above conditions cannot be fulfilled.

Many anthropologists tend to use the terms "stratum" and "class" rather loosely, and do not normally restrict the latter to groups and their relations to means of production, or indeed to any functional groups capable of self-mobilisation. In most cases what they are describing are either relationships of superordination-subordination only or else differences of rank and prestige. The first instance may be little more than a form of patronage, and the second an example of status groups in Weber's sense. Ranking is thus based not on control of economic resources so much as on conceptions of honour and a shared style of life.

The so-called "consensus" theorists of stratification (e.g., Barber 1959; Shibutani and Kwan 1965) and those concerned with situations of high social mobility (e.g., many anthropologists in new nations), assume the existence of shared society-wide values to which there is merely differential access. This enables the observer to construct schemes of gradation as defined by Ossowski (1963:41 ff.). The schemes may either be concerned with access to one dominant resource, ("sample" gradation); or multifactorial ("synthetic" gradation). Patronage systems of stratification can probably be regarded as gradations. In the case of ranked status groups, however, consensus over desirable goals and resources may be less complete.

The whole issue of stratification, however, is often clouded by the factor of the popular ideology of stratification within a given society. It over this question that some of the African researches have foundered, and which has caused some of them to assert that, despite the existence of an elite, because there is no class consciousness, social classes are "more analytic than real" (Tuden: 21). Dumont also claims that social ranking can only be adequately understood through knowledge of the ideology supporting it, although this is not to say that "ideology is necessarily the ultimate reality of social facts and delivers their explanation" (1961:?8). Southall (1970:256) also makes a plea for distinguishing subjective and objective or realist and nominalist aspects of social stratification.

Pluralism

The Furnivallian heritage of the plural society concept, with its image of two or more socio-cultural sections, each possessing its own parallel set of values and institutions and a substantial degree of institutional self-sufficiency and completeness, still provides a starting point for most discussions of pluralism. Later writers have developed the concept further. Although there is disagreement as to the essential features of a plural society,[1] most writers would agree upon the following broad points. First, plural groups may be based upon any one, or a combination of, such particularistic criteria as race, language, religion, place of origin or culture, but is most often ethnic (e.g., Geertz (1963). Second, the typical plural society is seen as one in which the respective segments each have their own set of values, and pursue their life interests and goals more or less independent of one another. Following Van den Berghe, (1969: 69) pluralism may take one or more of three possible forms: cultural pluralism (sufficient heterogeneity of values that makes meaningful interaction across cultural boundaries difficult or impossible); social pluralism, marked by the existence of relatively closed social communities (which may or may not be based on cultural pluralism and structural pluralism, characterised by distinct and incompatible institutions, and sometimes also by differential civil and legal status of the component groups (a variable which has long pre-occupied M.G. Smith, e.g., 1965, 1969). Van den Berghe also makes a point of distinguishing between subjective pluralism and more objective reality, for as he recognises, the two may diverge considerably (1969: 70).

When it comes to locating the integrating mechanisms of plural societies there is less agreement. In the post-colonial world, however, it no longer seems reasonable to follow Smith (1969) or Kuper (1969; 1970) and confine the concept to "white dominant" or "white settler" societies where integration is achieved through coercion. Economic interdependence is clearly more important in those poly-ethnic societies of the new nations where the white population is negligible.[2]

"Ethnic Stratification"

It is in attempting to manage the twin variables of pluralism and stratification that the theorists have been most uneasy. If we accept the "consensus" view of stratification, and see the essence of pluralism as a general absence of consensus with the wider society by members of the different sections, obviously the two are logically quite distinct. Here we may find stratification within the individual segment of the plural society, but each of these segments will exhibit a pattern of ranking unique unto itself and ungeneralisable across its boundaries. Thus it will be virtually impossible for either the observer or a member of the society to construct a broadly acceptable overall continuous ranking system for the society as a whole (cf. Rex 1970). By the same token, as cross-segment consensus increases, so the pluralism decreases. In "non-consensus systems of stratification on the other hand, whether the separate goals, values and life-chances are determined by ethnic (or other particularistic) factors or not, the primary interest would seem to lie in structural relation and the lack of mobility i.e., the stratification aspect (as implied by Morris 1967), and secondarily in the cultural features by which they are distinctive. Thus, what is termed "ethnic stratification" should not be confused with pluralism *per-se* (cf. Kuper 1969) which in such situations would seem to be a redundant concept[3] (Benedict 1970).

Other situations have been documented (e.g. Smith 1965) in which pluralism and stratification intersect in particular ways. Smith's Grenada material shows, for example, how plural segments may exist within major strata, each segment maintaining a more or less separate cultural, social and institutional life. If we consider each of the plural sections to be a particular form of status group (in Weber's sense), then every Grenadian is judged by a "double standard" his class or stratum and his cultural or ethnic group membership. Objectively, the first may appear to be more important in a structural analysis of the overall society; but subjectively, the second may provide a powerful and conflicting principle of evaluation. Still regarding ethnic (and other particularistic) sections as status groups; in a society which is also stratified by status-rank, there is room for some play of status uncertainty and selection of status reference group according to circumstances. Here is where the subjective element becomes particularly crucial, as will be exemplified below.

Juxtaposing some of the concepts briefly introduced above,

we may now begin to apply them to a concrete situation. A complex society like Malaysia could be approached from a number of different angles, but a combination of stratification and pluralism concepts appear to provide a useful initial perspective. For the external observer a form of class stratification cross-cutting ethnic boundaries is increasingly apparent, although most Malaysians show little awareness of class distinctions in the western sense of the term. Perception of social differences in an ethnic idiom is more common. Provisionally it may be said that Malaysian society is subjectively more plural than objective reality might warrant. This means that the "folk model" of Malaysian social structure and the social scientist's rendering of it may diverge considerably. Furthermore, each of the three major component ethnic groups of the country (see below) besides having its own internal status system, manifest different perceptions of Malaysian social structure such that a correspondence or equivalence between particular statuses in two ethnic communities is often hard to establish. Moreover, these ethnic-specific status systems are not overty of a "class" type, as will be shown.

One of the most salient issues of Malaysian society therefore is under what conditions ethnic status overrides status derived from other (stratification) sources, particularly in the modern sector. From the standpoint of the overall society, there may be some justification for viewing the ethnic group as a special kind of status group (in Weber's sense). For it is usually community of an amorphous kind and associated with a particular evaluation of honour and ideal style of life (Gerth and Mills 1958: 186-7). All members of the group are judged by a similar yardstick and it is assumed that all are "playing the same game" (Barth 1970:15). This would subsume Weber's idea of "honour". What counts here, however, is not just the "objective" behaviours of cultural traits observed by the researcher, but the interpretation and significance such behaviours have for the actors in given situations. Thus, one item of behaviour (or occupational category) can have a different meaning according to context, and in this flexibility lies one of the mechanisms by which ethnic boundaries are raised or lowered as needed (cf. Nagata 1974b). In a poly-ethnic society where modernisation is creating a growing number of new status indices upon which the interests of all groups are beginning to converge, ethnic boundaries (as expressions of ethnic status) can still be maintained, at the expense, it seems, of class consciousness (cf. Enloe 1968:9). It is the manner in which objectively similar occupations and activities are given the "ethnic stamp" that forms much of the substance of this paper. Some comprehension of why this is so, however, can only be gleaned from a knowledge of the structure and organisation of Malaysian society at its widest, and possibly even beyond. For the immigrant populations in particular (see below) an awareness of their foreign heritage and separate history must be counted as part of the relevant and ongoing tradition of these groups in Malaysia.

Historical and Social Background

The Federation of Malaysia[5] is distinctive among its fellow Southeast Asian nations for the relative proportions of its immigrant "minorities", who are almost as numerous as the indigenous Malays and aboriginal tribal peoples combined.[5] The most massive immigration of both the Chinese and Indian minorities was originally stimulated by British colonial interests, which required their labour and skills in exploiting fully the potential mining and agricultural resources of the peninsula. Little opportunity or encouragement was offered by the colonial masters for members of the three groups to interact socially, and indeed their separation was preserved and enshrined in the deliberate colonial policy of maintaining a division of labour along ethnic lines. Thus, the Malays provided the basic agricultural force and source of rice for the rest of the population; the Indians were recruited as indentured labour for the rubber plantations; while the Chinese quickly assumed a dominant position in the mining, manufocturing and commerical sectors which also tended to cluster around urban centres. In practice the ethnic comparisons and confrontations which most prominently divide Malaysian society, upon which popular and political attention focuses, are between Malay and Chinese. For demographic and historical reasons, the Indians do not weigh so significantly in the balance.

In the political realm, many traditional Malay institutions

were preserved by the practice of indirect rule. Each of the sultans and rajahs along with a traditional aristocracy of the nine originally independent states which were eventually incorporated into the Federation, retained his formal position and title within his own state over matters of the Islamic religion[6] and Malay custom. The creation of a Malaysian Civil Service which now provides nearly all the senior administrative officials of the Federal government, abrogated most of the sultans' real power, but not from the Malays, since the latter play an important role in this bureaucracy through a series of preferential quotas. Since Independence (in 1957) the government has consisted of a fairly stable coalition of three ethnic-based parties known as the Alliance.[7] Although it is often said that in Malaysian society the malays are in the ascendant politically that the Chinese dominate commercial life and the Indians constitute the rural proletariat, this statement must immediately be qualified, for there are numerous exceptions in every case. Not the least is the large proportion of poor, landhungry Malay peasants with no access to sources of power. Nevertheless, it is a popular stereotype model of Malaysian social structure held by members of all ethnic groups about their own soeiety, and on the basis of which many everyday judgments are made.

Since Independence and the disappearance of collective unity versus the colonial power, ethnicity has assumed great salience in Malaysia's social life (Freedman 1960). As mentioned above, the most important political parties are ethnic-based, while those whose banners are more universalistic (e.g., in attempting to appeal to what we would call class sentiments) muster but little support. Likewise many voluntary associations are the vehicles of particular ethnic groups, even many of the religious organisations which would be expected to provide at least inter-religious inter-ethnic interaction, e.g., between Malays and Indian Muslims. Further, each ethnic group supports its own educational institutions, and although some children from each attend "neutral" English-medium schools 89 per cent of Malay, 85 per cent of Chinese and 67 per cent of Indian children are educated in vernacular schools at the primary level (Department of Statistics 1962:63). Finally, the administrative organisation and political policy of Malaysia is still couched in ethnic terms. All official forms, registrations and identy cards require the statement of the bearer's "race". The Second Malaysia Plan, a five-year development programme, embodies a plan for "restructuring society" along ethnic line (1971), by redistributing different sectors of the economy more evenly between different ethnic groups. One of its principal aims is to increase the involvement of the Malays in the commercial sector. None of this of course encourages universalistic thinking or action, but merely perpetuates an ethnic particularism which is a major obstacle to the development of class awareness in Malaysian society.

All this, however, must not be allowed to obscure two facts. The first is that internal differentiation within each of the ethnic groups, Malay, Chinese and Indian, is succh that they cannot be considered as "groups" in the sociological sense. Great disparities of wealth and power exist in all the communities: the Malay royalty and politicans versus poor peasants; wealthy Chinese businessmen versus the impoverished proletariat; and Indian political and business leaders versus indigent labourers and rubber tappers.

Second, there is evidence objectively to demonstrate the existence of certain occupational and functional strata across ethnic lines, popular ideology notwithstanding. At this stage, however, it is probably more appropriate to refer to them as "quasi-groups" (Dahrendorf 1959). Figures indicate that, despite the Malay preference quotas for higher civil service positions, in comparison with the composition of the population at large, in 1968 the Malays in fact held fewer Division I posts than the other groups (Gibbons and Zakaria 1971: 336-7). It is true that the proportion of Malays in the overall Malaysian Civil Service is higher than for other groups, but this is balanced by the clear predominance of non-Malays in the technical and professional service (*ibid*:338). It is apparent that within ihe government, political and business elities, a symbiosis exists between members of all communities, whereby licenses to do business for example, are traded for directorships (cf. Evers 1973:128). Again, the extent to which such alliances and quasi-group formation succeed in dissolving ethnic boundaries is open to question, as will be shown.

At the other end of the scale, in the labour force the

TABLE 6.1

Ethnic Representation in Division I Posts in Malaysia, Comparison with Proportion in Total Population

	(% in onarall population	(% in Division
Malays	46.8	36.3
Chinese	34.1	36.1
Indians	9.0	31.5
Tribals	8.7	—
Other	1.4	—

Source: Gibbons and Zakaria (1971).

unemployment rate for Malays and Chinese is not significantly different: 5.8 per cent of Malays and 6 9 per cent of Chinese. Among the Indians, however, it reaches 10.3 per cent (Department of Statistics 111). In urban areas alone, figures for the same year show 11.7 per cent of Malays, 8.5 per cent of Chinese and 12.6 per cent of Indians actively unemployed (*ibid*: 133). In the field of education, the Chinese have a slightly lower proportion (but not strikingly so) of members who have never received formal education: 15.8 per cent, compared with 17.0 per cent of Indians and 20.2 per cent of Malays (*ibid*: 60). In the distribution of occupations by sector, certain ethnic imbalances clearly occur, showing a heavier Malay concentration in agriculture and such services as the police/army/fire brigade; the Chineses predominate in sales and commerce, mining, clerical and medical services; the Indians in agriculture and labour and in senior administrative and medical services. When on the other hand we compare the percentage of each ethnic group in particular occupational categories and status levels (which takes into account the different ratios wlthin the total population), somewhat smaller differences occur along ethnic lines. Thus among high professionals (including physicians, dentists, medical technicians and other specialists) are found 0.1 per cent of the Malays, 0.4 per cent of the Chinese and 0.4 per cent of the Indians. In the teaching profession we find 3.4 per cent of the Malay work force, 2.9 per cent of the Chinese and 3.0 per cent of the Indians. Administrative and executive positions occupy 0.7 per cent of the employed Malays, 2.8 per cent of the Chinese and 1.2 per cent of the Indians. 3.2 per cent of the Malays, 3.7 per cent of the Chinese and 4.4 per cent of the Indians are occupied in transport and communications, Finally, in the category of labourers are found 5.7 per cent of Malays, 6.3 per cent of the Chinese and 10.4 per cent of Indians (Department of Statistics 1968: 100). And even in the realm ot high finance, by virtue of the elite alliances referred to above, a growing number of company directorships are moving into the hands of the Malays, some of whom hold multiple positions of such kinds. One individual, scion of a sultan's family, sits on the board of 14 different eompanies. Given the ethnic cross-section in each occupational and status category, lack of total balance notwithstanding, the differences are not of sufficient magnitude for a simplistic claim of ethnic stratification on a completely pluralistic division of labour to be substantiated.

Perceptions of Stratification in Malaysian Society

While three parallel and more or less independent systems of ranking and prestige between traditional Malay, Chinese and Indian sections can be clearly shown to exist, there is in all cases a demonstrable variation within each group by level and language of education. Members of each of the ethnic groups also tend to evaluate "modern" ranks and occupations differently according to whether the referent is "Malaysian society" as a whole or whether that of the ethnic community alone. Particular attention will be devoted here to the Malay system, with illustrative contrasts from the Chinese and Indian communities.

In order to discover how people in Malaysia perceive stratification in their own society, both formal and informal methods were used. Formal questionaire surveys, in which respondents were asked about "the people at the top of our society" and "the people at the bottom", were employed to elicit general categories. More specific questions were then asked about the identity of leaders and elites, from which some assessment could be made concerning the qualities of, and qualifications for high (and low) status, Since for most respondents this is an artificial way of thinking about their own society, greatest attention was paid to informal situations in which individuals spontaneously judged others, placed them in categories and provided some expression of social distance or solidarity between speaker or actor and referent. This proved to be a more difficult method practically and far less quantifiable, but had the advantage of taking into account the dynamics and inconsistencies of real situations. Ultimately, this is probably the more reliable approach despite its qualitative nature.

The Malay Status System

In the traditional Malay status system there were two major criteria of rank: an ascriptive secular system revolving around royalty and aristocracy; and a religious hierarchy, both ascribed through descent from the Prophet, and achieved through religious learning and piety. Members of the former group comprised a closed stratum[8] (Gullick 1965). Thus, even the most remote relative or descendant of a sultan or rajah may use a royal title. Descendants of a royal female and a non-royal male could (and can) claim special intermediate titles, which vary according to state, e.g., *wan* or *megat* in Perak, Kedah and Selangor, *ungku* in Johor, and *mik* in Kelantan and Trengganu. There was also a series of aristocratic titles, e.g., *datuk* and *tun* which are still used and can now be achieved through service to the nation. The values associated with government, "nablesse" and non-manual "clean" occupations have been carried over from the royal era into the modern sector as the ideal of most Malays (cf. Alatas 1968).

With the high evaluotion placed on the Islamic faith, religious titles also carried great weight. As a result of early Arab trade and immigration to Malaya, a number of Malays claim not only Arabic descent, but even descent from the Prophet Mohammed which entitles the males to the honourific *Syed* and females to that of *Shrifah*. Other terms like *Sheikh* are also deemed to indicate Arab origins. Rank in the religious domain could also be achieved in various ways. One was by making the pilgrimage to Mecca, whereby the pilgrim was permitted to append the title *Haji* (female *Hajjah*) to the name. Otherwise, recognised religious leaders and teachers commonly assumed one of a variety of possible titles, e.g., *imam*, *ustaz*, *munshi*, *lebai*. Generally speaking, Malays are extremely sensitive to all opportunities to express rank, from any source, traditional or modern, religious or secular, ascribed or achieved, indigenous or immigrant, from an inventory of which the above is but a limited sample. In the present day may be added such new honourifics as "doctor", "professor", "inspector" or "captain", derived from (just one more) immigrant, achieved secular, modern status sector.

It is partly on the basis of the traditional system of ranked statuses that perceptions of stratification by modern Malays must be viewed, both of the ethnic community and of wider Malaysian society. In a number of surveys I conducted, in which informants were asked to rank certain occupations and statuses, and reinforced by observation of attitudes and behaviours, significant differences emerged depending upon whether the referent was Malay or Malaysian society. When the ranking is interpreted as pertaining to the Malay community alone, royalty is still said to be at the apex. Where Malaysian society is the focus, on the other hand, government officers are normally seen as the elites, the ones with the "real" power. Indeed, as the new rulers, they tend to receivc a similar kind of respect as the traditional rulers,[9] and for upwardly mobile Malays civil service is analogous to a more ancient feudal-retainer service in the household of a sultan (Alatas 1968). Within the ethnic status framework, individuals of high religious standing are generally claimed to rank second to royalty and aristocracy, while for Malaysian society as a whole, businessmen and professionals, particularly those with high (western) education, are normally placed second.

Verbalised expressions of ranking, however, do not invariably correspond with attitudes and statements observed in actual situations. Despite the charisma (*daulat*) of royalty and old titles in the ethnic community, this frequently contrasts with the personal unpopularity of individual incumbents; further, the qualities of education and achievement of many royals are notably lacking in comparison with such distinctions on the part of many non-royals. Many Malays too resent the sizeable stipends and other privileges for which royalty are still eligible. What really seems to preserve the continuing respect which considered opinion still accords to the sultans is their symbolic position, representative of Malay history and identity, as many informants put it, "something the other races do not have". Otherwise, they are not remarkable for their contribution to modern society. In contrast, those who really receive the admiring attention, however, reluctant (see below), within Malay society today are the successful professional and business people, who are all the more respected for their achievements over what are considered to be overwhelming odds, in view of the stereotyped model of the social structure described above. In communities where they are found, Malays will single out, in tones almost of awe and reverence, those of their number who have reached these pinnacles of attainment in the modern sector of their society. And in communities where they are not to be found, the ideal is submerged by a retreat into the preserve of traditional ethnic status rank of royal and religious elites as a protective mechanism and boundary market.

Whatever the appearance to the outside observer, few Malays see either their own ethnic group or the wider society as divided into "classes", unless we use the term "class" in its loosest sense of "category" or "quasi-group" (Dahrendorf 1959). Indeed, for monolingual Malays, there is no word conveying the meaning of the English term in their vocabulary. Most Malays perceive Malay society in the form of two polarities, or dichotomously (Ossowski 1963: 24ff.). Among the polarities most commonly found are the "rich and poor" (*orang berada, tak berada*); "big people and little people" (*orang besar, orang kecil*); the educated and uneducated; and the religious and non-religious. These are hardly classes in a functional sense, since they are not closed or clearly bounded (sociocentric), but change according to the relative position of speaker and referent and the point the speaker wishes to make. Thus, when ego is comparing himself to a prince, the latter is a "big man" and himself a "little man". But in comparison to a poor peasant, his characterisation of himself may be in the direction of a "big man". The dichotomous view of society appears to be held most commonly among Malays of less and only vernacular education.

As far as Malaysian society is concerned, however, ethnic "class" distinctions predominate. The question as to who are at the "top" and "bottom" of society spontaneously evoked ethnic responses as the largest single category of all replies. Typically, Malays, or Malays and Indians were seen as the "bottom" (by over 30 per cent of informants) and Chinese at the "top" (by over 40 per cent of informants). Again, the ethnic perception of Malaysian society was more marked among Malays with less or only vernacular education.

Chinese Perceptions of Stratification[10]

Since their long detachment from China, and from access to the traditional high stutus positions of genetry and literati-bureaucrats, overseas Chinese communities have developed new status systems and their own internal social structure within the wider society of which they are a part. Ranking is based heavily upon the attribute of wealth. Wealth has become a social solvent which can mitigate humble origins in a way not possible either in traditional Chinese of Malay society. Political or governmental positions do not receive such universally high evaluation as among the Malays, nor do any religious positions. There is also a tendency among the Chinese to view most rural occupations as the least desirable, and to be relegated to the "bottom of society", both Chinese and Malaysian. The professionals, whom the Malays would place (in practice, if not in word) nearer to the "top" of society, are more often placed by the Chinese in a middle or upper middle category, but secondary to businessmen, particularly when the latter is re-inforced by wealth.

As far as Malaysian society is concerned, the sultans and Malay aristocracy are often acknowledged to beat the apex of the structure, but in a category by themselves, in a sense almost detached from "real" society. Among the Chinese, as among the Malays and Indians, the vernacular educated more commonly perceive Malaysian society in ethnic terms. Thus, the political elites are identified as the Malays, while the Chinese feel they have no elites at the national level. In the political domain, however, even many Chinese who are English-educated and of higher status (from the standpoint of the observer) perceive an exclusion from positions of power and authority (seeing these as the preserve of the Malays). At the other end of the scale too, Chinese of all social and economic levels see the "bottom" of Malaysian society in ethnic terms, viz., the rural Malays. Wealthy Chinese rarely seem to recognise the existence of the Chinese poor, in keeping with their stereotypes of the "lazy Malays" and "industrious Chinese". Interestingly, they also see the Malays at the top, in their capacity of royalty and government leaders. Although the Chinese have a term (and a character) corresponding to the English world "class", they are more likely to see the inlernal divisions of their own community in the form of dialect or region of origin lines than those of class.

In general, those occupations and statuses commanding the highest respect among the modern Chinese in Malaysia are those in commerce, urban-oriented and of western origin, for which English language education is an important qualification, and this accords with the growing westernisation and modernisation of Malaysian society as a whole.

Indian Perception of Stratification[11]

Within the Indian community in Malaysia, the deepest internal division is undoubtedly religious, and secondly according to regional and linguistic affiliation. Cleavages by major religious groups, Muslims, Hindus, Sikhs and Jains, are far more salient than those of any pan-Indian hierarchy, including caste.[12] Within certain religious groups, sub-divisions corresponding both to regional and occupational specialisations are also found. For example, the Muslims are divided into: the Chulias who are largely Hindi and Tamil-speaking cloth merchants and jewellers; the Kakas from the Malabar region, also merchants; the Tankasi from Southern Benares who are mainly breadsellers and labourers; and the North Indian Muslims from Gujarat and what is now Pakistan, who are largely traders. Religious elites tend to rank highly in all groups, those of the Muslims being approximately the same as among the Malays.

In contrast to traditional Malay society, however, Indian Muslims always placed a greater value upon business as an occupation and wealth as a source of status, and this is maintained both within the Indian community and in Malaysian society at large. Government and professional occupations, with English language education as a qualification, are also highly respected and sought after. Among the Indians as a whole, the stereotype of Malaysian society is represented most strongly as one in which the Malays are the political and the Chinese the economic elites, while the Indians are "at the bottom" of society. Again, the concept of "class" is poorly understood, save in English and highly educated circles, the Indian role in the labour union organisation notwithstanding (see below).

In their perceptions of the importance of modern governmental and political positions, of professional occupations, of the instrumental value of the English language and higher education, and of the increasingly high evaluation of business and commerce (as enshrined in the Second Malaysia Plan). the Malays, Chinese and Indians in Malaysia are all subscribing to a status system which is becoming more uniform throughout much of the world. This is accompanied by a growing emphasis on the material perquisities in the form of modern suburban homes, and an urban-oriented, consumer-based style of life, with cars, TV's, servants and lavish entertainment, by members of all groups, despite any Malay misgivings over conflict with religious or residual peasant values (cf. Mokhzani 1965: 155; Kahar Bador 1973).

Perceptions of Inequality in Inter-Ethnic Situations

Probably the most telling way of actually demonstrating an absence of class consciousness, and concommitantly, perception of individual and group conflicts and resentments in other idioms on the past of Malaysians, is through a series of situations which in other societies or environments might well have generated the growth of strategic groups or class antagonisms. In recounting these situations, however, care must be taken not to lose sight of the broader picture, i.e., of the overall structure and organisation of Malaysian society, and of the political and historical environment in which is exists.

Given the facts of growing convergence of status evaluation in many spheres, especially in modern achievement-based occupations, and of the shared desire for political, economic and educational resources by members of all the ethnic sections of Malaysia, and in conjunction with the fact that there is less maldistribution of these resources than is popularly believed, the interest of the observer focuses upon an apparent social and cultural "lag". That is, the extent of universalism in judging individuals of the same objective status levels and pursuing similar styles of life, is still relatively limited. Particularistic ethnic-based criteria still modify what would otherwise appear to be converging values and equivalent social rank categories. Even in the face of similarities of occupations and the aknowledged desirability thereof, internal ethnic differentiation within these positions is commonly preserved. Within the merging process there is a drawing apart, a constant awareness of individuals as incumbents of another, cross-cutting status-role system, that of ethnicity. Partly this signifies a persistence of traditional status values alongside and in opposition to those of a modernising system (a classical case of status incongruence), but in Malaysia it would seem to be more than just that. It is more a case of "sense of group position" (Blumer 1958) in a complex social environment in which ethnic attributes play an important role in structuring social situations. Inevitably this involves the frequent invocation of ethnic stereotypes, both of self and other, although not uniformly favourable to self or negative to other. Such stereotypes are not necessarily immutable, and may be used variably according to the nature of the distinction intended. Finally, within the growing competition for similar occupations by all Malaysians, it is apparent that the same occupations are sometimes valued for different reasons and adapted to different ends by members of various ethnic groups.

Absence of Class Awareness in Intra-Ethnic Relations

A striking feature of most situations where individuals exploit others of the same ethnic group or where there is a marked superordinate-subordinate distinction, is the rarity with which it is perceived as a class phenomenon. Rarely is it viewed or generalised as the product of a basic social inequality or different set of life chances within the group. Although it would be naive to claim no resentments at all, mostly such cases are seen as individual or person-specific only. The examples which follow were largely drawn from fieldwork in which the point of orientation was the Malay community in which the research was concentrated.

One response to inequality, particularly of inferior to superior, which is characteristic of Malays, is a form of jealousy recognised by the Malays themselves and called by them *denki.* This underscores the ambivalence with which persons of higher status or success are viewed by those of lower, thus tempering the respect otherwise accorded. Expressions of *denki* are found from simple situations of envy in "keeping up with the Jones" to professional patron-client relations over services of the latter. Often there is an element of resentment that some of their group have "made it" whereas they themselves did not, for example in obtaining university scholarships. The assumption normally mode and implied is that the favoured ones merely had more effective patrons or some other hidden relationship not available to the speaker. Similar sentiments are frequently heard from small Malay entrepreneurs who are unable to obtain any of the much-vaunted special loans or training earmarked for the Malays under the Second Malaysia Plan. They allege that all the privileges fall into the hands of the rich Malays who are "political wheelerdealers" (*kaki politik*), self-interested (*kepentingan sendiri*) or "climb on the backs of others" (*naik atas belakang orang lain*). Such sentiments usually arise out of individual actions or particular incidents and are therefore personal. They do not normally exist as part of a coherent body of generalisations from which an incipient class awareness could be adduced. But herein lies the ambivalence: the strong latent respect for all elites (and titles), royal, governmental, professional; while the strength of ethnic pride may still be sufficient to counter the personal unpopularity of certain incumbents of those positions.

Denki is also found in ethnic institutions, where leaders are accused of not paying due attention to the rank and file or even of going against the interests of the latter. One example concerned the Malay Chamber of Commerce, an institution designed to protect and foster the interests and needs of Malay traders and businessmen. In practice, its membership in one large Malaysian city includes only a fraction of those eligible by their occupation. Most of the Malay entrepreneurs who have not joined the Chamber of Commerce claim that its leaders are too self-interested and proud (*sombong*) hence the former derive no benefits from membership. They claim that the leaders do not help their own people as do the Chinese, a negative self-stereotype. On the other hand, some dissatisfied members and non-members of the Chamber prefer to use sub-ethnic epithets to characterise the Chamber's officials, calling them "Arabs" (which some of them are by descent) instead. By dissociating themselves from a common ethnicity some individuals attempt to minimise the divisive implications of intra-ethnic exploitation translating it instead into an ethnic idiom. One newly-formed small group of Malay petty traders which organised itself outside the auspices of the Chamber of Commerce in the same city, spent many of its initial meetings, not in creating a force in opposition to the Chamber's elitism, but in wrangling over sub-ethnic identities (Indonesian, Arab, Indian-Muslim) (cf. Nagata 1974b) within its own ranks.

Potential class unity or formation of strategic or action groups in the form of trade unions across ethnic lines is also weak. Partly, this is due to the weakness of the unions themselves. This in turn may be directly related to their emasculation by a government still mindful of the experiences of the 1930's when allegedly Kuomintang organised labour movements from China created a measure of political upheaval at the time. As a result many of the modern union leaders behave more in the manner of obedient civil servants than true representatives of their constituents. Another reason for the ineffectiveness of the unions arises out of the predominantly agricultural base of the economy and limited development of manufacturing and a true "labour market". A third reason has to do with the pervasive ethnic structuring of most social organisations, which reaches even to the trade unions. In some cases this is a consequence of the identification of certain occupations with particular ethnic groups, e.g. Malay taxi-drivers or Indian rubber tappers. In other cases, parallel ethnic unions have emerged within an occupation. Thus, there are ethnic branches of the Teachers' Union, each acting independently. Finally, any idea of the union as a meaningful pressure group seems to have been submerged by the demonstrated effectiveness of the political party as a more viable alternative. Again, most political parties in Malaysia are either overtly or covertly largely ethnic institutions. In sum, it is estimated that only about 10 per cent of Malaysia's labour force is union organised (Pillai 1972: 15). The prognosis for any emergent class consciousness through unions in the near future is therefore slim.

Circumvention of possible intra-ethnic "class" problems is sometimes achieved in other ways. A noticeable reticence on the part of Malays in particular to use the professional services of members of their own community centres around the assumption that such relationships are fraught with possibilities of mutual dissatisfaction and disagreements which are more appropriate or more tolerable between members of different ethnic groups. Thus, Malays feel fewer constraints in a quarrel over prices or poor service with say, a Chinese contractor, but distinctly uncomfortable in haggling or quarreling with a member of his own community. By extension it may be said that among Malays in general there is often an aversion to employing or being employed by fellow Malays. Outside the traditional royal or neo-traditional government/civil service, personal dependence and subordination is a condition at best ambivalent, but often potentially dangerous. While reflected glory can be acquired from such associations, the burdens can be onerous. Thus. many Malays are quite explicit in stating their preference for a non-Malay employer, saying the latter are lets demanding or exploitative, more generous, and are less likely to take the employee for granted. Conversely, the employee feels less personal loyalty or obligation to commit himself beyond the call of contractual duty to his employer hence unbound by the multiplex ties of an all-embracing patronage which limit his freedom. This helps to explain the common preference for non-Malay (although Muslim) house-servants on the part of Malays. Usually this dilemma is resolved by hiring a Muslim Indian, or else rationalised by the device of ascribing either to the servant or to the employer a distinct sub-ethnic status, e.g., by calling the former "Indonesian" or "Indian", or transforming the latter into an "Arab" in order to structure the situation in more acceptable terms and to avoid the encombrances of ethnic obligation (cf. Nagata 1947b). This process frequently involves the invocation of a negative ethnic self-image: Malays are said to be lazy and to gossip in-ordinately about their employers' affairs, or to take advantage of their favoured position to waste time. On consideration, however, the prime factor appears to be the need to express status distinctions in the form of ethnic difference, thus avoiding the knotty question of intra-ethnic sub-ordination or inequality. Thus, the unity of ethnic group and its status-honour system is preserved.

Among the Chinese likewise, the objectively quite clear distinctions between rich and poor fail to generate the heat of resentment and awareness that for example, the popular identification of Malays with political power and privilege eommonly produces. Preference for utilising the services of their own group by the Chinse, however, is justified less on tolerance of super-ordinate-sub-ordinate relationships within the group than by the fear of retaliatory sanctions for failing to do so, due to the highly organised nature of the community. Here, the continuing salience of certain historical events and a tradition long underground, cannot go unmentioned. This is the residue of the labour-organising activities of the 1930's, continued in a different form in the Emergency (1948-60), and probably simmering beneath the surface in some segments of the Chinese community today. While such stirrings may have many of the trappings and heritage of a true class struggle, its current manifestations seem to represent more an expression of Chinese chauvinism, an ethnically defined discontent, despite its official ideological characterisation (as "Communist").[13]

In a similar vein, it may be said that the strongest labour union in Malaysia, carrying 30 per cent of all union membership viz., the plantation workers, is largely an Indian movement, unable to mobilise the interest of non-Indian workers in the same industry (Pillai 1972: 15-16). The latter continue to operate through other institutional channels, usually the ethnic political party. Otherwise within the Indian community, occupational and other status differences tend to be phrased with reference to such particularistic considerations as regional, linguistic or religious origin, especially where these closely correspond, as with the Chulias and Tankasis (see above).

Ethnic Perceptions of Social Difference

It is impossible to deal with the weakness of class awareness in Malaysia without facing the very tangible reality of ethic consciousness which dominates most perceptions of social inequality in Malaysian society. Not only in lelatively abstract questioning on leadership and on the nature of those people "at the top" and "at the bottom" of society, but also in daily action, ethnic boundaries are erected and maintained, even within similar occupations and statuses. Although a number of "modern" occupations, are now uniformly (by all ethnic groups) considerd good and desirable, that goodness and desirability tends to be moulded within an ethnic format and hedged around with ethnic symbols. Where quasi-groups with common latent interests (Dahrendorf 1959) exist in the perception of the observer, these have not become manifest and mobilised as the basis of conflict groups or incipient social classes. Instead, vertical status groups continuously cross-cut and override potential horizontal one of stratification, as numerous incidents show.

One such incident[14] involved a predominantly "working class" urban Malay community, part of whose land was threatened with expropriation for purpose of the construction of a petrol station by an unknown company. In practice, those behind the plan were Malays and other leaders of the Malay Chamber of Commerce, but very few of the threatened community knew this. When the plan to re-zone the land was announced, it was immediately assumed that the project must be Chinese-sponsored, and although the anonymity of the planners remained intact until the end, it was consistently regarded as a Chinese conspiracy. Significantly, the channels activated by members of the community in an attempt to counteract the "plot" were all particularistic in nature. First, (somewhat ironically) they tried the Malay Chamber of Commerce; later Muslim religious and voluntary associations, and finally the ethnic political party (UMNO). An appeal was even sent to the king (a Malay sultan). Although complete satisfaction was not obtained through these channels, there was never any suggestion of neglect or obstructionism by class superiors.

The interpretation remained that it was an ethnic plot and the whole affair was played out in these terms.

Quasi-Groups—Businessmen

The merchant and entrepreneur has long been regarded in social science as a crucial functional group in the classic class hierarchy. A capitalist group, largely in control over their own means of production, they are seen as the original bourgeoisie, at least in the west. As bourgeois they share common interests and a similar life style, and are thus members of a single status group. In modern Malaysia, with its official ideology as reflected in the Second Malaysia Plan, business and commerce receive high respect and are lauded as the goals to which all presently under-privileged Malays should aspire. This is publicly supported with references to the Koran and the Prophet Mohammed's role as a merchant, and the fact that trade has always been a respect occupation in the Islamic world is stressed. The Chinese and Indians, of course, have long regarded business and trade as respectable and desirable. In an objective sense therefore, business success (and the wealth it brings) can be said to be giving rise to a functional group transcending mere sectional interests. Subjectively, however, ethnic segregation within the class still dominates most business activities, evaluations of its role in society and the selection of individual with whom to do business.

In certain contexts there is, not surprisingly, a preference for doing business with members of one's own ethnic community. Thus, the Malays have a battery of folk sayings about the honesty (*kejujoran*) and trust (*amandh*) of which only fellow Muslims are capable, and constantly excoriate the deceptive practices (*tipumenipu*) of the Chinese. In the same vein, they defend the little niceties of Malay custom (*adat*), such as politeness to customers (*melayan pelanggan*) as being more important than making a larger profit. Likewise ths Chinese prefer their own kind for reasons of efficiency and better service. Indians also feel that other Indians, Muslim or Hindu, are more efficient and better-organised than the Malays, although Indian Muslims are somewhat more tolerant of Malays for religious reasons. Non-Malays further are often resentful of the Malays' current special position, and even should a Malay become an indubitably successful entrepreneur, he will always be regarded as having "made it" unfairly, and as a likely candidate for failure in the future.[15]

There are occasions, however, when negative ethnic self-images take over and other considerations dictate the choice of business partner or evaluation to be made. Malays, for example, will avoid trading with other Malays because of their ineffeciency, poor service and contacts, and even it is sometimes alleged, because they capitalise on their "race" and religion for custom but without providing the appropriate service or competitive prices expected. The latter, of course, retaliate by claiming that the lower prices of the non-Malays are only possible through their habit of cheating, while Malay customers also try to take advantage of their "race" by demanding excessive credit which is not honoured. Some Malays even go as far as to suggest that the aspiring Malay businessman should become "more like the Chinese", a sentiment one increasingly hears among the Malay government elite and successful Malay entrepreneurs themselves (cf. Poppenoe 1970). Thus, even within the growing alliance between Malay and non-Malay at the highest levels, perceptions of each other are most commonly phrased in ethnic terms, even when positive. Finally, in business transactions, as in the case of professional services, where it is anticipated that haggling or unpleasantness might be necessary, the preference is to transfer this hostility to a member of another ethnic group where fewer particularistic constraints operate.

The disjunctions between the business communities of the three ethnic groups are reinforced by the existence of three separate Chambers of Commerce which do not co-operate with one another.

Despite a tendency for members of different ethnic groups but of similar social or occupational status to converge in the same suburban residential areas, the possible effects of this on strategic group formation are limited. First, many entrepreneurs still prefer to reside close to their place of business, e.g., in shop-houses, and even these often follow lines of residential segregation by ethnicity. Second, even within modern "mixed" housing settlements, private social activities are still largely intra-ethnic. As yet the "business community" in Malaysia more closely resembles Dahrendorf's quasi-group only.

Quasi-Groups—Professionals and Civil Servants

As among businessmen, professionals of different ethnicity do not commonly align themselves as a single interest or pressure group vis a vis other social groups, as we have seen with respect to the teachers' unions. While a uniformly high esteem is placed upon higher (and often English-medium) education as the means of achieving professional status, educotion has become one of the most active arenas of ethnic competition (Enloe 1970), as a means of "showing one race what the other can do". Little parables containing equivalents of the latter message are now frequently heard, for example in speeches and sermons to Malays by religious teachers and community leaders on special occasions. Finally, members of different groups view professional status as a means to different ends. Whereas many Chinese, for example, would become a doctor for material reward, a Malay might see it as one stepping-stone to political mobility. Indeed, it is significant that of the approximately one dozen Malay doctors in the entire country, at least half are active politicans and not practising medicine at all.

Civil servants, another quasi-group which might be expected to become an effective strategic group in a modernising society, are in Malaysia ethnically divided. Although meeting and co-operating in the public (i.e., the work) sphere, in the private sphere, even when residing in the large, multi-ethnic "middle-class" or "upper middle class" suburban settlements of the capital wherein dwell many civil servants, low ethnic interaction and even lower intermarriage is found. Rather than forming groups with recognised and manifest interests, the latter remain latent and subordinate to the manifest interest of the ethnic group, as shown in such activities as lobbying over ethnic quotas in the civil service. The instrumental value of the civil service is seen by Malays as a source of titles and association with royalty and aristocracy, by the non-Malays as an avenue to wealth and power.

Quasi-Groups—Workers

Even among the workers, the strategic group which has per-empted so much of the attention of western stratification theorists, there exists in Malaysia little sense of commonality acrose ethnic lines. In areas where inter-group mobilisation might be expected, as in labour unions or in unemployment grievances, in fact no such action occurs, as we have seen. Although the rate of unemployment for each group is approximately similar, it is usually perceived as a zero-sum situation by the disaffected, who atribute their own misfortune to the machinations or special privileges of another group. Indeed, the major communal riots in Malaysia over the past few years have been largely "working class" phenomena. The weakness of the trade unions has already been discussed. Most workers' associations, e.g., those for hawkers, trishaw and taxi-drivers, cluster within specific ethnic communities. Potential solidarity of Malaysia's workers is further weakened by the nature of the economy. Due to the under-development of the manufacturing and commercial sector and consequent lack of total dependence even of many urban dwellers on an industrial economy, the focus of the poor is not inevitably directed to worker-employer opposition. Individuals and groups are cloaked in other roles more salient than the functional or occupational, and very often ethnic.

Although the work arena forms one of the most common areas of interethnic interaction, this interaction rerely seems to spill over to other spheres of activity. Workers tend to see work opportunity as a "limited good" and their competitors as members of other ethnic groups. These are the people who most frequently characterise the "top" of society as dominated by members of another group, while the "bottom" consists largely of their own kind. Thus, Malays see themselves (and sometimes themselves and the Indians) at the "bottom" and the Chinese "on top". Many Indians express the same view. Chinese on the other hand will invariably focus on Malay elites at the "top", and while recognising the existence of the Malay peasantry, quite clearly see themselves as a discrimiated working majority, particularly in the urban areas. So strong is this feeling among the working Chinese indeed, that some have attempted to improve their working chances in certain fields by converting to Islam, in what they see as a quasi-ethnic shift or change in ethnic status, at least publicly. Conversely, a number of ambitious Malay (and Indian) families who wish their children to rival the Chinese in certain trades, are sending them to Chinese vernacular schools in the expectation that this will thereby improve their commercial chances.

Conclusions

The Malaysian material illustrates that there is clearly a trend from what might be described as a Furnivallian type of pluralism with distinct systems of status ranking for each ethnic section to a form of objective stratification in which there is increasing competition for the same statuses and resources by members of all ethnic groups. Modern Malaysian society therefore is more stratified than plural. On the subjective level, however, this process is obscured, with the result that a form of "subjective pluralism" may be said to exist. This involves persistent behefs by members of all groups that, a) the division of labour and valued resources is ethnic-based, and b) where the above is patently not the case, perceptions of similar occupations and statuses and their incumbents are cloaked in ethnic terms, as are evaluations of their performances.

At all social levels attempts are made to maintain complementary ethnic differences even within the same occupational and status group, and choices of patrons, clients, employers and characterisations thereof are tailored accordingly. Thus, ethnic groups resemble vertical status groups, which precludes the formation of effectional or strategic groups. Members of a single occupational or status category of diverse ethnic origins correspond to Dahrendorf's quasi-groups only. As yet there is a very underdeveloped sense of class consciousness in Malaysian society, either within its component ethnic segment or for the country as a whole. What sense of class there is tends to be more frequently verbalised among those with higher or English medium education, and projected on to other ethnic groups.

The factors involved in such perceptions of inequality must

be sought, not at the individual or personal level, but in the order of the wider social structure. This would include the residue of traditional status ranking ideals of each of the communities—"left-overs" from the true "pluralist" period, when separate and parallel status systems were the norm. Account must also be taken of the perpetuation of ethnic idioms in most public and officlal statements and policy, the weakness of the industrial economy and lack of total dependence on the urban market by much of the working population, and the limited development of labour unions. Under the impact of modernisation, many changes are impinging upon Malaysian society without any clear stabilisation having yet set in (cf. Evers 1973). Hence there has been insufficient time for meaningful strategic groups or class-like sentiments to crystallise. Finally, the total self-image of a society by its members includes its historical antecedents as well as external events impinging upon it. Clearly the existence of the parent nations of the immigrant Malaysians and the shadow of earlier union and other activities as well as the colonial past will colour this image. Thus, within the growing stratification of Malaysian society, what Dehrendorf terms latent interests have not yet become manifest, and a somewhat anachronistic ethnic model still widely prevails.

NOTES

1. Part of this may be due to the simple reason that it is as much a descriptive as a theoretical construct, developed inductively in many cases by each writer to suit the characteristic of the society in which he studied.
2. I have conveniently omitted all reference to "race". It is true that in many countries, particularly in the colonial era, physical differences were often as important as, if not more so, than cultural in determining life chances in the overall society. In Malaysia however, physical characteristics are *indubitably* secondary to ethnic/cultural differences in all matters of status determination.
3. Somewhat confusingly, however, the political scientists and some sociologists, e.g. Dahrendorf (1959) adhere to a definition of pluralism which is almost the reverse of that of most anthropologists and sociologists. For the former, the larger the number of cross-cutting allegiances of individuals to different institutions regardless of

particularistic ties, the greater the pluralism. Thus, individuals can be of high status in one system and low in another.

4. Formed in 1963 out of the previous territories of Sarawak and Sabah in North Borneo on the one hand, and the Malay peninsula on the other. Singapore seceded in 1965.
5. The ethnic breakdown of the population of Malaysia in 1970 was as follows:

Malays	46.8%
Chinese	34.1
Indians	9.0
Aboriginals	8.7
Others	1.4

(Department of Statistics, 1972:24)

6. All Malays are of the Muslim faith (as are also some Indians). The majority of Indians of course are Hindu, and the Chinese a combination of Buddhist, Confucianist and Taoist.
7. These are respectively the United Malays National Organisation (UMNO); the Malaysian Chinese Association (MCA); and the Malaysian Indian Congress (MIC).
8. A major exception to this rule was the traditional state of Negri Sembilan, where the unilineal (matrilineal) kinship basis of the political system created vertical cleavages along lineage lines, and these frequently overrode distinctions of status or class (Gullick 1965).
9. It is instructive that even the modern word in Malay for "government" is *kerajaan,* whose etymology clearly links it to rajahs and royalty. That some of the new officials are not necessarily considered as their equals by members of the royalty themselves, however, is also true, althongh a somewhat peripheral issue here (cf. Kahar Bador 1973).
10. I am indebted for some of the information on Chinese attitudes and values to some of my students and their research at the University Sains Malaysia, Penang.
11. My knowledge of the views of the Indians regarding internal stratification of their own society owes much to the information provided by some of my sudents at the University Sains Malaysia, Penang.
12. The role of caste in Malaysian Indian society is most important in certain religious ceremonies where particular caste specialists are required to officiate, but decreasingly so in matters of marriage and occupation.
13. It is unfortunately just not possible to document these statements with any solid evidence, due to the sheer lack of information and the sensitivity of the problem. This is a view, however, held by many informed and aware Malaysians of all ethnic backgrounds and communicated personally to the writer, but must at best remain impressionistic.

14. See Nagata (1972) for a fuller account of this incident.
15. We cannot ignore here a category of business alliances called "Ali Baba", in which (usually) a Malay uses his special position to obtain a licence for a particular business and finds a Chinese partner to put up the capital, e.g., in taxi-driving. With some exceptions among the elites, this kind of arrangement does not normally result in a particularly close relationship developing between the two partners. Generally the relationship remains purely instrumental contractual and singlestranded, without the subsequent development of any multiplex ties to reinforce it.

REFERENCES

Alatas, Syed Hussein, 1968, "The Grading of Occupational Prestige amongst the Malays in Mglaysia", *Journal of the Malayan Branch of the Royal Asiatic Society*, XLI, Part 1: 146-157.

Arensberg, Conrad M., 1961, "The Community as Object and as Sample", *American Anthropologists*, 63 (2) Part 1: 241-264.

Barber, Bernard 1959, *Social Stratification*, New York: Harcourt, Brace and World.

Barth, Frederik, 1970, *Ethnic Groups and Boundaries*, London: Allen and Unwin.

Benedict, Burton, 1962, "Stratification in Plural Societies", *American Anthropologist*, 64(6): 1235-1246.

Benedict, Burton, 1970 "Pluralism and Stratification" in Plotnicov, L. and A. Tuden (eds.), *Essays in Comparative Social Stratification*, Pittsburgh: University of Pittsburgh Press.

Blumer, Herberi, 1958, "Race Prejudice as a Sense of Group Position", *Pacific Sociological Review*, 1: 3-7.

Dahrendorf, Ralf, 1959, *Class and Class Conflict in Industrial Society*, London: Routledge and Kegan Paul.

Department of Statistics, 1968, Socio-Economic Sample Survey of Households—Malaysia, 1967-1968. Kuala Lumpur: Government Printing Press.

Department of Statistics, 1972, *1970 Population and Housing Census of Malaysia—Community Groups*, Kuala Lumpur: Department of Statistics.

Dumont, Louis, 1961, "Caste, Racism and 'Stratification'." In Louis Dumont and David Pocock (eds.), *Contributions to Indian Sociology*, V: 20-43. The Hague: Mouton.

Enloe, Cynthia, 1968-69, "Issues and Integration in Malaysia", *Pacific Affairs*, 41: 372-385.

Enloe, Cynthia, 1970, *Multi-Ethnic Politics: The Case of Malaysia*, Berkeley: Center for South and Southest Asia Studies, University of California.

Evers, Hans-Dicter, 1966, "The Formation of a Social Class Structure: Urbanisation, Bureaucratisation and Social Mobility in Thailand". *American Sociological Review*, 31 (4): 480-488.

Evers, Hans-Dieter, 1973, "Group Conflict and Class Formation in Southeast Asia", in Evers, H.-D. (ed.), *Modernization in Southeast Asia*, Singapore: Oxford University Press for Institute of Southeast Asian Studies: 108-132.

Freedman, Maurice, 1960, "The Growth of the Plural Society in Malaya", *Pacific Affairs*, 33: 158-168.

Geertz, Clifford, "The Integrative Revolution", in Geertz, C. (ed.), *Old Societies and New States*, Glencoe: Free Press: 103-157.

Gerth, H. and Mills, C.W., 1958, *From Max. Weber*, New York: Oxford University Press, Galaxy Books.

Gibbons, David S. and Zakaria Haji Ahmad, 1971, "Politics and Selection for the Higher Civil Service in New States", *Journal of Comparative Administration* (November): 330-348.

Gullick, J.M., 1965, *Indigenous Political Systems of Western Malaya*, London: Athlone Press, London School of Economics Monographs on Social Anthropology, No. 17.

Kahar, Bador, 1973, "Social Rank, Status-Honour and Social Class Consciousness Amongst the Malays", in Evers, H.-D. (ed.), *Modernization in Southeast Asia*, Singapore: Oxford University Press for Institute of Southeast Asian Studies: 132-149.

Kuper, Leo, 1970, "Stratification in Plural Societies: Focus on White Settler Societies in Africa", in Plotnicov, L. and A. Tuden (ed.), *Essays in Comparative Social Stratification*, Pittsburgh: University of Pittsburgh Press: 77-95.

Kuper, L. and Smith, M.G., 1969, *Pluralism in Africa*, Berkeley and Los Angeles: University of California Press.

Lloyd, Peter, 1966, *The New Elites of Tropical Africa*, London: Oxford University Press.

Mokhzani, B.A.R., 1964, "The Study of Social Stratification and Social Mobility in Malaya", *East Asian Cultural Studies*, 4 (1-4) (March): 138-161.

Morris, H.S., 1967, "Some Aspects of the Concept Plural Society", Man N.S. 2 (2): 169-184.

Nagata, Judith A., 1972, "Social Perspectives, of an Urban Village in a Malayo-Muslim Community", *Western Canadian Journal of Anthropology*, 3 (2): 65-84.

Nagata, Judith A., 1974a, "Tale of Two Cities: The Role of Non-urban Factors in Community Life in Two Malaysian Towns", *Urban Anthropology*, 3 (1): 1-27.

Nagata, Judith A., 1974b, "What is a Malay? Situational Selection of Ethnic Identity in a Plural Society", *American Ethnologist* I (2): 331-350.

Ossowski, Stanislaw, 1963, *Class Structure in the Social Consciousness*

(Translated from the Polish by Sheila Patterson), London: Routledge and Kegan Paul.

Plotnicov, Leonard and Tuden, Arthur (eds.), 1970, *Essays in Comparative Social Stratification*, Pittsburgh: University of Pittsburgh Press.

Pillai, Chandrasekaran' 1972, "Trade Unions as Pressure Groups", in Proceedings of a Seminar, *The Present and Prospective Roles of the Labour Movement in Malaysia*, 15-17.

Poppenoe, Oliver, 1970, "Malay Entrepreneurs: An Analysis of the Social Backgrounds, Careers and Attitudes of the Leading Malay Businessmen in Western Malaysia", Unpublished Ph.D dissertation, London School of Economics and Political Science.

Rex, John, 1970, *Race Relations in Sociological Theory*, London: We,denfield and Nicholson.

Schwab, William, 1961, "Social Stratification in Gwelo", in Southall, Aidan (ed.), *Social Change in Modern Africa*, London: Oxford University Press.

Second Malaysia Plan, 1971, *The Second Malaysia Plan, 1971-75*, Kuala Lumpur: Government Press.

Shibutani, T. and Kwan, K.M., 1965, *Ethnic Stratification: A Comparative Approach*, New York: Collier Macmillan.

Smith, M.G., 1965, *Stratification in Grenada*, Berkeley and Los Angeles: University of California Press.

Southall, Aidan, 1970, "Stratification in Africa", in Plotnicov, L. and Tuden, A. (eds.), *Essays in Comparative Social Stratification*, Pittsburgh: University of Pittsburgh Press: 231-273.

Tuden, Arthur and Plotnicov, L. (eds.), 1970, *Social Stratification in Africa*, New York: Collier Macmillan.

Van Den Berghe, Pierre, 1969, "Pluralism and the Polity: A Theoretical Exploration", in Kuper, L. and Smith M.G. (eds), *Pluralism in Africa*, Berkeley and Los Angeles: University of California Press: 67-81.

7

Social Organisation in Sri Lanka

Even as the family is the biological unit the village may be considered the social unit of the Sinhalese national organisation. It is not self-sufficing functionally, economically or socially but it can be so if hard-pressed to it. The united appearance manifests itself in large-scale undertakings. A sentimental attachment binds the members of each village. This gives rise to loyalties in the maintenance of which bitter feuds take place between villagers. This unity is clearly expressed during festival occasions and religious processions. In games, in processions (*peraheras*), and calamities the group consciousness predominates. The fact that whole villages were bestowed on nobles and brave leaders in recognition of services proves the realisation of its unity.

As stated earlier, for harmonious functioning each village was bound ap with one or more villages either in the vicinity or at a distance. Such a mutual interdependency regulated the needs and maintained co-operation and association. The strongest of these bonds was marriage. Other functional groups living in other villages fulfilled certain functions such as laundering and devil dancing. These duties belonged to certain castes. Certain villages are still in the habit of intermarrying to such degree as to establish strong reminiscences of a system of dual organisation.

People of the same caste inhabited a village. It is not possible to say how this practice originated. Was it due to one original settler, or founder or settlement of the same caste of people giving birth to a village? Migration of a few families from another site may have later resulted in the growth of a whole village which, though long separated, maintained their former relations despite the distance.

Caste, in the Sinhalese social structure is an ancient institution which today has lost both the rigidity and shades of distinction as found in the Indian system. Possibly the four main Aryan grouping into Brahmin, Warrior, Trades and Slave was accepted in early Ceylon. Later, other influences reacted in eliminating the ancient stigmas and helped to forget them. A change in values ushered in new distinctions that appeared under euphemistic titles or foreign linguistic words.

Caste has been organised on the principle of function with the king or chief as the central head. Certain people who were originally grouped together and followed a certain art, function, or profession came afterwards to be known by the name of the art, function or profession. The respectability, superiority and precedence attached to each case fluctuated with the importance and value affixed to each by social convention or regal auihority. From times of old Sinhalese society consisted of agricultural peasants, the chief farmer being nominally the king himself. The Brahmins assisted in spiritual, constitutional and advisory capacities. The merchants of diverse kinds were also known. The fourth class consisted of slaves and menials. The agriculturists since they tended to be possessed of economic power increased their numbers and acquired power. They became the warriors and hence the rulers. With political authority and majesty there developed a superiority of the persons belonging to these circles. These became the chief castes.

Below is a list of the main castes as they function today:

1. Badahela
2. Bedde
3. Bandara
4. Batgama
5. Berawa

6. Durawa
7. Durayi
8. Embetta
9. Gadi
10. Gahala
11. Gattaru
12. Goigama
13. Hakuru
14. Halagama
15. Hinna
16. Huluvali
17. Hunna
18. Karawa
19. Lokuru
20. Navandanna
21. Nekati
22. Oli
23. Padu
24. Panna
25. Panikka
26. Patti
27. Porokara
28. Rada
29. Rodi
30. Salagama
31. Vanni
32. Vahampura
33. Bharata
34. Lansi
35. Miko
36. Eurasian
37. Kapiri
38. Mukkaru

39. Paravaru
40. Anikuntaka
41. Waggai
42. Ja
43. Marakkala

The strict observances connected with caste tend to be forgotten in the cities and towns during social intercourse although in private life the details are observed. Specially in marriage[1] caste distinctions have to be observed. Yet among the lower classes such restrictions regarding commensality and and connubium are fast disappearing. Town life affords the best escape from despondency and depresssion due to caste inferiority in village circles.

The Government ostensibly discourages the perpetuation of caste observances under a cloak of secret preferential treatment for some castes in certain offices. This course of procedure may be justified on principles of democratic rule according to the majority wish. Law and order cannot be effectively maintained in a viliage if the people come to realize the social position of the official is lower than their own. On this score the Englishman (*European*) has been at an added advantage in that he belonoed to the ruling class, had no obvious caste inferiority and was generally a higher official than the Ceylonese.

In the village caste is even now an active force deciding and controlling its affairs. Since each individual knows each other's caste distinctions each one expects preferential and respectful treatment according to the rank. That the system is in such active force could be known from the following. During the many tours of ethnological research into the rural parts of the land the writer has miserably failed in his attempts to make also called lower caste individual sit down on a chair in the presence of the Goigama neighbours.

In spite of all such embarrassments and awkward situations the distinct functions of the different castes are carried out without upsetting the balance of village life. Other villages co-operate. There is co-ordination between the different functions of each caste. The respective caste comes in at the due time and place. Traditional functions should never be overlooked on occasions of a ceremonial nature. The society expects it of them and the people invite the functionaries to undertake such obligations. The dhobies drummers, and other craftsman render the essential services of the village organisation and each of these constitutes an integral part of the whole system. With the march of time and progress modern ideas are quickly spreading in villages where the traditional manner of life prevailed until very late. The establishment of new institutions and the encouragement of western methods are combining to disintegrate the older system. The ideas of eqaulity are loosening the firm ties of mutual regard. Political demagogy has removed the last remaining psychological predisposition for a continuity of the harmonious cycle of ancient village life.

Caste or "*Varga*"[2] can be best understood if one's family name (*cognomen*) is known. This is the *ge* name of family name.[3] It has very little significance today but in ancient times the *ge* name had a real meaning and gave one the idea of a man's family history. Caste and family command great respect and position in every village.[4] There are various grades[5] in the same caste; some being higher and others relatively lower. Besides there are a hundred minor shades of difference. There are families who are believed to belong to or descend from the same ancestor. Yet during the course of years the fluctuations of fortune affect some families as to be of no consequence in society. Finally the superiority of caste alone remains. Most of the families, who presume to belong to the nobility owe their social position to political changes that ushered in a new or foreign dynastic rule. These have been treacherous and disloyal to the old government and consequently found favour with the new. But for their opportune exploits they would still be classed as humble peasants or low caste inferiors.

The *ge* name (*vasagama*, *pelentiya*, *mulnama*) preserves an historical record of the succession of titular ranks, and honorifics added to a family in the course of its long descent. By an examination of these family names it may be possible to trace connections between scattered groups. Their chief role today is in marriage when the family names help to identify the respectability of the new party. These names are also being used as sur-names. A man may marry a girl lower than himself in caste gradation but the girls are alway given aways to superior caste men. Higher social status and family connections can be won by the peculiar system of dowry whereby the rich girls are married to men of good social standing, the majority of them being highly-salaried government officers. The enables the rich girls to get married easily and well whilst their educated, good-looking poor sisters are left at times to pine away and die as spinsters despite their high caste and aristocratic bearing.

The feudal system[6] of the Sinhalese is a thing of the past. Slight traces of it may be evidenced in ancient temples and Kandyan provinces. Caste can function effectively only within such an enforced system where a central authority must be able to exercise full dictatorial power. When this person is the king himself it becomes very easy. Today few families still function as serfs attached to temples or families in return for certain privileges enjoyed by them; these being the use of land or incomes from it. No trace of this is left in the lowlands except where successive families serve certain others as their masters. The annual Kandy Perahera is still organised according to the feudal system.

The Sinhalese kinship terms are designed to suit a classificatory system in which persons who stand in the same relationship to another are addressed by the same terms by him. For example the mother's sisters will all be called by the same term by her children. But for purposes of identification and convenience of reference in their absence various descriptive epithets are added to the names. They are the names of the village or adjectives like small, medium, big, light, fair or dark. Sometimes also a pet name comes to stay.

The juniors are not allowed to address the senior relatives by name. By custom certain relations are forbidden to intermarry. Such relationships could be at once discerned by the term of address. Although legally there is no objection to persons marrying one's mother's sisters' children or father's brothers' children the social organisation disapproves of such unions as being incestuous. Such an act is condemned as the marriage between brothers and sisters since in the opinion of the Sinhalese the same blood flows in the veins of these parties. However, the ortho-cousin marriage forbidden by custom and tradition is entered into by relations either out of love without the parent's consent or with parent's connivance for retaining property and money in the same family.

The following is a short list of relationship terms:

1. Self	*Mama*
2. Father	*Piya*
3. Mother	*Mau*
4. Father's father	*Mulhtha*
5. Father's mother	*Achchy*
6. Father's younger brother	*Baappa*
7. Father's younger brother's wife	*Punchi Amma*
8. Father's younger brother's son	*Sahodaraya*
9. Father's younger brother's son's wife	*Nena*
10. Father's younger brother's daughter	*Sahodari*
11. Father's younger brother's daughter's husband	*Massina*
12. Father's elder brother	*Mahappa*
13. Father's elder brother's wife	*Mahamma*
14. Father's elder brother's son	*Sahodaraya*
15. Father's elder brother's son's wife	*Nena*
16. Father's elder brother's daughter	*Sahodari*
17. Father's elder brother's daughter's husband	*Massina*
18. Self's father's elder sister	*Nenda*
19. Self's father's sister's husband	*Mama*
20. Self's father's elder sister's daughter	*Nena*
21. Self's father's elder sister's daughter's husband	*Sahodaraya*
22. Self's father's elder sister's son	*Massina*
23. Self's father's elder sister's son's wile	*Sahodari*
24. Self's father's younger sister	*Nenda*
25. Self's father's younger sister's husband	*Mama*

26. Self's father's younger sister's son	*Massina*
27. Self's father's younger sister's son's wife	*Sahodari*
28. Self's father's younger sister's daughter	*Nena*
29. Self's father's younger sister's daughter's husband	*Sahodaraya*
30. Self's mother's mother	*Achchy*
31. Self's mother's father	*Atha Muttha*
32. Self's mother's younger brother	*Podi Mama*
33. Self's mother's younger brother's wife	*Podi Nena*
34. Self's mother's younger brother's	*Massina*
35. Self's mother's younger brother's son's wife	*Sahodari*
36. Self's mother's younger brother's daughter	*Nena*
37. Self's mother's younger brother's daughter's husband	*Sahodaraya*
38. Self's mother's elder brother	*Loku Mama*
39. Self's mother's elder brother's wife	*Loku Nenda*
40. Self's mother's elder brother's son	*Massina*
41. Self's mother's elder brother's son's wife	*Sahodari*
42. Self's mother's elder brother's daughter	*Nena*
43. Self's mother's elder brother's daughter's husband	*Sahodaraya*
44. Self's mother's elder sister	*Loku Amma*
45. Self's mother's elder sister's husband	*Mahappa*
46. Self's mother's elder sister's daughter	*Sahodari*
47. Self's mother's sister's daughter's husband	*Massina*

48.	Self's mother's elder sister's son	*Sahodaraya*
49.	Self's mother's elder sister's son's wife	*Nena*
50.	Self's mother's younger sister	*Kudamma*
51.	Self's mother's younger sister's husband	*Baappa*
52.	Self's mother's younger sister's son	*Sahodaraya*
53.	Self's mother's younger sister's son's wife	*Nena*
54.	Self's mother's younger sister's daughter	*Sahodari*
55.	Self's mother's younger sister's daughter's husband	*Massina*

Marriage between cross-cousins is preferred to any other. In fact it was obligatory through not enforced now-a-days. In fact it is a union between a Nena and Massina, *i.e.*, between father's sister's children and mother's brother's children that constitutes the ideal marriage in Sinhalese society. Now-a-days marriages are arranged between unrelated families by friends as go-betweens or professional brokers.

Little that could be called Sinhalese in the sphere of law and custom[7] remains now-a-days. It is true that Kandyan law[8] is still recognised and applicable. Nevertheless, Roman-Dutch law and English law apply to most of the cases. The customs are also fast disappearing. Land tenure in the uplands is settled according to Kandyan law. Certain local institutions like Gansabhas for deciding smaller cases are being employed, and even oath by ordeal is sometimes practised.

NOTES

1. At marriage the parents and even the most educated partners are concerned about the distinct caste grade of each other, Parents often ostracise the children who violate the rules and traditional customs regarding favourable unions.

2. Perera, E.W., *Sinhalese Names, Clans and Titles—Ceylon Antiquary*, Octboer 1908.
3. Reimers, E., *J.R.A.S.*, Vol. XXXI, No. 83, p. 437.
4. Very few of the present generation live up to it.
5. There are 12 main divisions of Goigama, 9 Karawas, 10 Durawas.
6. Reimers, E., *J.R.A.S.*, Vol. XXXI, No. 83, p. 437.
7. Parnatella, T.B., *J.R.A.S.*, Vol. XXI, 1908.
8. Hayley, F.A., *Laws and Customs of the Sinhalese*.

8

Social Change in an Emergent Nation

B. WENDELL

The emergence of politically new and economically developing nations has been one of the major features of change since World War II. Among former colonies, increasing internal self-government has culminated in political independence, and the creation of large-scale programmes, often government-sponsored and government-encouraged is resulting in economic and social development. In these emergent nations, elites of various kinds are in relative short supply; there are comparatively few persons possessing highly differentiated technical and professional skills and often there are few indigenous "entrepreneurs" who think and act in terms of large-scale innovative operations, either in or out of government.

Of course, the elites in any society have an importance for the society far exceeding their numbers. In a preface to the Stanford University comparative study of elites, it was stated that:[1]

> "The ways of a society are largely fixed by the myths and doctrines of a ruling few. Democracy differs from oligarchy not in the presence or absence of an elite who wield most

influence, but in the closed or open, representative or unre-presentative, responsible or irresponsible character of the elite. Who these elites are, how they live, what training they get, how they circulate, are among the most significant facts of the history of a society".

In the new and developing nation-states, elites may assume even more importance by their sheer scarcity than in the older and more developed countries. Even though few a numbers it is they who lead and facilitate change, or oppose and hinder new developments. Their talents and initiative are crucial in getting new ideas accepted in the society, yet their function is also to maintain a continuity with the past and to preserve social integration. They are mediators and communicators, interest articulators and aggregators, creators and disseminators of culture, preservers of values, change leaders, and standard makers for the general population. Thus, with the transformation of former political dependencies into new states, the development of indigenous leaders having adequate training and experience becomes of great importance. Political change formally transfers political power from on old colonial elite, often intertwined with an indigenous traditional elite, to an emergent national elite and at the same time, planned economic and social changes place a premium on new skills and talents, and demand new personnel possessing them.[2]

Of course, the social composition of elites is inextricably linked to political, economic, and social developments in the emerging nations. Increased governmental functions, the development of responsible self-government, new patterns of elite recruitment and socialization, the changing modes of interest articulation and aggregation, economic advancement, increased social welfare and educational opportunities, the spread of national citizenship, and other developments are changing the social characteristics of elites as well as changing the nature of elite positions themselves, and their interrelationships. In turn, the changes in elites affect the direction, tempo, and content of future political, economic, and social changes.

One purpose of this paper is to understand some of the changes in the social composition of elites during a country's transition from colonial status to political independence, and to describe the social backgrounds of the elites who are leading a country into independence. We know a good deal about the polity and economy of the new states, but we know considerably less about related social changes within them. Thus, this paper is addressed to the following questions: As progress toward political independence and economic advancement has been made, how have the elites changed? What are the social characteristics of the emergent elites when compared to the elites of the late colonial period? What distinctions have developed between the occupants of different types of elite positions? In the social base from which elites are recruited changing? If so, in what why? Have shifts in the locus of political power changed the super-ordinate-sub-ordinate relationships between different types of elites? What positions are held by the most influential persons in an emerging nation?

A second purpose of this paper is to understand the recent changes in elites and the present social characteristics of elites by relating them to the context of social change in which they have occurred. Certain long-term social trends that summarize an aspect of the entire history of the new nation under consideration are discussed. Thus, the facts and figures given on elites are not simply descriptions, but they also represent an underlying theory of social change. This theory derives most directly from the work of Godfrey and Monica Wilson[3] and uses, as its key concept, the nation of "scale". My thesis is that social change in the emergent nation under consideration can be understood as a long-term trend toward an increase in the scale of society, that is an increase in the range of relations, an increase in the scope of social interaction and dependency. Space does not permit a full exposition of this thesis here, but one aspect of it, the increase in the internal inclusiveness of society, or more particularly, the evolution of human rights, is discussed in some detail.

Jamaica: A Nation Emergent

Jamaica is a country of over 1.6 million people, a mountainous island about 146 miles long and 50 miles across at its widest part, located just 90 miles south of Cuba in the Caribbean Sea. Discovered by Columbus in 1494 during the explorer's second voyage to America, Jamaica was first settled by the Spanish in 1509. However, the British captured Jamaica in 1655 and have held the island for three centuries, until the present political transition to independence. The original inhabitants of Jamaica at the time of discovery, a branch of the Arawaks known as the Tainos, have contributed practically nothing to the present population. Little remains today of the 146 years of Spanish rule. A few sites and decaying buildings are left, place names of headlands, bays, rivers, mountains, etc., have remained, and there still are a few everyday terms which are left from the Spanish period.[4]

Oversimplifying, one can say that the people of Jamaica were imported from Africa while the dominant ideas and institutions of Jamaica were imported from England. For example, between 1655 and the end of the British slave trade in 1808 between 736,000 and 759,000 slaves from the west coast of Africa were brought to Jamaica in excess of those exported.[5] Throughout most of the history of Jamaica since "Discovery", black men and women have been numerically superior while being socially inferior. In 1943, 78 per cent of the population was classified as black, 17.5 per cent coloured, about one per cent white, one per cent Chinese, two per cent East Indian, and less than one per cent was classified as "other races".[6] Very small, but socially significant, numbers of Jews and Syrians were also ethnically differentiated.[7]

Although "Africanisms" are still apparent in one form or another in some aspects of lower class life in Jamaica, especially in religion and magic, dancing and singing, folklore and women's hair styles, the dominant institutions of the socicty are generally English in form and content. African-style political institutions, systems of justice, economic organization, and family life did not survive the plantation system of slavery, although slavery itself has left its mark in more or less subtle ways on modern Jamaican life, especially among members of the lower classes. In addition to the black lower classes, there is a small, predominantly white, upper class which[8] "... represents the culture of mid-twentieth-century West European society", and a brown intermediate section which "... is culturally and biologically the most variable, and practices a general mixture of patterns from the higher and lower groups".

Also, there have emerged distinctive Jamaican (or West Indian) cultural forms which are often mixtures or combinations of past forms from all classes and which, with the coming of independence and the stirring of national pride, are achieving a new unity.[9]

Modern political changes may conveniently be viewed as beginning during 1937-38. During that time strikes, riots, and other disturbances, and the Royal Commission report which resulted, called attention to the political, economic, and social deprivations of the vast majority of Jamaicans and helped to set in motion changes toward increasing self-government, representative democracy, economic development, and social reform.[10] World War II stalled political developments in Jamaica temporarily, but universal adult suffrage was first introduced, along with limited self-government, in November, 1944. Since then, there has been steady constitutional advance during a period which can be described as "tutelary democracy"—with less tutelage and more democracy having come in 1949, 1953, 1956, 1957, and 1959. During 1958, Jamaica became part of the West Indies of Federation, along with other British territories in the Caribbean. However, a referendum held September 19, 1961 resulted in a Jamaican decision to "go it alone". Today, a new constitution has come into effect, and on August 6, 1962 Jamaica shook off the last remnants of colonial dependence and donned the new garb of a politically independent nation-state within the British Commonwealth of nations.

Although it is too early to tell for certain, there is much evidence to indicate that sometimes during the mid-1950's Jamaica entered the stage of economic growth which W.W. Rostow calls the take-off into self-sustained growth.[11] Recent economic changes have transformed Jamaica from an underdeveloped to a partially developed country, although by comparison with developed economies Jamaica remains a relatively poor country. Agriculture is of great importance to the Jamaican economy, with almost half of the gainfully employed persons being engaged in agricultural work, but manufacturing has increased in recent years and now rivals agriculture in size of its contribution to the domestic product. Furthermore, Jamaica suffers from unemployment and poverty;

its land is often wasted or poorly used; it has a growing population; it lacks capital, although capital resources have increased; it has relatively low, although increasing, per capita productivity; it contains a relatively large, though diminishing, proportion of illiterates compared to developed countries; and its people are poorly, but increasingly better, educated.[12] Thus, Jamaica is moving out of a past not only of political independence, but also of economic deprivation, into the modern world.

The Increasing Scale of Society

The changes that have taken place in Jamaica during the last two decades are striking, but they are further extensions of events that can be traced back as far as the discovery of the island by Columbus. There are certain continuities and trends which suggest developmental changes. These can be conveniently summarized as *increases in the scale of society.* The ideas of increasing scale is not suggested as a cosmic principle; but as a theory that can usefully be applied to different times and places. Jamaica represents since discovery, and perhaps even before that, a society which is expanding in people, in degree of organization, in total power, in internal inclusiveness, in space, and in time. This is not to say that there have never been contractions in scale in the course of Jamaican history, but the long-term non-repetitive movements of the time series—the *trends* not the cycles nor apparently random fluctuations—have been toward the increase in the scale of society.

At least from the time of discovery Jamaica has increasingly been drawn into a network of relations that have been expending territorially. At first, interaction and interdependence involved parts of Europe, Africa, and other places in the "new world". Although the densities of communication vary with different parts of the world, Jamaica has become part of global society. With independence, the links of economics and government necessarily binding Jamaica to a metropolitan power are no longer enforced by colonial domination. Jamaica is now free to establish wider territorial ties, both economically and politically through agreements, treaties, and alliances.

Jamaican society has expanded through time by the spread of literacy, increasing education, and most recently an increasing emphasis upon a Jamaican (or West Indian) perspective to Jamaican history. Not only are more contemporary Jamaicans "in touch" with more of their own past, but their thoughts and actions are increasingly informed by the accumulated knowledge of Western civilization and by other civilizations as well.

As Jamaican society has increased in scale, it has increased in complexity and has become organized into manifold hierarchical levels of skill, income, and prestige. The organization of human effort has become more intricate, and managerial and supervisory personnel both in and out of government, occupying positions of co-ordination, control, and direction, have increased in importance. Differentiation of function, specialization, rationality and impersonality have increased.[13]

Jamaican society has increased in total power. I am not referring here to technological advance, although it is related, but to *social power*. The ability of the Jamaican people to achieve their collective goals has increased immeasurably. This is partly due to technological advance, but it is also due to increasing differentiation of function, increasingly complex organization of effort, and increasing social mobilization. The application of a zero-sum concept of power—the nation that power is limited and a scarce commodity—is simply inadequate to describe the *changing* total power of Jamaican society—and probably other developing societies as well. However useful the zero-sum concept of power may be to describe the competition over the distribution of power *at any given time*, it is more accurate to view power as a resource which can be developed when describing *changes in total power through time.*

Belief in ancestors and local spirits, in magic and witchcraft has declined greatly, and is now of little practical importance. There has been a spread of universal religions with membership in world organizations. The aboriginal culture has been wiped out; although *obeah* men still exist, their influence and their clientele have declined greatly.

An increasing consciousness of the widening relations and dependence on past and contemporaneous groups among more and more Jamaicans has followed the increase in the scale of society.

Although social stratification increased as Jamaican society increased in scale, there has been a reduction of hereditary privilege. As will be pointed out in detail later, the circulation of elites has increased, and the elite has expanded in relative size and has become less exclusive. Elites are recruited from a wider range of social origins than before—although they may eventually be more homogeneous in origin with respect to one characteristic, country of birth—and recruitment of elites is increasingly based upon universalistic criteria of achieved skills. Elites have become more accessible to the masses, and the masses have become more accessible to the elites.

As Jamaican society increased in scale, an increasing diversity occurred with the resulting isolation of subgroups which were functionally significant for the total society. Jamaican society was a heterogeneous aggregation of individuals of diverse origins resulting from migration, by choice and by force. However, the contacts between diverse groups were preconditions for the reduction of heterogeneity, for an increase in the *internal inclusiveness of the society.* This process has not yet run its course, but the trend is in the direction of the reduction of ascriptive barriers which have in the past prevented the association of some persons with other persons in the society and the institutionalization of equal opportunities for the mutual access to facilities and services. It is the process of repeated redefinitions of society to include more and more people within it on a more equal basis in some respects with the formerly more favoured members of the society. In part, this is an aspect of increasing mobility, in that the size of the group within which any Jamaican may move freely has increased in social as well as in geographical distance.[14]

The trends toward increasing mobility and circulation, more equal opportunities, and the reduction of ascriptive barriers have occurred *pari passu* with the trends toward increasing social stratification. The spread of equality and increased stratification are sometimes viewed by writers, when they don't simply ignore one or the other, as a dilemma in that the two trends seem opposed to one another. However, they both can contribute to an increase in the ability of members of a society to achieve their collective and individual goals and in this sense, at a higher level of abstraction than before, they appear, not opposed, but alike in their consequences. Increased stratification can contribute added power, more effective organization of effort, and higher levels of social mobilization. And the trend toward equality can result in more people in the society being more committed to it, in more people being more highly motivated to achieve, in a greater overall development of human resources, and in a more effective distribution of talent and skills in the most important positions in the society.

The Evolution of Human Rights

The trend toward the increasing internal inclusiveness of Jamaican society can be identified by the extension of rising minimums of human rights, universally applied to an increasing proportion of persons in Jamaica. Following the United Nations' usage, I include civil, political, economic, and social rights[15] by the term, human rights, as defined as follows:

Civil rights—freedoms from torture and slavery; freedoms of religion, expression and assembly; the right to security of person, equality before courts and tribunals, a fair and public hearing by competent and impartial tribunals established by law, presumption of innocence until proved guilty, and the right of everyone to be considered a person before the law, among other such rights.

Political rights—freedom to take part in the conduct of public affairs, voting, and equal access to public service as well as others which define the people's rights to participate in the political system on the basis of equality.

Economic rights—the right to fair wages and equal remuneration for work of equal value, safe and healthy working conditions, equal opportunity to be promoted subject only to considerations of seniority and competence, rest and leisure, reasonable limitation of working hours and periodic holidays with pay, ownership of property either alone or in association with others, the right to form and join a trade union for the promotion and protection of one's economic interests, and the right to strike, among others.

Social rights—the right to marry and establish a family, to the free choice of a marriage partner, to enjoy the highest attainable standard of physical and mental health, to free primary education and equal access to secondary and higher education, to an adequate standard of living including adequate food, clothing, and housing, and the right to take part in the cultural life of the nation, among others.

From the point of view of the historical extension of these rights, it is accurate to describe much of the social history of Jamaica in terms of the changing, that is *rising* status of the lower classes be they white, brown, or black or be they slaves, indentured bond servants, agricultural labourers, urban workers or unemployed poor people. The Jamaican lower classes have emerged as participants in the society on the basis of more equality than they have enjoyed in the past. The gradual extension of civil, political, economic, and social rights—*rights* which are embedded in law not simply benefits deriving from benevolent paternalism that may be granted in exchange for personal subservience and submissive gratitude—to the lower classes in Jamaica can be easily documented. Unfortunately, no Jamaican has as yet come forward to do the necessary research and to tell the story with the relevance to present aspirations, and with the vigour and vision that the story deserves.

This is not to say that gross inequalities of status and opportunities do not exist in Jamaica today. Although it is true that there is equality of civil and political rights, as these are expressed in law, such equality is partly irrelevant and partly nominal when actual practice is considered. The laws against *obeah* and the use of *ganja*, for example, apply *equally* to the upper and middle classes, who generally consider these practices to be foreign, and to the lower classes, for whom such practices have been part of accepted cultural patterns. Furthermore, the high costs of legal advice, differential unfamiliarity with the law, and differential participation in legal administration reduce the power of the lower classes to implement and realize their civil rights.

Since 1944, equality of political rights has been more fully achieved than equality of civil rights. However, the inequalities of social and economic stratification in Jamaica result in some reduction of real equality in the political arena. Money buys election propaganda and thus may influence the election outcome, the conferral of prestige coopts some elected political leaders to some degree, and the differential distribution of skills by classes tends to restrict the formulation and administration of governmental policies to members of the middle and upper classes.

Economic and social inequalities in Jamaica are even greater than civil and political inequalities. As social facts rather than as legal statements, economic and social equality and equality of opportunity do not exist. In his analysis of Jamaican social structure, M. G. Smith[16] accurately highlights the present inequalities in Jamaica. The white upper classes, the brown middle classes, and the black lower classes are grossly unequal with economic and social advantages accruing most to the upper and least to the lower classes.

The present inequalities with respect to civil, political, economic, and social rights, however, have a past during which the inequalities were far greater: and the long-term term trends in these rights have been toward increasing equality, toward rising minimums applied to more and more people. The new constitution of Jamaica entrenches a comprehensive set of human rights to apply equally to all Jamaicans.[17]

Also, as the internal inclusiveness of Jamaican society has increased, there has been a decreasing reliance on brute force for the maintenance of social cohesion and an increase in social integration based on consensus. This process has not yet run its course either. In fact, serious problems of the creation of more social unity now face Jamaica, but the trends are clear.[18] Consent has increased and naked power has decreased in importance.

There is interaction between scale in space, in time, and in internal inclusiveness. One type can occur without the others, and instability may result. For example, increase in territorial scale can occur with very little internal inclusiveness such as may occur with the emergence of empires. As a result, the integrative institutions may be inadequate to maintain the geographical scppe of the society and contraction in territorial scale may take place. Such scale contraction has occurred, usually in connection with other discontinuities, several times in the history of Jamaica.

Finally, there is interaction between demand for and achievement of civil, political, economic, and social rights. Although the long-term trends show that the direction of change is toward the application of an equal set of rights to all adults in the society, at any given time there may be a substitution rate of one type of right for others. That is, certain rights can be gained at the expense of others. For example, with emancipation, new civil rights were obtained, but certain traditional economic rights were lost. The former masters of the former slaves no longer were obligated to prevent economic deprivation among their workers, although taday new and more thorougzhgoing economic rights are enjoyed by all Jamaicans.

Of course the identification of a long-term trend toward equality, toward the rising minimums of civil, political, economic, and social rights to an increasigly large number of persons, does not mean that the continuation of the trend is inevitable, nor that it will continue automatically without definite actions being taken. Also, mathematicaly speaking, one can write a number of formulas which would each adequately fit the known past trend but which each extrapolate the trend in a different direction: that is, each would predict a different future from the same past. In addition, the trend has not always occurred without agitation and violence, and it may not continue without further disorder. Thus, the future of human rights in Jamaica may be problematical, but the analysis of social trends suggests that the trend toward equality of rights has been no accident and may reflect some underlying principle of change.

A Dynamic Mechanism of Change

How has the trend toward equality of rights come about? What has been the dynamic mechanism underlying the changes in the nature and application of civil, political, economic, and social rights in Jamaica? Tentatively, the answer seems to be the resolution of problems of legitimacy. Changes in human rights have occurred as a result of refolution of anomalies between structures and practices on the one hand, and ideas about what is legitimate on the other. There has been a demonstrable interplay between ideas and institutions throughout the history of Jamaica. Institutions fostered certain ideas about what is right or wrong, what should or should not be; and ideas, often exogenous to Jamaica itself originally, have led to organized social action which often resulted in changing, eliminating, or creating institutions. For example, ideas about the social inferiority of Negroes were fostered in and diffused from Jamaica and elsewhere in the West Indies during one period of history when a justification of an important institution, slavery, was needed. The currency and spread of these ideas were in some sense "caused" by the institution, and validated it. On the other hand, ideas emerging in Europe raised questions of legitimacy concerning slavery, and social action based on these ideas eventually resulted in the disappearance of an institution: the slave trade was abolished and the slaves were freed.[19] From this viewpoint, social change in Jamaica to be understood more fully, should be set against the background of developments which have taken place in Europe and in the United States since the breakdown of feudalism. The rise of the modern state in Europe, the formation of a national citizenry (which implied equality for all adults in some respects), the American and French revolutions, the industrial revolution in England, the trade union movement, the formulation of new ideologies—political, economic, and social, the spread of mass education, and the growth of the welfare state are each relevant to political, economic, and social changes in Jamaica. Available evidence supports the contention that ideas, usually imported from Europe and to some extent from the United States, have, over the course of Jamaican history, led to social action which has resulted in the reduction of anomalies between such ideas and institutions. Usually, the result has been structural change toward more equality, and what might be considered "progress"; that is, more equality was created by giving more people more rights. (But not always. One of the more interesting examples occurred in 1865 when the white ruling oligarchs created more equality by giving away some of their own political rights because it was no longer, after emancipation, legitimate for one section of the citizenry to have such rights without the newly-created citizens, the former slaves, having the same rights too.)

Ideas regarding human rights of various kinds often have been expressed in lower-class demands, discontents, disaffection, and alienation. Before 1944, when universal adult suffrage was begun, lower-class collective protests took the form, as

Reinhard Bendix says of Europe before the formation of the modern political community, "...of millenarian movements, social banditry, and direct outbursts of violence, which ranged from an inchoate venting of accumulated grievances to a cunning or righteous insistence upon the customary rights even of the most sub-ordinate groups".[20] Such patterns of protest remain in Jamaica today, but their frequency and significance are greatly diminished because in recent years major protests have been expressed by participation of the lower classes in the new national political community. Legitimate political action and legal trade union activity account for the expression of many modern demands.

The elites, of course, have played a crucial role throughout the whole process of circular causation between ideas and institutions. The actions or inactions, their ideologies, attitudes and beliefs have contributed toward expansion or contraction of internal inclusiveness or helped maintain existing barriers of exclusiveness. Upon occasion, they have boldly led scale-increasing change, and on others they have, as Tawney points out in a similar connection, walked reluctantly backwards into the future, as other European governments did after the levelling doctrines of France, doing from above what is sometimes accomplished by revolution in spite of their contrary ideologies and attitudes, but because of their belief that, if they didn't, something far worse than a change toward equality might befall them.[21]

There is ample evidence of lower-class discontents, disaffection, and alienation today. Many lower-class persons say that their interests are not being served. They raise questions about the civil service ("a middle-class preserve"), the new office buildings for the Ministries ("why not more housing?"; "The brown men take care of themselves!"), they see new factories and a new air terminal, buty the see their circumstance improved less than they expect. Some member of the new Jamaican elite realize that, although Jamaica has experienced considerable economic growth on the basis of conventional criteria, not enough of Jamaica's increased wealth has yet trickled down to the mass of the population. They hope to spread available resources wider than in the recent past. But some of them also realize that the lower-class Jamaican can be a recalcitrant tool of action, usually uneducated and perhaps illiterate, suspicious of change, often actively resisting efforts of field workers to change his ways, shorttempered in his expectations for government to do something for him, being only half a citizen in that his duties and obligations are not clear to him, while his rights are increasingly in his consciousness, and increasingly alienated if his expectations are not met if his obligations are pointed out to him.[22]

Jamaica today may have reached another stage where a new anomaly has emerged between the current ideas concerning human rights and the elites' ability or willingness to provide for them. New problems of legitimacy have arisen; new solutions are being sought. The formulation and implementation of such solutions is an important part of elite functions. With the political developments which led to an independent Jamaica, the social composition of elites has been changing, a new leadership group has been forming—especially since 1938. The decisions that will mold future social change in Jamaica are in the hands of this new Jamican elite.

Top Governmental Elites, 1939-1954

In 1939, Jamaica had a modified Crown Colony government little changed since 1884 and faced five more years before the beginning of tutelary democracy. Although there were elected members in the Legislative Council, the electorate was limited and generally uninterested in politics. For the most part, the elected members played the role of an irresponsible opposition, and they had special powers over finance that often made governance difficult. The Governor had great powers which included the reserved right to override the elected members in case of necessity. In addition to the Governor, the Legislative Council contained a number of *ex officio* and nominated members equal to the number of elected members.[23]

In contrast, Jamaica had been ten years on the road to self-government by 1954, the most recent political change at the time being the introduction of the ministerial system in 1953. The Legislative Council then was composed of only official and nominated members and its powers had been reduced with a few exceptions to the consideration of legislation passed by the new House of Representatives. The latter body consisted of 32 members elected on the basis of universal adult suffrage from the 32 constituencies into which Jamaica had been divided. At the general election in 1949, "... 477,107 votes were polled out of a total of 732,217 persons eligible to vote, or 65.2 per cent".[24] The Executive Council was the principal policy-making body and had become a kind of quasi-Cabinet (and a schoolroom for full-fledged Cabinet members-to-be): Thus, it included eight elected members from the House of Representatives, who were Ministers with responsibility over the work of the government departments, in addition to the official and nominated members. Although the element of tutelage was still present in the Governor's reserved legislative power, which could be exercised without the consent of the Executive Council, there was considerable responsible self-government regarding internal affairs under the 1953 Order in Council. In fact, political power had shifted significantly, although not completely, into the hands of the elected representatives of the Jamaican people.[25]

Table 8.1 shows some of the changes in the social characteristics of the top governmental elites during this transition period. Included among "top governmental elites" for each year are members of the executive and legislative branched of the government, the directors, permanent secretaries, and other important civil servants of all governmental departments (and in 1954 of the new Ministries as well), and the custos (a nominated person) of each parish. In other words, elected political leaders, higher civil servants, top officials, and occupants of certain nominated positions are included among the top governmental elites. As fas as possible, persons occupying functionally equivalent positions were selected for both times, although this was not a simple thing to determine because of the proliferation and change in governmental positions between 1939 and 1954. The data are based upon information on such persons available in the *Handbook of Jamaica* and in *Who's Who, Jamaica* for 1939 and 1954.[26]

From Table 8.1, note that about half of the top governmental leaders were Jamaican-born in 1939, but by 1954 the percentage had increased to 75. Thus, from the point of view of Jamaicans, the top governmental leadership positions were less exclusive in

1954 than they were in 1939, with Jamaicans having a greater chance of occupying such positions in 1954.[27] There was a relative reduction of non-Jamaicans (mostly English) in these roles. During the period under consideration, this was accomplished in part by the replacement of Englishmen by Jamaicans in given leadership roles, and also by the creation of new roles (e.g., an increase in elected political leaders from 14 to 32) which were filled by Jamaicans for the most part. This process of increasing the total number of leadership roles in government has continued as the functions and services of government have expanded, and the replacement of foreign personnel in existing roles since 1954 has increasingly contributed to an increased access to such leadership positions on the part of Jamaicans. Still more new roles for Jamaicans have been created in defense and foreign affairs with the coming of independence.

The top governmental elites are subdivided further in Table 8.2. For each type of elite the trend is the same—an increase in the percentage of Jamaican-born persons from 1939 to 1954. The smallest increase was for the elected political leaders, but for 1954 the percentage of Jamaicans among them was 93 per cent. The largest increase was in the case of the higher civil servants, yet in 1954 about a third of such persons were still non-Jamaicans. This large increase for the civil servants reflects the results of a deliberate policy to "West Indianize" the civil service[28] and the steps which had been taken to promote opportunities for Jamaicans (and some other West Indians) to receive formal, technical, administrative, professional and other specialized training. They also reflect the facts that comparatively few Jamaicans possessed the necessary skills and experience to perform top civil service roles expertly in 1939 and that, although the increase in Jamaicans in these positions has continued since 1954, Jamaica, as other new nations, may be in part dependent for some years on the distribution of specialized and differentiated skills available in technologically more advanced societies. Officials and nominated persons (for convenience designated "appointees") increased from 54 to 70 per cent Jamaican-born.

Of the person born in Jamaica, 29 per cent were urban-born (in Kingston, Spanish Town, or Montego Bay) in 1939 compared with 34 per cent in 1954 (see Table 8.1). Thus, the

TABLE 8.1

Percentage of Top Governmental Elites Having Selected Social Characteristics, 1939 and 1954

Selected Social Chracteristics	Elites Having Selected 1939 (N=63)* Per Cent	Characteristic in: 1954 (N=126)* Per Cent
Jamaican-born	53	75
Urban-born (Jamaican-born only)*	29	34
Holds at least one non-governmental elite position	62	41
Elementary education or less	20	12
Secondary school education	44	54
Some university or more	36	34
Upwardly mobile	70	71
Age 55 or older	40	34

Source: 1939 and 1954, *Who's Who Jamaica.*

* The number of cases are only approximate because of a few cases in which no information was available for some of the variables. The percentage of urban-born persons are based upon the Jamaican-born elites only and i 31 for 1939 and 90 for 1954.

1954 top governmental elites were slightly more urban with respect to place of birth than the 1939 elites. The elites were more likely to be urban-born than the entire Jamaican-born population. In 1943 about 12 to 14 per cent of the population was urban-born.[29]

However, the general comparison on urban birth is somewhat misleading, since the different types of elites did not change in the same way. The elected political leaders increased in percentage of urban-born forn 0 to 20 per cent, while the appointees and the higher civil servants had reductions in the percentage of urban-born (from Table 8.2). In 1939, the differences between the three types of elites were greater than in 1954 with the civil servants most urban, the appointees next, and the elected political leaders least urban. The rank order was the same in 1954, but the differential changes resulted in the different types of elites being more alike in 1954 than in 1939 in this respect.

The study of governmental elites becomes increasingly meaningful as the relationships between such elites and other institutional sectors of the society are specified. One such relationship is revealed by an examination of the relative number of top governmental elites concurrently holding elite positions in other social institutions. The simultaneous occupancy of elite positions in different institutions creates networks or circles of communication and influence that transcend particular institutional structures, and the number of non-governmental elite positions held by top governmental elites is one indicator of the range of their influence in the larger society. For example, top governmental elites who also occupy an elite position in the private economic sector are able to extend their influence into the economic life of the nation in ways that would be impossible if they occupied only their governmental roles. Also, governmental elites who are simultaneously economic elites may have their performance in their governmental roles affected by economic interests in ways that would otherwise be impossible.

The percentage of top governmental elites who hold at least one elite position in an institution other than government (mostly economic) is given in Table 8.1. From 1939 to 1954, the percentage of top governmental elites holding at least one non-governmental elite position declined from 62 to 41 per cent.

However, from Table 8.2 it can be seen that the different types of elites did not change in the same way. Consistent with the general trend, the higher civil servants were less likely to hold non-governmental elite positions in 1954 than in 1939, the percentage decreasing from 36 to 20. At both time periods, the civil servants were most likely, compared to elected political leaders and appointees, to have their authority confined to their governmental roles. This finding is consistent with the fact that the civil service has been increasingly professionalized while the governmental bureaucracy has increased in size and functions.

Also consistent with the general trend is the change in elected political leaders. Changing more than any other type of top governmental elite, the elected political leaders had 100 per cent who occupied at least one non-governmental elite position in 1939 but only 45 per cent in 1954. Thus, although the elected political leaders had much more formal responsibility and authority in 1954 than in 1939 as a result of conistitutional changes which redefined their duties, their authority was more confined to purely *governmental and political* roles at the later time.

A bifurcation—or at least a partial bifurcation—of power is reflected in this trend. As the economic and social elites lost direct control over the elected political positions, representatives and spokesmen of the labouring classes gained. Both major political parties in Jamaica—the People's National Party (PNP) and the Jamaical Labour Party (JLP)—are in a sense labour parties. Each is linked to a particular trade union, and although each has middle and upper class supporters, both must depend upon the lower socio-economic groups for the bulk of their support at the polls. Increasingly committed to economic and social development, the new Jamaican popular government has taken an increasingly larger part in economic and social life. Thus, whatever decline in the total power of the elected political leaders may be indicated by the confinement of their authority to purely governmental and political roles may be somewhat offset by the increase in the authority of such roles themselves over certain aspects of the Jamaican economy and society.

Contrary to the general trend is the change in appointees. The dual occupancy of governmental and non-governmental roles increased among them from 63 to 83 per cent from 1939 to 1954. Thus, while constitutional changes reduced the formal responsibilities and authority of the role of the appointees, the occupants of these roles in fact were more likely to be persons who had a wide range of influence due to interlocking elite positions in governmental and other institutional sectors. In other words, the established economic and social elites grasped more firmly the diminishing powers of the nominated positions.

Returning to Table 8.1, fewer of the 1954 elites had only an elementary school education than the 1939 elites, and more of them had a secondary school education. However, there was

TABLE 8.2

Percentage of Top Governmental Elites Having Selected Social Characteristics by Type of Elite Position, 1939 and 1954

Selected Social Characteristics	Type of Elite Position*					
	Elected Political Leaders		Appointees		Higher Civil Servants	
	1939 (N=14)+ Per cent	1954 (N=32)+ Per cent	1939 (N=27)+ Per cent	1954 (N=29)+ Per cent	1939 (N=22)+ Per cent	1954 (N=64)+ Per cent
Jamaican-born	85	93	54	70	32	68
Urban-born (Jamaican-born only)	0	20	38	26	57	48
Holds at least one non-governmental elite-position	100	45	63	83	36	20
Elementary education or less	29	36	13	3	23	3
Secondary school education	57	46	35	54	46	58
Some university or more	14	18	52	43	31	39

Upwardly mobile	83	93	58	35	79	76
Age 55 or older	27	23	63	63	23	26

Source: 1939 and 1954, *Who's Who, Jamaica*.

* The percentages represent the relative number of persons in each type of elite position having a particular social characteristic.

† The number of cases on which the percentages are based is given for each type of elite. It is approximate for some variables since a few cases did not have full information. The urbanborn percentages are based upon the sub-universe of Jamaican-born only. These N's are: elected political leaders 11 (1939) and 29 (1954); appointed officials 13 (1939) and 19 (1954); and higher civil servants 7 (1939) and 42 (1954).

little difference between the two groups with respect to the percentage who had university education. The elected political leaders were the least educated of all the top governmental elites both in 1939 and 1954 (from Table 8.2). Also, unlike both the appointees and the higher civil servants, they had a larger percentage of their number who had received no more than an elementary school education in 1954 than in 1939. Since educational levels are rising generally in Jamaica, one cannot expect this particular change to reflect a trend. Also, many educated persons were somewhat reluctant to risk their positions in society by standing for elected office before a generally black, lower-class, and poorly-educated electorate—especially in the years of limited self-government when the element of tutelage still restricted to some extent both the authority and prestige of elected positions, and when many members of the highly educated groups were still suspicious and uncertain about domination by what they thought of as "mob-rule". With full self-government and complete independence and with the chance of becoming an honourable member of the recently created Cabinet, elected political office should be somewhat more enticing to members of the educated groups.[30]

Even though the elected political leaders, with 36 per cent of their number having no more than an elementary school education in 1954, were more like the general population than they were in 1939, and even though they were more like the general population than either the appointees or the higher civil servants with respect to education, they were still considerably better educated than the average person in Jamaica. In 1943, 95 per cent of the Jamaican population over age 25 had received no more than an elementary school education, and in 1960 the Provisional figure was 92.5 per cent.[31]

The higher civil servants were more highly educated in 1954 than in 1939, and they were more highly educated on the average than the elected political leaders at both times, especially in 1954. Afther the ministerial system was introduced in 1953, this fact (and correlated differences in outlook and behaviour) apparently resulted in friction between some members of the two types of elites in their day-to-day working relationships, the higher civil servants sometimes chafing under the rule of a less-educated politician and a politician in turn sometimes overly asserting himself in an effort to validate himself in his new role as head of a ministry. Of this problem, one informant told me the following:

"The political leader is looked upon as a real leader of the country. At public functions he is the top man. He has dominated the scene from a power point of view in the public mind. At the same time, the civil servants in the governmental bureaucracy in some senses have become the real rulers and they have assumed too much importance in the actual making of policy. Take a politician who has power that derives from the formal position that he occupies, but he is surrounded by high powered civil servants who have benefited from higher education, special courses of various kinds, etc. This government has, by the way, done a great deal, has invested a great deal, in giving civil servants and others the opportunity to receive high powered technical training. The politician represents the will of the people since he was elected by them. And yet, the high powered technical advice he gets tends somehow to submerge the will of the people. As you know, high powered technical people can do great damage in the policy-making process. Policies may have no relation to the ordinary conditions of the life of people of the country if the technical people play too much of a role in either formulating a policy or in a non-supervised implementation of it. . . . Sometimes a Minister is so intimidated by his civil servants, by what he assumes is their superior technical skill and higher education, that he may seek refuge in Cabinet to turn down his own recommendation. That is, he was afraid to tell his civil servants that he didn't want to recommend something because he couldn't think of the definitive reasons for his action. But he could go back to the civil servants in his ministry and say that Cabinet had turned it down and that was that."

Of course, as the same informant pointed out later in the interview, the civil servants have legitimate complaints too. What appear to be correct policies to them in terms of the economic and social development of Jamaica are sometimes not adopted by the politicians for "political reasons", that is because the politicians must be concerned with the public reaction to their policy. Perhaps this would be acceptable if the "public reaction" involved were the responses of the general public, but it is often some special group, especially some articulate and already favoured minority.

This conflict between politicians and civil servants, however, should not be overemphasized, and few other new nations are in as enviable a position as Jamaica. One of the distinctive features of Jamaica's transition to independence has been early and sustained efforts to develop a governmental bureaucracy containing an increasing number of qualified Jamaicans at all levels. A competent and experienced bureaucracy composed of Jamaicans gives Jamaica considerable advantage over some of the other new nations in achieving stability and effectiveness in efforts to attain the national goals of a newly independent country. England has been, perhaps, the most enlightened of the colonial powers during the dismantlement of its empire, and Jamaica may be the best example of adequate preparation for independence among the former British colonies, although the Colonial Office bungling which led to the collapse of the West Indies Federation has had deleterious consequences for the smaller islands.

As expected, the appointees were the most highly educated type of governmental elites at both time periods, although the higher civil servants were almost as well educated on the average in 1954. Although the percentage of appointees having no more than an elementary school education decreased from 1939 to 1954, so did the percentage having a university education.

One might expect the governmental elites to be more upwardly mobile in 1954 than in 1939, since the constitutional changes opened up new routes to power and influence, and included the participation of the lower socio-economic classes in the political process. However, no such trend is apparent from Table 8.1. Both in 1939 and in 1954, the elites were highly mobile with respect to upward occupational mobility, 70 and 71 per cent respectively were upwardly mobile.[32]

However, the percentages for upward mobility in Table 8.1 are averages of differential changes for the different types of elite groups. As one would expect, the elected political elites were more upwardly mobile in 1954 than in 1939, and they were the most upwardly mobile of the three types of elites (from Table 8.2). The higher civil servants had about the same rate of upward mobility at both times. However, the appointees were the least upwardly mobile group both in 1939 and 1954, and contrary to the change for elected political leaders, they were considerably less likely to be upwardly mobile in 1954 than in 1939. Considering the fact that these persons are elites, one can assume that about 65 per cent of the appointees (the non-mobile persons) had elite backgrounds.

Thus, while the predominantly black lower-classes were obtaining representation through their elected leaders and the elected political positions were becoming somewhat more accessible to the "average Jamaican", the predominantly light or white persons representing the established interests were increasing their hold over the nominated positions. This is consistent with the findings concerning joint occupancy of governmental and non-governmental positions discussed earlier. However, since 1954, changes increasing the participation of the leaders of the political parties, while decreasing the descretion of the Governor in making nominations to these offices, have resulted in a decrease in the exclusiveness of the group. In the new constitution for an independent Jamaica, the Legislative Council is replaced by a Senate, all members of which will be political appointees. Thus, the appointees can be expected increasingly to approximate the social characteristics of the elected political elites, although differential campaign contributions and other favours to the political parties and the differential distribution of skills by social classes may still result in the representation of some members of the highest socio-economic groups among the appointees.

In Table 8.1 note that the 1954 elites were slightly younger than the 1939 elites, 34 and 40 per cent respectively being 55 or older. However, none of the types of elites actually changed in age even as much as six per cent. Rather, this average reduction of six per cent was due to changes in the differential proportions each type of elite represented at the two times. That is, at both time periods the elected political leaders and the higher civil servants were much younger on the average than the appointees (see Table 8.2), and there were relatively more of them compared to the appointees in 1954 than in 1939. In fact, none of the three types of elites change much in the percentage of those 55 or over. The appointees were exactly the same, with 63 per cent.

The appointees were much older than the average adult in Jamaican society, but the elected political leaders and higher civil servants were much nearer in age to the general population. Of all Jamaicans age 25 and over, 20 per cent were age 55 and over in 1943. In 1960 the percentage was 23 per cent.[33]

Comparison of Different Types of Elites, 1958

A more complete description and analysis of the social composition of Jamaican elites requires a more inclusive definition of elites than that so far employed. Persons occupying the "command posts" in institutions other than government need to be considered. Leaders in business, religion, education, law, medicine, and other institutional sectors also exert influence on public affairs in Jamaica and perform a variety of elite functions. Additionally, the transition to independence continued beyond 1954, with the introduction of more self-government and less tutelage in 1956 and again in 1957. By the summer of 1958, Jamaica had nearly achieved full internal self-government.

A sample of all Jamaican elites was selected and their social characteristics determined by reference to *Who's Who, Jamaica.* A description of this sample is given in Appendix I. These characteristics are given by type of elite position in Table 8.3 The categories of "elected political leaders", "appointees", and "civil servants" are not strictly comparable to those same categories in Tables 8.1 and 8.2, but are somewhat more inclusive. Elected members of the then-new Federal Parliament, mayors and some parish councilors were added to the elected political leaders. Also, the then-newly-appointed Senators to the federal government were included among the appointeess. And the civil servants in Table 8.3, although excluding judges, doctors, and teachers who are categorized separately, include some fairly low ranks in the civil service, in addition to the higher civil servants considered earlier. Thus, one must be cautious about attributing trends to these data in comparison with the 1939 and 1954 top governmental elites. However, by logical elimination of alternatives, one will note that most trends noted earlier are borne out by the 1958 data.

Since many elites hold more than one elite position simultaneously, it would be possible to categorize them more than once in Table 8.3 However, a given individual has been classified only once, as before. Arbitrarily, governmental elites who held other elite positions were classified only by their governmental positions. That is, governmental positions were given priority over other types of elite positions, the only exceptions being among civil servants who were professionals. For non-governmental elites, an attempt to determine their major activity was made.

Country of birth. There was a wide range of differences between the various types of elites with respect to country of birth in 1958. Nearly three-fourths of the religious leaders were foreign-born. They continued in the tradition of the missionaries of the nineteenth century, who did much to spread humanitarian values in Jamaica, and throughout the world. Their relative role in Jamaica today has been greatly reduced in many ways, and is far less militant compared to the role that their predecessors played in spreading ideas of equality and freedom' They have been in part displaced by change-leading, national elites, especially elected political leaders and higher civil servants who man the policy-making and administrative positions of a growing welfare state. Also, they have had to make room for a growing number of other professionals and voluntary workers who are promoting economic and social development through secular organizations.

Social welfare elites (workers and administrators) were more likely to be Jamaican-born than religious leaders, but over half were still foreign-born originated from technologically originated from technologically more advances societies—in this case primarily from England and the United States.

Sixty-three per cent of the judges were born in Jamaica, and full 94 per cent of the barristers and solicitors were. Of course, the foreign-born among he judges were mainly English. Related to this is the fact that one of the highest percentages of foreign-born among any type of civil servant was among the higher officers of the police. Also, in 1958 there were only a

TABLE 8.3

Percentage of Jamaican Elites Having Selected Social Characteristics by Type of Elite Position

Selected Social Characteristic	Type of Elite Position: Elected Political Leaders (N=52)*	Appointees (N=34)	Civil Servants (N=185)	Economic Elites (N=269)	Religious Leaders (N=33)	Educational Leaders (N=35)	Judges (N=9)	Medical Elites (N=71)	Barristers and Solicitors (N=36)	Social Welfare Elites (N=7)
Per cent Jamaican-born	98	91	82	69	28	71	63	76	94	43
Per cent residing in metropolitan Kingston-St. Andrew	23	47	87	66	64	63	78	75	81	71
Per cent with highest occupational rating	94	100	45	73	94	29	100	93	100	57
Per cent upwardly mobile	83	31	79	62	57	51	56	35	52	57
Per cent male	100	94	96	96	100	66	100	87	97	43
Median age in years	50	61	46	49	50	48	53	46	46	50
Per cent Anglican	38	73	58	47	25	55	57	53	57	29
Per cent Protestant	49	19	30	23	44	34	29	25	17	72
Per cent Roman Catholic	9	8	9	20	28	3	14	18	13	0
Per cent Jewish	0	0	1	8	3	0	0	2	3	0
Per cent atheist, agnostic, or independent	4	0	2	1	0	7	0	3	3	0

Per cent elementary education or less	27	0	2	13	0	0	0	0	0	0
Per cent secondary school education	42	61	52	64	6	31	22	0	58	43
Per cent some university or more	31	39	47	23	94	69	78	100	42	57
‡ *Of those with some university or more* † the percentage whose university was located in:										
Jamaica	7	0	4	0	3	4	0	3	0	0
British Isles	53	92	69	40	53	78	86	59	93	75
Canada	0	0	12	23	3	13	14	11	0	0
United States	40	8	11	30	40	4	0	20	0	25

Source: *Who's Who, Jamaica.*

• Except where indicated (‡), the approximate number of cases on which the percentages are based is given in parentheses.

† Does not always add up to 100 per cent, because of a few elites educated in countries other than those shown.

few top military officers in Jamaica, but expatriates controlled the top ranks with minor exceptions. Of course, the position of the military reflects the constitutional situation at the time which still left the defense of Jamaica to the former imperial power. However, the interpretation of the law and especially the legal use of force within Jamaica was more controlled by expatriates than might have been expected considering the constitutional developments. This reflects in part a preoccupation of the established economic and social elites with the problems of order as self-government increased and complete independence came nearer. They considered the black lower-classes increasingly to be a threat to order as the British withdrew and the Jamaican government, with more limited resources for controlling civil disorder and with fewer commitments to the old established elites, took over. With independence, a new commanding officer, born in the Bahamas, but identified as a "local" has been appointed to the new Jamaica Regiment.

Almost a third of the Jamaican economic elites, including commercial, agricultural, and others, are foreign-born. This seems relatively high, but may be accounted for in part by a colonial attitude toward commerce. For example, Broom says:[34]

"It is ironic that British colonialism, which historically has been so heavily influenced by commercial interests, should have implanted a disdain of commerce among many colonial peoples This may be in part because a colonial may seek recognition in two places, in the colony and in the metropolitan 'home'. The dual striving is apparently achieved without conflict of ends most readily in the public service and, of course, some immediate status is acquired by the very identification with official functions."

However, it may be less ironic in this way than Broom thinks. Like so many things in Jamaica today that are identified as being colonially-induced backwardness and debilities, "a disdain of commerce" my be not so much a result of colonialism *per se* but more a British trait, a transplanted English tradition. As David Granick has recently pointed out, businessmen in Enland, in contrast to those in other European countries and the United States, are regarded more or less as second-string civil servants.[35]

However, the nature of enterprise in Jamaica, the problems of capital formation and investment, and the scope of economic development, have each contributed to maintaining, in some instances increasing, expatriates among the economic elites.

Education and health are two important areas in which expansion is necessary to bring about change in Jamaica as directed by the emergent national elites, thus an increasing need for skills in these areas has developed since 1944. It is not surprising, then, to find that Jamaicans constitute only about three-fourths of the educational and medcial elites. For example, the founding of the University College of the West Indies (now University of the West Indies) in Jamaica in 1948 and the development of the medical school and a university hospital have contributed to the number of (non-West Indian) expatriates among these elites. However, at the rate Jamaicans and other West Indians are being trained in these areas, the relative number of expatriates will probably be reduced within a decade even though educational and health facilities will continue to expand.[36]

The rank order of the governmental elites with respect to Jamaican birth, as shown in Table 8.3, is the same as shown earlier for the top governmental elites in 1954. However, in each case the percentage for 1958 is even larger than that for 1954. This may show a continuation of the trend for the reduction of foreign-born persons among these groups, but the categories for 1958, as earlier stated, are defided somewhat differently that in 1954. However, it is interesting to note that the elected political leaders in 1958 were nearly as likely to be Jamaican-born, with 98 per cent so classified, as was the general population of Jamaica, 98.6 per cent of whom were Jamaican-born in 1960.

Metropolitan residence. The percentages of different types of elites residing in the metropolitan Kingston-St. Andrew area serve to illustrate the concentration of elite functions in Jamaica's major city. About half or more of the different types of elites, wirh the exception of the elected political leaders, live in the metropolitan area. These percentages range from 47 per cent for appointees to 87 per cent for civil servants, and compare with about 24 per cent of the general population of Jamaica who live in the Kingston-St. Andrew metropolitan area as of 1960. Only the elected political leaders, with 23 per cent residing in the urban area, approximate the distribution of the general population. Mayors and chairmen of the parish councils, of course, were located in the areas in which they held office. Also, members of the House of Representatives (MHR's) had to stand for election in the constituencies into which Jamaica was divided geographically, and their official residences were generally retained in them.[37] However, the House meets in Kingston and the MHR's spend a considerable amount of their time in the city. A few MHR's listed two addresses in *Who's Who*, one in the parish in which their constituency is located and one in the Kingston-St. Andrew metropolitan area.

Occupational rating and mobility. The occupational ratings of the different types of elites are shown in Table 3. The rating scale uscd is the same as that used earlier. The largest percentages having the highest occupational ratings are appointees, judges, barristers and solicitors. Each of these groups have 100 per cent of their members in the highest occupational rank. Next are elected political leaders (94%), religious leaders (94 %), and medical elites (93 %). Seventy-three per cent of the economic elites are in the highest occupational rank, followed by the soclal welfare elites with 57 per cent. Then come the civil servants with 45 per cent in the highest occupational ranks. Finally, the educational leaders have the fewest in the highest occupational rank with only 29 per cent so classified.

With respect to upward mobility, the most mobile group were the elected political leaders, 83 per cent of whom were upwardly mobile. They are closely followed, however, by the civil servants 79 per cent of whom upwardly mobile. Thus, although over half of the civil servants were not of the highest occupational rank, they are a group with one of the highest rates of upward occupational mobility. Appointees are the laest likely of any elite group to be upwardly mobile with only 31 per cent so classified. This lends support to the discussion of the findings reported earlier for the 1954 top governmental elites, and shows further that elected political office and the civil service comprised new routes of access to the achievement of higher socio-economic positions for Jamaicans of relatively humble socio-economic origins, while the *ex officio* and nominated positions tended to go increasingly, until 1958, to the already entrenched higher socio-economic classes.

With the exception of the appointees and medical elites, each of the other types of elites have over 50 per cent of their number who are upwardly mobile. This shows little about new channels of upward mobility for Jamaicans in the case of religious leaders, since so few religious leaders are Jamaican-born. But it shows that the upper classes, although greatly over-represented, do not have a monopoly over the high positions in the economy, education, the judiciary, law, and social welfare.

Sex. With the exception of two types of elite groups, 87 to 100 per cent of each type of elite is composed of men (see Table 8.3). The dominance of men over the important roles in public affairs and business is so well known as to require little further comment here.[38] The two exceptions are educational leaders 66 per cent of whom are men, and social welfare elites, 43 per cent of whom are men.

Age. Supporting the conclusions for the 1954 elites given earlier, the appointees are older on the average than either the elected political leaders or the civil servants. Also, they are older than any other elite group, their median age being 61. The youngest groups are the civil servants, medical elites, and barristers and solicitors who have median ages of 46. The other groups are as follows: educational leaders, 48; economic elites, 49; elected political leaders, religious leaders, and social welfare elites, 50; and judges, 53.

Religion. In 1960, 19.8 per cent of the general population of Jamaica were Anglicans. Yet among the different types of elites, the percentage of Anglicans was much larger (see Table 8.3). Seventy-three per cent of the appointees were Anglican, another reflection of the high social status and the centrality to the "established interests" in Jamaica of this type of elife at this time. The percentage of Anglicans in other groups is: civil servants, 58; judges and barristers and solicitors, 57; educational leaders, 55; medical elites, 53; economic elites, 47;

and elected political leaders, 38. Closer to the general population are social welfare elites of whom 29 per cent are Anglican and religious leaders themselves, of whom 25 per cent are Anglican.

Roman Catholics are a larger proportion (28%) of the religious leaders than they are of only other elite group. In descending order, according to the proportion of Catholics, are the economic elites (20%), medical elites (18%), judges (14%), barristers and solicitors (13%), elected political leaders and civil servants (9% each), appointed officials (8%), educational leaders (3%), and social welfare clites (none). With exception of educational and social welfare elites all of the elites contain a larger proportion of Catholics than would be expected by chance alone since only 7.2 per cent of the general population of Jamaica is Catholic.[39] One reason for this is that the Catholic Church has offered secondary school educational opportunities which have been a route to the attainment of elite positions for some persons.

Jews, who are only about 0.04 per cent of the general population, are most overrepresented among the economic elites of whom they constitute 8 per cent. They are also overrepresented among barristers and solicitors and religious leaders themselves (3%). Although they constitute only 2 per cent of the medical elites and 1 per cent of the civil servants, the Jews are somewhat overrepresented among these groups as well.[40]

Educational leaders have the largest percentage, 7.0, of atheists, agnostics, and independents, followed by elected political leaders, 4 per cent, medical elites and barristers and solicitors, 3 per cent each, and civil servants, 2 per cent. However, atheists, agnostics, and independents are underrepresented even among these elites, since the constitute 11.4 per cent of the general population.

There are some types of religions adhered to by members of the general population of Jamaica which are not present among the elites shown in Table 8.3 to any extent, if at all. Some of these are Hindu, Moravian, Pocomanian, and Ras Tafari brethren, among others.

Education. As can be seen from Table 8.3, by 1958 the elected political leaders were still less educated than the appointees and the civil servants, but they were more educated than they had been in 1954. Comparison of this variable between 1958 and 1954 can lead to a reliable conclusion since the 1958 group, being more inclusive of the lower rungs of the various hierarchies in the cases of elected political leaders and civil servants, should show a lesser educated group than the 1954 group unless there had been some real changes toward higher education. Alsh, the civil servants appear to be better educated in 1958 than they were in 1954; and in 1958 they were more likely to have attended a university than were the appointees.

The different types of elites ranked with respect to percentages, who have had some university education (from high to low), are: medical elites, religious leaders, judges, educational leaders, social welfare elites, civil servants, barristers and solicitors, appointees, elected political leaders and economic elites. However, the elected political leaders were the least educated group when the entire educational distribution is considered, having 27 per cent who had no more than an elementary education. Thus, the politicians were most like the general Jamaican public in this regard.

Table 8.3 also shows the percentage of persons with at least some university education who received their university training in a given country. The dependence of Jamaica for higher education on external areas is clearly seen in the very small percentages of persons who had received university training in Jamaica. Of course, the University College of the West Indies had just begun ten years before, so its effects in providing trained elites had not yet realiy begun to be felt. Britain is the place where many Jamaican elites received their higher educations. Three-fourths or more of the barristers and solicitors. appointees, judges, and social welfare elites went to universities in the United Kingdom. However, of those who attended a university, 40 per cent of the elected political leaders did so in the United States; and 53 per cent of the economic elites, 31 per cent of the medical elites, and 23 per cent of the civil servants did so in Canada and the United States combined. With the predominance of imported English laws in Jamaica, barristers, solicitors, and judges will probably continue to be educated in Britain for some time, but for the other types of elites it is safe to predict a considerable decrease in the proportions attending universities in Britain. Not only the University of the West Indies, but also American universities will make inroads. In the case of UWI, the reasons are obvious; and in the case of American universities, they are closer, the education they offer is increasingly recognized as being more practical and useful, given the needs of a developing nation, and an increase in educational grants from sources in the United States seems likely now that Jamaica is independent.

One of the more interesting and important developments in future years will be the impact of the University of the West Indies. Aside from the obvious academic implications and the advantages of having classroom examples and illustrations selected for a West Indian student body with greater emphasis on West Indian events and conditions by West Indian instructors, there are other consequences. What will be the effects of UWI in instilling general attitudes toward government and the political system, toward Jamaica, Trinidad, and other new nations in Africa and elsewhere, toward the world situation, toward alternative modes of political organization, etc.? The intellectual climate of Jamaica—and the West Indies generally—may change as more and more of the future elites are trained at UWI and as Jamaican and other West Indian intellectuals become a larger, more locally trained and less European-oriented group.[41]

It is difficult to overemphasize the importance of the growth of a West Indianizing West Indian university. In addition to the obvious skills that it can impart, it can contribute importantly to the resolution of certain ambivalences and dilemmas which are characteristic of many Jamaican and other West Indian intellectuals. For example, among UWI students today there is considerable effort, deliberate and self-conscious and often quite sophisticated, to achieve intellectual freedom. However, this may be more difficult to attain than political independence. Despite the emergence of Jamaican and West Indian cultural forms and unities, the West Indies represent a particular cultural hybrid which has developed under the cultural hegemony of England. England—the great power—hangs over intellectual life like a spectre. As Scott Greer has said,[42] Jamaica is "... not only itself, it's a shadow of England, but not England, the Empire, but not the Empire—high noon, Victorian time". When searching for their own identity, West Indian intellectuals often appear to be a mixed bag of contradictions, all neatly internalized to maximize agonizing self-recriminations. Alternately, they denounce England, defend England, and pounce on each other with accusations of having a "colonial mentality". They write poems, stories, and plays celebrating Jamaica's awakening and nationhood, but at the same time give voice to words which are reminiscent of England's modern "angry young men" and which are more appropriate to the sorrows of a declining nation with a golden past than to the joys of a former colony facing a new and better future. Some are finding intellectual freedom, but some still turn to England, denying part of themselves and aspiring to be a shadowy substance of what they never could have been, never can be, and to what few Englishmen are anymore. The University of the West Indies can help to create new alternatives, Jamaican and West Indian models.

Elites and Influence

Objective indicators of scope of influence. Table 8.4 shows the percentage of the different types of Jamaican elites having certain amounts of influence in addition to their major elite positions. Two objective indicators of the scope of influence were used. The first is the percentage who occupy elite positions in three or more different institutional sectors simultaneously, the interpretation of which was discussed earlier. According to this indicator, the different types of elites rank as follows with respect to the scope of their total influence from highest to lowest: appointees, elected political leaders, barristers and solicitors, economic elites, medical elites, educational leaders, civil servants, and finally religious leaders, judges, and social welfare elites, who were tied for last place.

Note that the rank order of the three types of governmental elites is the same as that given for 1954, the appointees having the most, and the civil servants the least scope of influence. In addition to the appointees and elected political leaders, only the barristers and solicitors and the economic elites had more

TABLE 8.4

Percentage of Jamaican Elites Having Certain Amounts of Influence by Type of Elite Position

Objective Indicators of Scope of Influence	Type of Elite Position									
	Elected Political Leaders (52)*	Appointees (34)	Civil Servants (185)	Economic Elites (269)	Religious Leaders (33)	Educational Leaders (35)	Judges (9)	Medical Elites (71)	Barristers and Solicitors (36)	Social Welfare Elites (7)
% with three or more elite positions	37	56	1	22	0	3	0	10	25	0
Vverage % based on formal association indicators which are given below	51	73	31	35	33	42	19	26	41	48
% with at leost one membership in formal associations	87	94	69	71	61	77	56	65	81	100

% who hold at least one office	46	71	19	20	24	40	0	10	22	29
% with membership in six or more formal associations	19	53	6	13	15	9	0	3	19	14

* The approximate number of cases on which the percentages are based is given in parentheses.

than one-fifth of their numbers with wide influence according to this indicator.

The second objective indicator is membership and office-holding in formal associations (excluding business concerns and government and including mostly voluntary associations ranging from social and recreational clubs to professional organizations).[43] The three indicators used (membership in at least one association, holding at least one office in an association, and membership in six or more associations) were averaged in order to construct an index of participation in the organizational membership structure. Such an index shows the relative access to organizational networks of influence and communication, and are taken as a further indication of the scope of a leader's influence.

From most to least inffluence, as measured by participation in the organizational membership structure, were the following types of elites appointees, elected political leaders social welfare elites, educational leaders, barristers and solicitors, economic elites, religious leaders, civil servants, medical elites, and judges. The rank order is fairly similar to that given for simultaneous occupancy of three of more different eiite positions with appointees heading the list, followed by elected political leaders. Civil servants ranked considerably below the politicians, thus the governmental elites retained their relative rankings as shown earlier. However, social welfare elites and educational leaders rank much higher by the formal association indicator than they do by the indicator of simultaneous occupancy of elite positions in different institutional structures.

The nominations to appointive office in part have shown the accomodation of the new representative government to the economic and social elites of Jamaica by giving them a voice in government which most of them could not have obtained by running for elective office. Also, a position in the top circles of influence in Jamaica, while not a pre-condition to appointment, was certainly a consideration of importance in the selection of appointees. However, judging from the appointments made in 1958, political considerations and the radical characteristics of members of tne Legislative Council were also taken into account. Three appointments made at that time included an influential man of high reputation from the economic-commercial sector who was ethnically identified as a Syrian, a second-echelon reputational influential man from the economic-commercial sector who was ethnically identified as being light to medium brown, and a retired educator and civil servant who was not among the reputational influentials at all (although he occupied several elite positions simultaneously and belonged to several formal associations) who was ethnically identified as dark brown or black. Appointments made since 1958 further show the increasing importance of political considerations in these appointments.

It was reported earlier that the elected political leaders had their power increasingly confined to the governmental structure from 1939 to 1954. Yet in 1958 they still rank higher by two objective measures of scope of influence than any other elite except for appointees. By 1958 the participation of the elected political leaders in the organizational membership structure and to some extent their interlocking occupancy of elite positions in different institutional structures had increased and was more the result of their governmental position than a cause of it—to the extent to which these can be unentwined in this context. That is, the elected political elites were in part being coopted by the pre-existing and established social and economic elities. This should not be overemphasized in that it has been a two-way flow of communication and influence—the old established elites recognizing the new power of the elected political leaders by including them in some of their associations, both formal and informal, and being subsequently affected by their membership. In turn, the elected political leaders have become somewhat circumscribed in new and unanticipated ways by their new associations. For example, a few social and recreational clubs had a near monopoly on the validation of certain kinds of prestige. Accommodating to the shifts in political power, they have included a few elected political leaders who would not have been acceptable before their rise to political power. This accommodation constitutes a change in the system of social stratification by altering the criteria of differential evaluation—by reducing the relative importance of family background and other ascriptive variables while increasing the relative importance of achieved characteristics. Also, some control over the new additions to the power elite—the politicians—may be exerted in return for this conferral of prestige. The elected political leaders are far from fully coopted, but there is some indication that some to a certain degree have been. Cooperation of the new political leaders contributes to social stability in that it reduces cleavages and antagonisms, while promoting cooperation, between different types of elites. But it produces potential instability to the extent to which it leaves inarticulate or unattended the discontents of the lower-classes.

Institutional sectors and reputational influence. During the late spring and summer of 1958, the basic sample of 803 Jamaican elites, whose selection has been described in Appendix I, were sent mail questionnaires. One of the questions asked was as follows:

> Considering all aspects of Jamaican life, who would you say are the most influential *individuals* on the entire island? That is, who are the people who can really get things done and who are really most important in influencing major economic and political decisions which affect all of Jamaica? In each case, does the person usually stay behind the scenes or is he in the forefront of affairs?
> (*Please list 10 individuals in order of their importance*)

One hundred-twenty-five persons were nominated as being among the top ten influentials of Jamaica. However, 41 of them were nominated by only one respondent each and 12 of them were nominated by only two respondents each. These were removed from the analysis and the remainder of 72—persons nominated by three or more respondents—are shown in Table 8.5 according to various social characteristics.[44]

From Table 8.5, nose that the two most highly ranked reputational leaders were elected politicians. Their high rankings in reputational influence are themselves significant indicators of the transfer of power and the shift in influence toward greater representation and participation of the mass of Jamaicans. For example, the first person is Norman W. Manley, then Chief Minister of Jamaica and Minister of Development, founder and president of the People's National Party, and founder of Jamaica Welfare, Ltd. The second person is Sir

TABLE 8.5

Selected Characteristies for Each Reputational Leader who was Naminated for Inclusion Among the 10 Most Influential Persons in Jamaica

No. of Times Nominated	Rank Order	Institutional Sector of Major Elite Position	No. of Elite Positions	No. of Memberships in Formal Associat ons	Percentage of Nominations Reputed to Work Behind the Scenes
1	2	3	4	5	6
194	1	Majority Party*	2	5	2
150	2	Minority Party	3	6	2
132	3	Economic—commerce†	7	8	42
122	4	Majority party	2	9	19
117	5	Economic—agriculture†	3	8	29
107	6	Majority party	1	0	1
73	7	Economic—commerce (federal Senator)	7	11	42
59	8	Economic—agriculture†	4	7	18
57	9	Majority party	1	1	4
48	10	Economic—agriculture	7	0	64
45	11	Economic—commerce	7	5	91
41	12	Religion†	2	0	48
31	13.5	Economic—commerce	7	0	77
31	13.5	Economic—commerce†	7	6	36

30	16	Economic—commerce	7	5	85
30	16	Economic—commerce	2	8	89
30	16	Economic—commerce	5	3	86
28	18	Education†	2	2	57
26	19.5	Minority party	2	1	5
26	19.5	H.E., The Governor	1	12	58
25	21.5	Economic—agriculture	3	10	57
25	21.5	Mass media	1	2	48
24	23	Labour	1	6	13
21	24	Economic—commerce†	6	10	53
20	25	Religion	1	2	75
19	26.5	Professions†	2	12	67
19	26.5	Civil Service	2	0	88
18	28	Majority party	2	7	27
17	29	Economic—commerce	7	8	93
16	30	Civil Service	1	2	100
12	31.5	Minority party (federal elected pol. leader)	3	2	27
12	31.5	Minority party	2	6	8
11	34	Economic—commerce (Privy Council)	7	2	100
11	34	Economic—agriculture (Custos)	4	3	73
11	34	Majority party	1	7	10
10	36.5	Economic—agriculture	5	2	100
10	36.5	Minority party	3	3	38
8	38	Arts	1	1	100

(*Contd.*)

TABLE 8.5—*Contd.*

1	2	3	4	5	6
7	42	Economic—commerce	7	8	100
7	42	Economic—commerce	4	9	83
7	42	Minority party (party officer)	2	0	33
7	42	Economic—commerce	2	8	43
7	42	Majority party	2	1	0
7	42	Religion	1	1	83
7	42	Religion	1	2	86
6	48.5	Economic—commerce	2	7	100
6	48.5	Social welfare†	1	1	67
6	48.5	Economic—commerce	7	10	75
6	48.5	Minority party (party officer)	1	6	17
6	48.5	Economic—commerce†	2	8	75
6	48.5	Economic—agriculture	2	6	60
5	53	Civil Service	2	1	80
5	53	Mass media	2	5	0
5	53	Education	1	6	100
4	56.5	Majority party (party officer)	2	3	100
4	56.5	Majority party (party officer)	1	3	100
4	55.5	Social welfare†	1	7	25
4	56.5	Majority party (mayor)	‡	‡	67
3	65.5	Majority party (party officer)	2	1	100
3	65.5	Economic—agriculture	3	1	67

3	65.5	Economic—agriculture	3	10	33
3	65.5	Majority party (party officer)	1	1	100
3	65.5	Professions†	2	9	50
3	65.5	Economic—commerce	7	5	100
3	65.5	Economic—agriculture	7	9	50
3	65.5	Professions†	2	12	50
3	65.5	Majority party	1	1	0
3	65.5	Economic—agriculture	3	7	33
3	65.5	Economic—commerce	7	5	100
3	65.5	Economic—commerce	6	3	100
3	65.5	Economic—commerce†	7	7	100
3	65.5	Economic—commerce†	7	3	33

* All persons who are shown to be part of the majority or minority parties are members of the House of Representatives except where otherwise indicated.

† These persons were also members of the Legislative Council.

† This person was not listed in *Who's Who* for owing to an oversight in the preparation, thus these data are unknown.

William Alexander Bustamante, then Leader of the Opposition, former Chief Minister of Jamaica, present Premier, founder and president of the Bustamante Industrial Trade Union (BITU), and founder and leader of the Jamaica Labour Party. These men are the two great Jamaican leaders who emerged from the riots, strikes, and disturbances of 1937-38 as spokesmen of the people. More than any other Jamaican leaders they have been associated with these significant events, and their efforts for 25 years have identified them with the trends toward the economic betterment of the general population, civil and political equality (including self-government), and equal access to facilities, services, and social institutions. The rankings of Manley and Bustamante can be compared to the ranking of the Governor of Jamaica who was tied for 19th place in reputational influence in 1958. Considering how much the Governor's formal powers had been reduced by 1958, one may wonder that the Governor was ranked as highly as he was. However, compared to the paramount importance of the Governor before 1944 under the Crown Colony form of government, his ranking in reputational influence in 1958 was relatively low. Since 1958, the formal powers of the Governor have continued to dwindle, and so has his reputational influence.

Because of the predominance of political and economic elites among the 72 top reputational leaders, a somewhat different classification of institutional sectors was used than was used earlier. The leaders of the then-majority political party (PNP) have been differentiated from the leaders of the then-minority party (JLP) and economic elites in agriculture have been separated from economic elites in other spheres (mostly in commerce). Also, members of the Legislative Council and other nominated persons were classified according to their major activity, and a few other changes have been made for convenience.

According to the percentage of top reputational leaders contained within them, the sectors rank as follows:

1. economic-commerce, 30.4 per cent;
2. majority party, 18.1 per cent;
3. economic-agriculture, 15.3 per cent;

4. minority party, 9.8 per cent;

5,6. civil service (including the Governor) and religion, 5 6 per cent each;

7. professions, 4.2 per cent;

8,9,10. mass media, education, and social welfare, 2.8 per cent each; and

11,12. labour and arts, 1.3 per cent each.

However, a better indicator of the relative reputational influence of each sector may be the percentage of total nominations contained within the sectors. Thus, a sector that had fewer persons who were frequently nominated might rank above a sector that had more persons who were infrequently nominated. Such does occur with respect to the relative ranking of majority political party leaders and the economic-commercial elites, as can be seen by the following ranking based upon the percentage of nominations contained in each sector:

1. majority party, 29.5 per cent;
2. economic-commerce, 27.7 per cent;
3. economic agriculture, 15.8 per cent;
4. minority party, 12.3 per cent;
5. religion, 4.1 per cent;
6. civil service, 3.6 per cent;
7. education, 1.8 per cent;
8. mass media, 1.6 per cent;
9. professions, 1.4 per cent;
10. labour, 1.3 per cent;
11. social welfare, 0.5 per cent; and
12. arts, 0.4 per cent.

Clearly, the most influential sectors by this measure are the four political and economic groups. Combined, they account for 73.6 per cent of the 72 reputational leaders and 85.3 per cent of the total nominations. Again the reader should be reminded that the low ranking of labour should not be interpreted as indicating little influence for this sector. Rather, labour is represented by the political parties. As indicated, the leader of the JLP was also president of a trade union and a son of the Chief Minister was first Vice-president of the National Workers Union (NWU). For many purposes the parties and unions line up: PNP—NWU and JLP—BITU.

The importance of the political and economic sectors is not entirely due to the use of the terms "economic and political" in the question which was used to elicit the identities of influentials. Key informants agreed that these sectors were the most important ones which affect all of Jamaican life, and the study done in 1961-62 by Charles C. Moskos, Jr. shows the same four sectors to be most important compared to other sectors, according to his respondents, even though "political and economic" were not specified in the question used by him to locate reputational leaders.[45]

In 1958, the economic elites in agriculture were not "playing politics nearly as much as the economic elites in commerce, an exception being in the rather narrow case of negotiations between management and labour in sugar where the implications of the PNP—NWU and JLP—BITU alignments have not been irrelevant. Sugar was the dominant industry in agriculture, and its importance to the economy was so well recognized that both political parties would see to it that the sugar industry survived. At the same time, although the economic-agricultural elites were powerful, they were confronted with a heavily unionized labour force and their influence could be counter-balanced by trade union activity. Also, the agricultural sector was already being squeezed by wage increases. On the other hand, the mercantile class had considerably more freedom within which to exercise influence. The labour force in the commercial sector was less organized than in the agricultural sector and the imposition of controls on the commercial elites had to be carried out more by the use of governmental authority rather than by labour-management negotiations. Also, the expansion of commercial and industrial activities, the angling for markets, and the importance of governmental policies for economic development spurred the commercial elites' interest in politics and government. In this situation, it is understandable that the economic-commercial elites were very active behind the scenes trying to protect their interest.

The economic-commercial elites shown in Table 8.5 were most influential according to the average number of elite positions which they simultaneously occupied (X=5.8) and they were higher than any sector, exeept for the professions, in average number of formal association memberships (X=6.3). The economic elites discussed earlier in connection with Table 8.4 did not show up as being so influential because they included quite a number of relatively small and middle-sized operators and because the appointees among them were given a separate category. The reputational economic-commercial elites as shown in Table 8.5, however, contain only the largest operators, and, as noted, they were very high on each of the three indicators of influence employed. Also, the then-chairman of the Board of Directors of The Gleaner Company, which owns the only two daily newspapers in Jamaica, is an economic-commercial elite as is every other member of the Board. Finally, of the 17 appointees shown in Table 8.5 eight are economic commercial elites.

These economic elites generally preferred the JLP to the PNP. It is true that each of the major political parties draws heavily on labouring-class and small-independent-farmer support with an edge perhaps to the PNP among the former and an edge to the JLP among the latter. Also, each party draws some support from among the members of every social class, notably so with respect to a few well-known top economic elites, but differentially so with respect to the proportion of support received from the different social classes. But the PNP has been known for having a good deal of support among middle-class intellectuals and professionals, and the 1958 mail questionnaire survey confirmed this, showing much more support for the PNP than for the JLP among lawyers, civil servants, educational leaders, social welfare elites, doctors, and religious leaders. However, among the economic elites (including both small and large operators) the PNP received little support. Only 21 per cent of the economic-commercial elites and 7 per cent of the economic-agricultural elites preferred the

PNP compared to 48 and 50 per cent respectively of the same groups who preferred the JLP.

Also from Table 8.5, note that the economic-commercial elites were generally reputed to work more behind the scenes than in the forefront of affairs, the average of such designations being 77.4 per cent. Civil servants, religious leaders, and educational leaders shown in Table 8.5 were also much more likely to work behind the scenes than in the forefront of affairs. Of the remaining large sectors, economic-agricultural elites were about as likely to work in the forefront of affairs as behind the scenes, and of course, elected political leaders worked almost entirely in the forefront of affairs. However, the party officers of the PNP were "back-room boys" who worked mostly behind the scenes.

Elites and Ethnicity

Historically, ethnic differences have been of considerable importance in differentiating Jamaican society into segments of persons having differential rights and duties. Colour, of course, differentiated slaves from free persons at one period, and nationality background and religion have been important differentiating factors also. Ascription on the basis of ethnicity has been reduced as has ascription on the basis of other criteria but ethnicity has not yet become completely irrelevant to the distribution of elite functions in Jamaica.

Table 8.6 contains distributions of the Members of the House of Representatives and the Legislative Council by colour for 1951 and 1958. Both in 1951 and in 1958 the members of the House were much less likely to be white or light than were the members of the Legislative Council. Conversely, they were much more likely to be dark brown or black. As Broom points out in his discussion of the 1951 data, the House of Representatives[46] ". . . is more representative of the colour characteristics of Jamaica than is any other high-status group. Even so, the darker elements are under-represented, if one's sole criterion is proportionality". This was still true in 1958.

For the House of Representatives in 1951 the colour of four members was unknown, so the differences between 1951 and 1958 can not be accepted without caution. However, it appears from Table 8.6 that the relative number of black MHR's increased while the relative number of dark brown MHR's decreased. But for both 1951 and 1958, the percentage of dark brown and black persons combined was about the same, about 50 per cent. Also, the percentage of white, light, olive and light brown MHR's combined stayed about the same.

TABLE 8.6

Percentage of Members of the House of Representatives and the Legislative Council According to Colour

Colour	House of Representatives 1951 (Per cent)	House of Representatives 1958 (Per cent)	Legislative Council 1951 (Per cent)	Legislative Council 1958 (Per cent)
White and light	11	9	86	47
Olive and light brown	36	41	7	29
Dark brown	42	28	7	18
Black	11	22	0	6
Total	100	100	100	100
Number of cases	(28)	(32)	(15)	(17)

Source: 1951 data adapted from Leonard Broom. "The Social Differentiation of Jamaica". *American Sociological Review*, 19 (April, 1954), p. 125. Unfortunately, Broom has data for only 28 of the 32 members of the House in 1951, thus the percentage distribution is approximate and has been computed here under the assumption that the "unknowns" were distributed with respect to colour just as the "knowns". All members of the Legislative Council are classified.

1958 data from personal observation or from informants or both. All members of both the House and the Legislative Council are classified.

There was a decrease in the percentage of white and light persons in the Legislative Council from 1951 to 1958, from 86 to 47 per cent. The largest increase was in the percentage of olive and light brown persons, from 7 to 29 per cent; but there were also increases in the percentage of dark brown persons, from 7 to 18, and an increase in the percentage who were black from 0 to 6 per cent. The latter appears to be accounted for by the addition of one person who was nominated to the Legislative Council in 1951 just after Broom had completed his classification of members by colour. In the sense of proportionality, the Legislative Council members were somewhat more representative of the general population of Jamaica in 1958 with respect to colour than they were in 1951, but they were still grossly dissimilar—and much more dissimilar to the general population than were the members of the House. However, as indicated earlier, trends detected in such appointments probably will make the members of the Legislative Council in the future still more similar in coloar and other social characteristics to the members of the House.

The distribution of the top reputational leaders by sector and colour is given in Table 8.7. No Chinese were among the reputed influentials despite the fact that they were differentiated in the larger society. Also, none of Jamaica's East Indians were nominated For all 72 influentials the distribution by colour was as follows: 11 per cent white (foreign-born), 40 per cent Jamaican white and practically white, 28 per cent light and medium brown, and 21 per cent dark brown and black. Thus, the observation must be made again that the dark brown and black segments were under-represented.

In addition, colour distribution by sector were quite dissimilar. For example, comparing the four most influential groups, one can see that the political elites of both parties were most like the general population with respect to colour as was the case with other social characteristics. None of them were foreign-born whites, only four were Jamaican whites or near-whites, eight were light or medium brown, and eight were dark brown or black. Thus, the constitutional changes increasing the number of elected offices, enhancing the power of the elected positions, and permitting the introduction of mass political parties, has meant a shift in power to the coloured and black segments of the population.

The economic elites were quite different. Although three economic-agricultural elites were dark brown or black, seven of the others were Jamaican whites or near-whites and one was foreign-born white. The economic-commercial leaders were even more unlike the general Jamaican population than the economic-agricultural elites. None of them were dark brown or black, only four were light or medium brown, fourteen were Jamaican whites or near whites, and four were foreign-born whites. Thus, economic power largely remained directly in the hands of whites or near-whites, although it was limited, as discussed earlier, by the power of trade unions, political parties and government which was in large part directly in the hands of brown-skinned leaders.

Additionally, the economic-commercial influentials were ethnically differentiated fıom the other types of influentials further in that two of them were Syrian, eight were Jews, and three had Jewish backgrounds. (These persons are classified as Jamaican whites or near-whites in Table 8.7). Unlike the

TABLE 8.7

The Number of Top-72 Reputational Leaders by Sector and Colour

Sector	White* (Foreign-born)	Jamaican White and Practically White	Light and Medium Brown	Dark Brown and Black	Total
Majority political party	0	2	6	5	13
Economic-commerce	4	14	4	0	22
Economic-agriculture	1	7	0	3	11
Manority political party	0	2	2	3	7
Religion	1	0	1	2	4
Civil service	2	0	1	1	4
Education	0	0	2	0	2
Mass media	0	0	1	1	2
Professions	0	2	1	0	3
Labour	0	0	1	0	1
Social welfare	0	1	1	0	2
Arts	0	1	0	0	1
Total	8	29	20	15	72

* Excludes a few foreign-born whites and near-whites who are known to have Jamaican parentage. Such persons are included with the Jamaican white and practically white.

Chinese, who were also over-represented in commercial activity (but more concentrated in retail trade—especially the retail grocery trade), the Syrians and Jews tended not to be ethnically exclusive in their associations, they performed many elite functions, and they were not isolated from the blacks, coloured, and the other ethnics of similar social-class levels. Also, their rise to economic prominence is itself a measure of increasing internal inclusiveness in that the Jews have been legally discriminated against in the past. As Broom points out:[47]

> "Like the Chinese, the Syrians are concentrated in commercial activity. Unlike the Chinese, at the turn of the century they entered into competition with the relatively well established dry goods and wholesale firms run by creole whites and coloured. In large part through the skill of a single family, the Syrians have become a major economic force, tightly integrated and with close ties to the Syrian community in North America and throughout the Caribbean.
>
> ". . . the Jews of Jamaica . . . have never exceeded a few hundred. They were originally of Spanish and Portuguese origin and were important in the entrepot trade with the Spanish Caribbean. Along with the Scots, they dealt in plantation stores, a large scale business in which sales were made in bulk. In the 17th and early 18th centuries Jews suffered from discriminatory taxation and civil disabilities. The special taxes were rescinded first, and then, early in the 19th century they were relieved of the remaining impediments. As the coloured population became urbanized and achieved some vertical mobility, intermarriage and concubinage with Jews, as well as with other whites, took place.
>
> ". . . the group is the most fully integrated of all the ethnic minorities into Jamaican society. Like the coloured, many of their number perform elite functions".

Two of the persons classified in Table 8.7 as civil servants were foreign-born whites. One was the Governor and one was a special UN economic and social advisor to the Chief Minister.

The latter person has now left the island, and with independence, a new Governor has been appointed who is a dark-skinned Jamaican.

Conclusion

I have described and analyzed the social composition of elites in a new nation, the former British colony of Jamaica. Recent political developments, economic transformations, and social changes have altered the leadership structure, and a new Jamaican elite has arisen. However, such recent changes have been viewed here, not as startling discontinuities with Jamaica's prior history, but rather as continuations of certain long-term social trends which can conveniently be summarized as increases in the scale of society.

Oversimplifying, one can say that Jamaicans have moved from slaves, to become citizens and leaders. The increasing internal inclusiveness of Jamaican society, one aspect of increasing scale, has resulted in the reduction of ascriptive barriers and the institutionalization of more equal oppornities. It has meant the extension of rising minimums of civil, political, economic, and social rights for every Jamaican. One manifestation of this, of course, has been the creation of a national citizenry on the basis of political equality, and another has been the transcendence of past economic deprivations and social limitations.

Another aspect of the increase in the scale of society has been the increase in the size and inclusiveness of the elite. Circulation of elites has increased as elites have become less exclusive. The recruitment of elites has been increasingly based upon universalistic criteria and achievement, resulting in a wider range of social origins than before. A new national elite has developed which is more aware and concerned about the welfare of the lower-classes. Elites have become more accessible to the masses, and the masses have become more accessible to the elites. Today, the descendants of the former slaves not only are fullfledged citizens of their own country but also are prominent among its national leaders.

Whether the trend toward equality of opportunities will continue now that Jamaica is independent is problematical.

Independence itself has been a spur to the further rise of the lower-classes and the further spread of equality in that it has dramatized the past struggle for equality and affirmed the present aspiration for more equality in the future as a national goal. Also, from data reported elsewhere,[48] one can conclude that the new elites of Jamaica are fairly equalitarian in their attitudes. The overall level of equalitarianism is relatively high and variations by elite subgroups generally support the contention that equalitarianism among the elites may increase in future years. However, it is not simply a matter of sitting back and letting an inevitable trend unfold. Policies must be formulated and effective actions must be taken. Although much progress toward it has been made, the ideal of equality has not yet been achieved.

NOTES

1. Harold D. Lasswell, Daniel Lerner, and C. Easton Rothwell, *The Comparative Study of Elites*, Stanford: Stanford University Press, 1952.
2. See, S.F. Nadel, "The Concept of Social Elites", *International Social Science Bulletin*, Vol. 8 (No. 3, 1956), pp. 413-424.
3. Godfrey and Monica Wilson, *The Analysis of Social Change*, Cambridge: Cambridge University Press, 1945. Also see the discussion of Albanian elites by Charles C. Moskos, Jr. in this volume, Chapter 7.
4. Most of the Spanish terms in present day use have been brought back from Cuba and Panama by migrant labourers during the last eighty years. See, R.B. Le Page and David De Camp., *Jamaican Creole*, London: MacMillan and Co. Ltd., 1960.
5. Le, Page and De Camp, *ibid.*, p. 74.
6. George W., Roberts, *The Population of Jamaica*, Cambridge: Cambridge University Press, 1957, p. 65.
7. Leonard Broom, "The Social Differentiation of Jamaica", *American Sociological Review*, Vol. 19 (April, 1954), pp. 115-125.
8. M.G. Smith, "The Plural Framework of Jamaican Society," *The British Journal of Sociology*, Vol. 12 (September, 1961), p. 250.
9. *Cf.* M.G. Smith, "West Indian Culture," *Caribbean Quarterly*, Vol. 7 (December, 1961), pp. 112-119. In this discussion, Smith stresses the divisive effects of the duality of the West Indian culture complex. His partitioning of West Indian culture into a dominant European-Creole component and a subordinate African-Creole com-

ponent is based upon historical and socio-logical facts, but it sights other facts: both components are shared to some degree by members of every social class at the present time and the trends in emergent West Indian culture increasingly transcend the dominance of the old European tradition, the subordination of the African tradition, and the gulf between the two. The cultural duality certainly exists, but it should be considered along with the fact that there is emerging a distinctive combination of elements in a new unity, although in Jamaica, this new unity is likely to be more "Jamaican" than "West Indian" and yet it is likely to be increasingly universalistic, that is, a part of the modern world culture.

10. *West India Royal Commission Report*, London: His Majesty's Stationery Office, Cmd. 6607, July 1945.
11. W.W. Rostow, *The Stages of Economic Growth*, Cambridge: Cambridge University Press, 1960.
12. *The Economic Development of Jamaica*, by a Mission of the International Bank for Reconstruction and Development, Baltimore, Md., 1952; *Economic Survey, Jamaica, 1960*, prepared by the Central Planning Unit, the Government of Jamaica, 1961.
13. Some of the generalizations given here closely follow Wilson and Wilson *op cit.*, or Eshref Shevky and Wendell Bell, *Social Area Analysis*, Stanford: Stanford University Press, 1955.
14. Of course, in one sense this trend seems to be contradicted by the dismantlement of empires and the creation of new nations. The resulting new "nationality" becomes a new ascriptive barrier, sometimes where little national identification existed before, between the peoples of the different new states and the peoples of other states, both old and new. However, the rise of the new nationalism has served to reduce many ascriptive barriers that used to stand between various social groups *within* the territory of the new states, and has provided a basis for a new and more thorough-going internal unity. Also, the transfer of highest loyalty and allegiance from traditional or primordial groups to the state may set the stage, as others have pointed out, for a further step in which political and other organizations may be developed, which transcend the nation-state in the priority of its claim on the individual and which are larger in geographical scale than presently existing nation-states. Among the older nations of Europe, this trend is already apparent. There, the growth of supra-national organizations and the consequent decline of some degree and aspects of national sovereignty can be clearly seen today.
15. I have included cultural with social rights.
16. Smith, "The Plural Framework of Jamaican Society", *op. cit.*, pp. 249-262.
17. Materials on human rights in Jamaica can be found in the following sources: W.L. Burn, *Emancipation and Apprenticeship in the British West Indies*, London: Jonathan Cape, 1937; W.J. Gardner, *A*

History of Jamaica, London: Elliot Stock, 1873: Douglas Hall, *Free Jamaica 1838—1865: An Economic History*, New Haven: Yale University Press, 1959: William Law Mathieson, *British Slave Emancipation 1838-1849*, London: Longmans, Green and Co., 1932; William Law Mathieson, *The Sugar Colonies and Governor Eyre 1849-1866*, London: Longmans, Green and Co., 1936; Mary Proudfoot, *Britain and the United States in the Caribbean*, New York: Frederick A. Praeger, 1953; Robert Worthington Smith, "The Conflict between Planter and Parliament over the Slave Laws of Jamaica", unpublished Ph.D. dissertation, University of California, Los Angeles, 1942; H.A. Wyndham, *Problems of Imperial Trusteeship: The Atlantic and Emancipation*, London: Oxford University Press, 1937.

18. A detailed investigation of change in relation to social unity in Jamaica is available in James A. Mau, "Social Change and Belief in Progress: A Study of Images of the Future in Jamaica", unpublished Ph.D. dissertation, University of California, Los Angeles, 1963.
19. Some of these points are documented in Elsa V. Goveia, *A Study on the Historiography of the British West Indies*, Mexico: Instituto Panamericano de Geografiae Historia, 1956.
20. Reinhard Bendix, "National Citizenship of the Lower Classes: A Comparative Perspective", unpublished paper, pp. 2-3. I am greatly indebted to Professor Bendix for the conception of social change is being constituted in part by changes in human rights. See his "Social Stratification and the Political Community", *Archives Europeennes de Sociologie*, Vol. 1, (1960), pp. 181-210; and "The Lower Classes and the 'Democratic Revolution,' " *Industrial Relations*, Vol. 1, (October, 1961), pp, 91-116.
21. R.H. Tawney, *Equality*, London: George Allen and Unwin, Ltd., 1952, pp. 97-98.
22. Lower-class conceptions of their duties and obligations are the subject of detailed research in Andrew P. Phillips, "The Development of a Modern Labor Force in Antigua", unpublished Ph.D. dissertation, University of California, Los Angeles, 1963.
23. Morley Ayearst, *The British West Indies, The Search for Self Government*, Washington Square: New York University Press, 1960; Charles Henry Kunsman, Jr., "Recent Developments in Representative Government in Jamaica, 1938-1953", unpublished M.A. thesis, University of California, Berkeley, 1955; C.M. MacInnes, "Constitutional Developments of the British West Indies", in *Developments Towards Self Government in the Caribbean*, The Hague, Bandun: W. van Hoeve Ltd., 1955; Hume Wrong, Government of the West Indies, Oxford: Clarendon Press, 1923.
24. *The Handbook of Jamaica for 1954*, Kingston, Jamaica: The Government Printing Office, 1954, p. 37.

25. It should be noted that Jamaica has moved slower and more carefully toward independence than many other new nations. There is no question but that this has been beneficial in many ways. A large cadre of Jamaicans have been trained for leadership in politics and the civil service and to a lesser extent in commerce and industry. However, one negative effect may be that the average person in Jamaica faced full independence in 1962 with less thrill and challenge than if independence had come rapidly rather than in gradual increments from 1944 to 1962. The drama of the political transformation was somewhat diffused by many little excitements rather than a single climax. Some members of the Jamaican masses felt that they had been told they were getting freedom from colonialism so many times since 1944 that they were a bit cynical when independence finally fully came. As a resut, the psychological impact of independence may have been less than it might have been.
26. *The Handbook of Jamaica for 1939*, Kingston, Jamaica. The Government Printing Office, 1939; *The Handbook of Jamaica for 1954*, Kingston, Jamaica: The Government Printing Office, 1954; *Who's Who and Why in Jamaica 1939-40*, Second Edition, compiled and published by L.A. Thoywell Henry, Kingston, Jamaica: The Gleaner Co., Ltd.; *Who's Who*, Jamaica 1954, edited by Clifton Neita, Kingston, Jamaica: The Gleaner Co., Ltd., 1954.
27. Of course from the point of view of non-Jamaicans, one can say that the top governmental elites are now more exclusive rather than less so in one way, since Jamaican nationality status, although in a sense being achieved by Jamaicans through political change, was emergent as an ascriptive criterion for membership in the governmental elite group. At the same time, the need for persons possessing certain specialized and differentiated skills in connection with economic and social development (e.g., in the bauxite industry and the University of the West Indies) increased the number of non-Jamaicans among some types of elite groups.
28. The facts are somewhat more complicated than this statement suggests in that for about two decades it was believed that Jamaica might become independent as part of a nation larger in geographical scale than the boundaries of Jamaica itself. An independent West Indies Federation was to include nine other British territories in the Caribbean as well. Thus, a few non-Jamaican West Indians also moved into elite roles in Jamaica as part of the transition to independence. Now that Jamaica has reached independence on its own, we can expect such roles to be further "Jamaicanized" rather than "West Indianized". However, this may be accomplished in party by some non-Jamaican West Indians opting to become Jamaican citizens under the new Constitution.
29. The 1943 percentages for the entire population are estimates based on data given in *The Eighth Census of Jamaica, 1943, ibid*, Table 10,

p. 6. Unfortunately, comparable data for the entire population in 1960 are not available.

30. Also, membership in the two major parties had become more acceptable to many educated people since at this time the PNP had deemphasized its early socialism and since the demogogic rule of the charismatic leader of the JLP had given ground to a more bureaucratic and democratic party organization. See C. Paul Bradley, "Mass Parties in Jamaica: Structure and Organization", *Social and Economic Studies*, Vol. 9. (December, 1960), pp. 375-416.
31. *Eighth Census of Jamaica and its Dependencies, 1943, op. cit.*, Table 70, p. 127; and *West Indies Population Census, 1960* (provisional), Bulletin No. 20 (Jamaica), Kingston, Jamaica: Department of Statistics, 1962, Table 6, p. 70, and Table 7, p. 86.
32. An intergenerational measure was used, if possible, which was based upon the relationship between an elite's occupation and his father's occupation. If the father's occupation was not given, a measure of career mobility was used based upon the relationship between an elite's first reported job and his present job. Where possible, both measures were examined in order to increase the validity of the measure. The occupational rating scale used was a modified version of that given in W. Lloyd Warner, Marchia Meeks, and Kenneth Eels, *Social Class in America*, Chicago: Science Research Associates, Inc., 1949, pp. 140-141; and in Carson McGuire, "Social Status, Peer Status, and Social Mobility", a mimeographed memorandum for research workers, Committee on Human Development, University of Chicago, Chicago, Ill., 1948.
33. *Eighth Census of Jamaica and its Dependencies, 1943, op. cit.*, Table 21, p. 22; and *West Indies Population Census, 1960*, Bulletin No. 18, Table 1, p. 1. For a more detailed discussion of the data given in Tables 1 and 2, see Emily Roberta Smith (Reed), "Self-Government and the Political Elite in Jamaica, 1939 and 1954", unpublished M.A. thesis, Northwestern University, Evanston, Ill., 1957.
34. Leonard Broom, *op. cit.*, p. 125.
35. David Granick, *The European Executive*. New York: Doubleday, 1962.
36. Since the University of the West Indies (U.W.I.) has been a co-operative service including not only Jamaica but each of the former territories of the West Indies Federation and British Guiana and British Honduras as well, "West Indianization" rather than "Jamaicanization" gives the appropriate frame of reference in this example. As of 1957, only 38 per cent of the entire University staff and even less, 26 per cent, of the University teaching staff were West Indians. Only in the non-teaching, administrative roles did West Indians outnumber non-West Indians where the former occupied 71 per cent of the positions, according to a mimeographed University report.

37. A summary of the qualifications of MHR's in *The Handbook of Jamaica for 1958* (p. 40) says that an MHR had to reside in the parish which contained the constituency in which he stood for election; however, the relevant clause in the constitution (p. 60 of *The Handbook*) states only that residence in the island of Jamaica is necessary.
38. For example, see Wendell Bell, Richard J. Hill, and Charles R. Wright, *Public Leadership.* San Francisco: Chandler Publishing Co., 1961, Chapter Three. "Male Dominance in Public Leadership", pp. 34-55.
39. *West Indies Population Census, 1960,* Bulletin No. 14, Table 8.4, p. 27.
40. There appears to be a discrepancy between the data given here showing the percentage of lawyears who are Jewish in 1958 as 3 per cent and data given by Broom for 1951 which shows 7.1 per cent of the lawyers as being Jews. It is likely that the apparent discrepancy is accounted for in part by the differences in the methods used to sample the lawyers at the two time periods. For 1951, Broom selected a sample from all barristers and solicitors in residence and in practice, listed in the Handbook of Jamaica, and then used informants to determine ethnicity. For 1958, I tried to select only those barristers and solicitors who were among the more powerful or prominent ones, and used *Who's Who* information to determine religion. Also, another difference is that I classified them by their major activity. Thus, some solicitors were not classified as solicitors but as economic elites since their major activity was in the economic sphere. In my data, Jews are overrepresented among people who are qualified solicitors whose major activity is not practicing law but engaging in commerical activities. *Cf.* Broom, *op. cit.*, p. 124.
41. James T., Duke has completed a study of students at UWI, "Equalitarianism Among Emergent Elites in a New Nation", unpublished Ph.D. dissertation, University of California, Los Angeles, 1963.
42. Personal communication.
43. For a discussion of the social participation approach to the study of influence see Bell, Hill and Wright, *op. cit.*
44. The validity of this list of top influentials was tested by going over the list with a few key informants who were themselves among the top 72 influentials. With two or three exceptions, there was general agreement that this list was an accurate ranking. Also, during the winter of 1961-1962, another list of reputational leader was compiled relying solely on interviewing and working with the entire list of names when a respondent was ranking influentials. If one makes allowances for deaths between 1958 and 1962 and for the rise of a few new influentials in 1962 who were not on the scene in 1958, the lists are quite similar. See, Charles C. Moskos, Jr., "The Sociology

of Political Independence: A Study of Influence, Social Structure, and Ideology in the British West Indies", unpublished Ph.D, dissertation, University of California, Los Angeles, 1963.

45. Moskos, *ibid.*
46. Broom, *op. cit.*, p. 125.
47. Broom, *ibid.*, pp. 123-124.
48. Wendell Bell, "Equality and Attitudes of Elites in Jamaica", *Social and Economic Studies.* Vol. 11, (December, 1962), pp. 409-432, and Wendell Bell, *Jamaican Leaders: Political Attitudes in a New Nation,* Berkeley and Los Angeles: University of California Press, 1964.

APPENDIX I

DESCRIPTION OF 1958 SAMPLE OF JAMAICAN ELITES

The first step in constructing a basic list of names to constitute a sample of 1958 Jamaican elites was to select a 25 per cent sample of names from *Who's Who, Jamaica, 1957*, Kingston, Jamaica: The Gleaner Co., Ltd., no date. This was done in May, 1958 by selecting every fourth name after a random start from 1 to 4 using page proofs from *Who's Who*, which was then in press. In this manner, 598 persons were selected. Of these, seven persons were eliminated from the analysis, because it was later learned that they had died, were critically ill, or had left the island permanently. Because the 1957 *Who's Who* was still being compiled and revised in 1958, these data are accepted as 1958 information and have been so designated throughout this paper.

The second step was to add to the 591 persons selected as part of the random sample from the *Who's Who*. New names were selected from the King's House Invitation List, which is a ranking of persons in Jamaica according to their official status, be they elected politicians, civil servants, religious leaders, bank officials, foreign trade commissioners, or what. Also, other lists were used to check the up-to-dateness of the Invitation List, such as the Civil Service Seniority List; the list of members in the House of Representatives and the Legislative Council; and the list of Chairmen of Parish Councils and Mayors. However, the King's House Invitation List was the basic frame of reference for the supplementary sample. Thus, for some groups (appointees and higher civil servants) the sample selected equalled the universe from which it was drawn.

However, lesser civil servants were sampled by means of the *Who's Who* random sample. For elected political leaders, the sample approached the universe, but parish councilors were included only if they occupied the office of Chairman or fell into the random sample. In this manner, 212 additional names were added to the basic sample of 591 Jamaican leaders drawn from *Who's Who*, making a total of 803 persons who comprised the basic list. The King's House Invitation List was used to obtain a complete list of top leaders and to compensate for any omissions of top leaders in the *Who's Who*.

Finally, of the 212 persons selected from the King's House Invitation List, 59 were not listed in *Who's Who*. Thus, the data shown in Table 8.3 are based upon 744 out of the 803 persons who constituted the basic sample of 1958 Jamaican elites, or the equivalent of a 93 per cent response rate.

9

A Study of Ethnicity in Indonesia

M.F. EDMUNDS

In the study of ethnicity the unit of analysis has shifted from the isolated ethnic group defined by its cultural content to the ethnic unit as a social category, a form of structure, embedded within a larger system. Behaviour which had formerly been regarded as traditional may now be seen as emerging as a response to patterns of interaction and communication among groups, and items of culture as well as ways of thinking and of evaluating oneself are intrinsically related to the structural position of one's group in the larger society. Gluckman, for example, explains urban tribalism in terms of the social context of the town rather than in terms of the persistence of rural culture patterns in the city.[1] M.G. Smith's studies of pluralism treat group relations as a function of cleavages and segmentation in the nation as a while,while Cohen focuses our attention on how particular tribal polities share in the allocation of economic and political power, and Barth views the maintenance of ethnicity as based upon interaction rather than isolation, and thus concentrates on the boundaries between groups.[2]

It is somewhat paradoxical, however, that despite such theorectical convergence on the larger system and despite the increasing number of field studies on the emergence of ethnicity in cities, little has been done to conceptualize those features of the urban system which are relevant for the understanding of urban ethnicity. The problem arose in striking fashion in my own investigations of the expression of ethnicity in two cities in Indonesia, a nation well-known in social science as the classie ease of the plural society.[3] I found that ethnicity is manifested and experienced very differently in the two cities, and a review of the literature did not prove to be particularly helpful in elucidating why this should be so. The expression of ethnicity varied as the urban context varied, and the city itself become a relevant unit of analysis. The problem became one of relating ethnic group interaction and other aspects of social life to urban structure and ecology.

Background Information

Indonesia, the world's largest island complex, extends 3,400 miles from east to west and consists of thousands of islands populated by 300 different ethnolinguistic groups.[4] There are approximately 128 million Indonesians but the population is very unevenly distributed. The island of Java and neighbouring Madura with only 7 per cent of the total territory of Indonesia contains 65 per cent of the population—an average density of 577 persons per sq. km. The population density of the rest of Indonesia, the so-called outer islands, is 19 persons per sq. km. The important aspects of the social demography of Indonesia are that one-half of the population belong to a single ethnic group, the Javanese, that the vast majority of Javanese live on the island of Java, and that most other Indonesians see themselves as engaged in a more or less continual struggle to keep from being Javanized.

Indonesia has a national culture in that there are national symbols and such national institutions as a civil service, a military organization, and other central government agencies. Every Indonesian, however, is also a member of an ethnic group, be he Javanese, Malay, Balinese, Minangkabau, or somethihg else. The national language, Indonesian, exists side by side with various local languages. Ethnic groups have ethnically homogenous home territories on one or another island; the mixing of peoples occurs primarily in border areas and in such modern contexts as army camps, government bureaus, and cities.

In such modern contexts, including the most intellectual circles in the national capital, Djakarta, I have asked literally hundreds of persons if they knew anyone who was just an Indonesian with no ethnic affiliation. My respondents replied that there are a few who do approximate that model, and many felt that the children of some families would eventually lose all ethnic identification. It was clear, however, that at present there is no readily identifiable community of Indonesians as such. Not that there is any opposition between being a member of an ethnic group and an Indonesian citizen at the same time. This is not only the normal state of affairs but there is no viable alternative.

An elaborate set of stereotypes define the characteristics attributed by the various Indonesian ethnic groups to one another. The Javanese and the Sundanese, for example, are known to be very polite and refined and as being careful to control their emotions while the Batak are considered as more expressive and volatile, and also as less refined. Some groups are regarded as good businessmen, others as morally puritanical, and there are four groups about whom it is said that in a dispute with any of their members one has to be very careful because they are likely to fight with knives. Members of two other ethnic groups have the reputation of being food poisoners. Ethnic labels deal with vital areas—emotions, aggression, sex, food.

The Two Cities

My first field study of ethnicity in Indonesian cities was conducted in 1957-1958 among one ethnic group, the Toba Batak, in both their rural homeland and Medan, a town on the east coast of Sumatra. Subsequently, as political conditions stabilized in Indonesia, I returned between 1969-1971 for a total of nine months in the field and initiated two different projects. One project involved a re-visit to Sumatra to examine the changes that had occurred among the Toba Batak in village and city, thirteen years after my initial research. The second project consisted of a study of ethnicity among four different ethnic groups, the Javanese, Sundanese, Batak, and Minangkabau, located in the city of Bandung on the island of Java.* These two approaches provided new perspectives. Indeed, it became apparent that my 1958 conclusions[5] although valid for Medan in Sumatra did not hold for cities in Java, and the question arose of how to explain the discrepancy.

The expression of ethnicity in Medan and Bandung is different not only in terms of the quality of social relationships between members of different groups but also in terms of such other features as the organization of voluntary associations, the performance of rituals, rates of intermarriage, and the extent of the differences between the older and younger generations. These seemingly isolated variables, though often investigated and treated separately, are interrelated and form a consistent pattern when viewed in the context of the larger urban structure.

Let us examine the structure of the two cities in the light of some previous urban theories. Louis wirth related a large number of social variables to the three criteria of population size, population density, and cultural heterogeneity.[6] Based upon 1861 census data, Medan, the fifth largest city in Indonesia, has a population of one-half million while Bandung, the third largest city has one million residents, so that both are within the same range as regards population size; both cities have comparable population densities (9339 persons per sq. km. for Medan and 12,010 for Bandung); and both are characterized by ethnic heterogeneity although the ethnic mix varies.[7] Wirth's criteria apply to all urban centers and are not differentiating.

* The research in Indonesia was supported at different times by the Center for Advanced Study, the University Research Board, the Center for International Comparative Studies, and the Center for Asian Studies, all of the University of Illinois; and by the Southeast Asia Development Advisory Group (SEADAG) of The Asia Society. New York. In Indonesia, the research was greatly facilitated by Dr. Koentjaraningrat and the *Lembaga Ilmu Pengetahuan Indonesia* whose assistance I would like to acknowledge publicly. In the Bandung project, I was assisted by three Indonesian anthropologists: Harsojo; Parsudi Suparlan, and Djuriah Utjah, and by three University of Illinois graduate students: Hiroko Horikoshi, Caroline R. Wood, and Robert Wessing. I wish to thank them for their many contributions and also M.G. Smith, whose comments were particularly helpful.

The familiar distinction which has appeared in may forms between old indigenous cities and new cities is not applicable as both Medan and Bandung developed during the colonial era and are products of colonialism. Other typologies could be cited which, for example, distinguish between industrial and preindustrial cities;[9] plantation, commercial, and capital cities; or between large primate cities and smaller provincial ones. One could, in fact, devise an infinite number of arbitrary typologies but in each case the problem for the social anthropologist is to link specific aspects of urban structure to speciffc aspects of social life.

It would seem appropriate to turn to Furnivall (1939, 1948) since he developed the concept of plural society based upon Indonesian data and is referred to so frequently in the literature on pluralism and ethnicity.[10] What is emphasized in his writings is the notion of different social orders within the same political unit existing side by side, integrated in the market place, but otherwise separate. But for Furnivall the viability of the political unit depended upon the interconnections between these separate social orders, and in any case he tells us very little about the ethnic groups of Indonesia. "In Netherlands India", according to Furnivall, "the European, Chinaman (sic) and Native are linked vitally as Siamese twins and, if rent asunder, every element of the union must dissolve in anarchy."[11] Although Indonesia has had serious problems in achieving economic and political stability in the two decades since independence, the country has not dissolved in anarchy and the Natives now appear to be doing reasonably well in conducting the affairs of the fifth largest nation in the world. For Furnivall, plural society in Indonesia refers to "the European, Chinaman and Native". and not to Javanese, Sundanese, Malay, Minangkabau, and other Indonesian groups. He does not, in other words, difierentiate within the category of Native and he displays a completely external or European view of Indonesian pluralism. The presence of the Dutch did change the relationships among the Indonesians, and had this been described it would have provided an invaluable comparative bas for later studies of ethnic relations in post independence Indonesia, but Furnivall did not do so and for our study his work has little value.

The Dominant Culture Hypothesis

My hypothesis is that the aspect of urban structure that differentiates Medan from Bandung, and that accounts for the varying pattern of ethnic group relations in the two cities is the absence or presence of a dominant majority culture.[12] Medan is a city of minorities and lacks a dominant culture while in Bandung the dominant culture group the second largest ethnic group in Indonesia, with a total population of approximately 20 million.

To place the hypothesis in a broader perspective, the concept of a dominant culture may be divided into three separate components of the larger system that are sociologically relevant to ethnic expression in any multi-ethnic group situation. The first component is the population ratio, the social demography. This refers not only to the fact of ethnic heterogeneity, but rather to the nature of the particular mix in a given context. The second component concerns the established local culture, if any, and the manner in which members of other groups relate to and articulate with it. The third component focuses on the locus of power and its distribution among the various ethnic groups. The three components of the dominant culture hypothesis are the social demography, the established local culture, and the locus of power. Since 1930 the European population has declined drastically, the Chinese have increased slightly, and the Indonesin population considerably. During the 1930-1961 period there has been a 600 per cent increase in population in each city, almost entirely due to migration of native Indonesians.

In Bandung we note that the Sundanese total 73.7 per cent of the Indonesian population, a clear numerical majority, followed by 21.1 per cent Javanese and then small percentages of many other ethnic groups. The table is misleading in that some categories such as South Sumatra are regions, not ethnic groups. A variety of groups originating in South Sumatra have been lumped together in the census data, so that there are even more small ethnic groups represented than indicated.

The city of Bandung is the provincial capital of West Java, the homeland of the Sundanese people. Surrounding the city are rural farming communities that are almost 100 per cent

Sundanese, and migrants to the city acknowledge that Bandung "belongs" to the Sundanese. As Sundanese are the most numerous peoples the migrants have more daily contact with them than with members of their own ethnic group. During the colonial period there were European, Javanese, and Chinese sections of the city; however, now the various ethnic groups are no longer residentially segregated.

The ethnic groups in Bandung are the Sundanese, Javanese, Batavia (Djakarta), Moluccan, North Celebes, Malays, Minangkabau, South Sumatra, and Batak.

The Sundanese are the dominant culture group in that they set the standards of appropriate behaviour in public places, and most urban institutions are controlled by them and operated in terms of their culture patterns. They occupy key positions of power in the city and it is understood that the governor of the province, the mayor of the city, the presidents of local universities, and the heads of major agencies and most branches of the national government will be Sundanese. With some exceptions to be discussed below all migrants adapt to the locally dominant culture. They conceive of this adaptation as a process of individual adjustment but they are responding individually to the larger structure of ethnic group relations in the city. Migrants takc a position in the urrban system with reference to the dominant culture group and they occupy economic niches made available to them or left vacant by that dominant group. In orienting their behaviour in reference to the Sundanese most migrant peoples change themselves and their culture in the direction of becoming Sundanese-like. This process operates on both conscious and unconscious levels and although it is a reflection of the larger political context it has consequences for individual and group identity, as we shall see.

The Ethnic groups in Medan comprise the Javanese, Minangkabau, Malays, Mandailing Batak, Toba Batak, Other Batak, Sundanese, Batavia (Djakarta), and a sprinking of others in neghtive members.

In Bandung the Sundanese are a numerical majority, are the dominant culiure, aud havc control of political power. The three components here converge but there are, of course, other cases in which a minority population with an alien culture may enjoy overwhelming power, e.g., in a colonial situation. To consider all of the possible variations of these three factors would be going beyond the limits of our data, but an interesting contrast is provided by Medan, where there is no ethnic majority, no locally dominant culture, and considerable competition among ethnic groups for economic and political power.

The Javanese of the Indonesian population are the most numerous group, although not a majority. The Javanese, however, are not indigenous to the area. Most of them came to Sumatra to work on the plantations as contract laborers. Native peoples such as the Batak refused to work as estate laborers because they considered it beneath their dignity. During the colonial era in North Sumatra the Batak regarded the Javanese as a lower segment of humanity, referring to the men as coolies and to the women as prostitues. A number of Batak who had visited Java in the colonial period and met aristocratic Javanese for the first time noted with surprise that they were so different from the Javanese laborers in Sumatra. The Javanese in North Sumatra, as lower class recent migrants, neither occupied positions of power nor served as a dominant culture model for other ethnic groups. The peoples who were indigenous to the Meuan region, and in whose home territory the city was located, were the Malays, the Karo Batak, and the Simalungun Batak, but within the city itself they totaled only 13.5 per cent of the Indonesian population in 1930.

Medan arose as a commercial city within a vast estate complex on the east coast of Sumatra to serve the interests of European planters. By the end of two decades, 46.1 per cent of the population were not Indonesians—thes were Europeans, Chinese, and other Asians. Among the Indonesian population almost 52 per cent were migrants from the island of Java. Since independence the percentage of Europeans, Chinese and Javanese has declined while there has been a large increase in the number, as well as in the percentage of native people of Sumatra, particularly the Batak. But the various Batak subgroups do not constitute a majority and they are divided among themselves. Each subgroup conceives of itself as a separate unit and there is an additional cleavage along religious lines between Christian and Moslem Batak.

It is instructive to examine Medan and then Bandung from the perspective of one ethnic group, the Toba Batak. The group was selected as a basis for comparison simply because I have field data on the Taba Batak communities, in each city but the results can be generalized. Subsequently, we shall examine Bandung from the point of view of the dominant Sundanese, but we begin with Medan.

Medan

R. William Liddle in a mongraph on local politics in Pemantangsiantar, a North Sumatran city very similar to Medan, concludes that "the most critical principle of differentiation among individuals is ethnic or ethnoreligious affiliation;" that "the most striking findings are the overriding importance of ethnicity".[13] "For at least the last few decades", he writes, "the inhabitant of Simalungun/Siantar has identified most strongly with his ethnic or ethnoreligious group, and local loyalties and hostilities have been heavily colored by this ethnic self-identification. Practically all aspects of social life—residence, educational and occupational opportunities, religious belief and practice, friendship, political organization—are today affected by the perception of ethnic differences".[14] Liddle notes that his findings "seem to be at odds with studies of urbanization and tribalism in Africa"[15] and he refers specifically to publications of the Rhodes-Livingstone Institute.[16] An analysis of the differences between North Sumatra and Central Africa would be beyond the scope of this paper, although one factor of importance may be that both Liddle and I have worked in a postcolonial situation in which the Europeans present were few in number and had almost no political power. A dominant alien European administration tends to solidify diverse indigenous ethnic groups under its jurisdiction. In any case, my findings in North Sumatra confirm those of Liddle as to the pervasive influence of ethnicity and tribal allegiances as opposed to class factors. By ethnicity is meant contemporary ethnicity that has emerged in modern urban situations and not a rural persistence. In North Sumatran cities most political leaders are dependent upon a support group consisting of members of their own ethnic group, and each urban politicol party does tend to represent an ethnoreligious group; the Parkindo party the Christian Toba Batak, the Masjumi party the Moslem Mandailing Batak, and the PNI the Javanese.

The interpersonal consequences of a competitive urban system are that relationships between members of different ethnic groups tend to be tense, lacking in trust, and based on ethnic stereo-types. Certainly close individual friendships do develop but there is always the possibility of the individuals finding themselves involved in a larger confrontation between ethnic blocks which puts a strain on their relationship. It is particularly in situations involving competition that ethnic polarization occurs. There are many such situations ranging competition in business to office colleagues vying for the same promotion to teenagers striving for the affections of a girl.

It is well known and widely accepted in Medan that if the head of one's office is, say, a Mandailing he will tend to favor the members of his own group in job assignments and in the recruitment of personnel. Occasionally in government offices one will find that almost everyone in a particular department belongs to the same ethnic group. Indeed, if the situation is too blatant it may be called to the attention of the newspapers and create a minor scandal. I asked one Batak department head why so many men in his office were Batak and he assured me that he really did not plan it that way. He was a close informant and we had talked about the difference between particularlistic and universalistic criteria. He explained that so many Batak relatives came to him asking for employment that he did not feel that he could refuse them all. Some were well qualified, and when he had to make a choice between an equally competent Batak and a member of a different ethnic group he would choose the Batak, in large part because he could trust him more. Trust enhances office efficiency and the individual decisions made by the department head were rational, although the cumulative effect adds up to nepotism.

The major line of sociol differentiation and cleavage in Medan society is undoubtedly ethnic, despite the fact that within each ethnic group members occupy a range of social structure slots in the urban system, differ considerably in level of income, and display a variety of individual life styles. If one plots the interaction network of Toba Batak in nonwork situations the majority of iies are with members of one's own ethnic group. Some persons even choose the option of encapsulating themselves within the confines of an all Toba Batak community by withdrawal from as many non Toba Batak contexts as possible, by full participation in their Toba Batak neighborhood mutual aid society and their city wide Toba Batak clan association, by active involvement in the affairs of one of the Toba Batak ethnic churches in Medan, and by attending as many as possible of the Toba Batak adat rituals in which they are entitled to participate by virtue of kinship rights.[17] Not all Toba Batak choose this alternative. Many, particularly in the elite, extend their ties widely across ethnic lines. But those who do choose to restrict their activities to the Batak community find the necessary ethnic organizations and voluntary associations readily available, and will be rewarded by other members of their ethnic community for their involvement in Batak affairs.

There are alliances, it should be noted, which crosscut ethnic boundaries. The indigenous peoples—the Malays, Karo Batak, and Simalungun Batak—have formed political action groups in opposition to the migrant Mandailing Batak, Javanese, Minangkabau, and especially Toba Batak, the most agressive reeent intruders; but the action group has not been successful. There is some antipathy between the Christians, mostly Toba Batak but also many Karo and Simalungun Batak, and the Moslems, the Mandailing Batak, Malays, Javanese, and Minangkabau. The various Batak subgroups have banded together during some of the sporadic open fighting among ethnic groups that erupted in Medan during the 1950's. These alliances, however, arose on an ad hoc basis and only lasted for the duration of the actual conflict.

All Indonesian groups in North Sumatra are united in their opposition to the large Chinese community with its extensive business and commercial interests and ties with the Chinese across the Straits of Malacca in Malaya and Singapore. And, finally, the people of Sumatra are together in their antagonism toward what they regard as Javanese control of Indonesia. A particular sore point is that so much of the foreign exchange earned by the Sumatran plantations ultimately ends up in the national treasury in Djakarta, one factor in the Sumatran rebellion of 1958-1961 against the central government. Cross-cutting ties develop, then, but they are temporary, based on particular issues, and do not generalize to other areas of social life.

The basic predicament in Medan and in the province of North Sumatra generally is that after the departure of the Dutch colonial administration no one indigenous group could gain control. This led to intense competition to fill the power vacuum. The situation was complicated by population shifts due to heavy migration from rural to urban areas, the political instability of the new national government, the sometimes reckless economic policies of Sukarno which led to an extremely high rate of inflation, the lack of a truly national, distinctively Indonesian culture pattern which could have served as an alternative to ethnic lifeways, and the uneasy relationship of Sumatran peoples to the perceived domination by the Javanese of the national administration located on the remote island of Java.

Our understanding of ethnicity in Medan will be enhanced by contrast with the Toba Batak community in Bandung, to which we now turn.

Bandung

The Batak and other migrants in Bandung realize that the Sundanese are the dominant culture and they adapt to the realities of the urban situation in which they find themselves. For example, if a vacancy opened for the position of supervisor in an office in Medan the Toba Batak would maneuver and plan so that one of ther own might be selected, as they would assess that thereafter they would be favored, and the other groups in Medan would act in the same way. If there were a similar opening in a Bandung office it would be assumed that the position would be filled by a Sundanese, or possible a Javanese, and the other ethnic groups would not enter the competition. The difference between the two cities has profound implications for social life and for ethnic group relations.

The 8,000 to 9,000 Toba Batak are a clear minority in Bandung, a city of one million. It is not possible for them to encapsulate themselves either residentially or socially, as they are too few and too dispersed. In Medan, each neighborhood has a mutual aid society consisting of the Toba Batak located in the area; other ethnic groups also have their territorially based welfare association. In Bandung there are also neighborhood associations but membership is not restricted to a single ethnic group. Everyone who resides in a given section of the city is eligible to join, regardless of ethnic affiliation. There are fewer Toba Batak adat rituals in Bandung than in Medan, and the clan associations are less active. Thus there are fewer opportunities for a Batak in Bandung to limit his activities to distinctively Batak contexts, and there are correspondingly many more occasions for relationships with Sundanese in the neighborhood, at school, at work, and elsewhere.

They key to understanding social change in Bandung is the process that I have referred to as "becoming Sundanese-like". To describe this process, we may adopt the perspective of a Toba Batak migrant who has just arrived from Sumatra. The majority of migrants enter the city through a Batak social network and indeed their arrival is usually known in advance. All Batak churches in Java publicly announce at each Sunday service the arrivals and departures of the Toba Batak in their area. The experienced Bandung Batak learn about the new migrant and there is always someone, often a distant clan relative, who welcomes him to the city and who provides a short course of instruction in Sundanese culture and behavior, designed to help him adjust to life in Java. Most of the instruction takes place over a period of time in informal context on a person-to-person basis, but sometimes it is more formally organized. During one period of especially heavy migration a Batak ethnic association met in a Bandung warehouse and held weekly instructional sessions, in seminar like fashion. The Batak upperclassmen at Indonesia's leading technological university in Bandung, ITB, regularly meet with incoming Batak freshmen as an extracurricular aspect of the orientation programme.

The content of the instruction varies from recipes for appropriate behaviour in particular situations to the presentation of general rules on such an abstract level that they would delight the most rigorous ethnoscience oriented anthropologist.

I witnessed one session on how to drink tea in Bandung. It was explained and demonstrated that in Sumatra the Batak drink all the tea in the cup with gusto while the Sudanese not only handle the tea cup with greater delicacy, but they will only drink slightly more than half the contents of the cup, then they place it down on the table announcing that they have had enough. The instructor noted with some surprise that the Sundanese never finish their tea; "what a waste, and when we Batak do so," he continued, "the Sundanese consider us impolite!" He added that, "although the people here may behave in strange ways, we are guests in Sundaland and we must adapt to their standards of tea drinking. After all, we Batak are emigres in an alien land who have come here to make a living, so we are the ones who must adjust". It was a concise lesson, well told, and to the point.

In the instructional sessions it is noted that the Sundanese consider themselves more refined and civilized (*halus*) than the Batak, so that one aspect of the adjustment process consists of learning to become less agressive, to soften the rough edges, and to talk in a lower tone of voice. Aside from the specifics, the covert communication is that in order to survive in Bandung, a Batak cannot behave naturally and be "himself". He becomes very sensitive to the local culture patterns and he becomes oriented to changing his behaviour.

The migrant to Bandung receives instruction from other Batak on how behave and he acknowledges that he must discard his village ways and become more refined. He finds it difficult, however, to generalize these prescriptions to all the new interactional situations in which he finds himself and sooner or later he will behave crudely or inappropriately, with the result that he will be laughed at, embarrassed, or "put down" by a Sundanese. This hurts, as the migrant quite understandably wants to be accepted in the new urban community to which he has come to make a new life, but the experience represents a new phase in his adaptation to life on Java.

If we take a Sundanese perspective we may better understand what has occurred in the interaction. Most Sundanese have not had much experience with Batak although all are familiar with the Batak stereotype of a rough and agressive persons. The Sundanese and the Batak each approach the initial interaction guided by their own customs and emotional set, and at first they judge the other by their own standards. What the Sundanese define as being crude the Batak define as being honest, straightforward, and strong. What the Sundanese regard as refined behaviour the Batak regard as being evasive, insincere, and feminine. Each group feels morally superior to the other and at least initially the behaviour of each tends to validate these stereotypic evaluations. Each group in doing what it thinks is right and pɹoper behaves in ways that the other feels are morally deficient.[18] The end result, however, is not an interactional standoff because the Sundanese change their strategy and the Batak change their behaviour.

Within their own cultural system the Sundanese find if difficult to deal with an agressive person and their initial reaction may be to avoid Batak people, but this is at best awkward if one has a Batak neighbor or office colleague. It becomes clear, however, that if one shows respect and politeness to a Brtak he will take advantage of the situation, or as the Suneanese say, "if you lower yourself in front of a Batak he will climb on your shoulder and sit on your head". The Sundanese learn that one way to handle the Batak is to speak lounder and to become more agressive themelves, and to engage in what they call "bluffing" behaviour. After all, they are secure in the interaction as they are the dominant power group operating in their home territory. Their main strategy, however, is to let the Batak know in a variety of subtle and not so subtle ways that he is acting in an improper and really rather barbaric manner, which the Sundanese sinccerely believe. Among themselves the Sundanese comment that the Batak eat dogs, which to them is repugnant enough, but they also note that Batak eat people. Cannibalism did exist in the Batak highlands in Sumatra a century ago and the Sundanese are not entirely convinced that the practice has been discontinued. The Sundanese can ignore a Batak neighbor, make life uncomfortable for the entire family, and bring considerable economic pressure to bear if necessary.

It rarely goes this far, however, as the Batak eventually becomes aware of what is happening, is oriented to change as we have noted, and begins to experiment with new ways of behaving. After a Batak understands the Sundanese better he accepts even more local patterns and may become quite skilled in perceiving what the Sundanese define as being refined. One Batak businessman who had lived all his adult life in Bandung took great pride in the fact that he had a deep understanding of Sundanese culture and that he really knew how to handle the Sundanese in any situation. In time, a Batak migrant learns to speak softly, drink tea appropriately, and he observes all the Sundanese rituals of respect. The Sundanese in turn then acknowledge that here is a Batak who is becoming civilized, so they begin to behave toward him in a more human, i.e. Sundanese, way by showing more deference. The process is mutually reinforcing.

With increasing self and cultural awareness a Batak will sometimes begin to manipulate the stereotypes. He fully realizes that the Sundanese regard him as crude and emotionally volatile, but he may raise his voice or even make threatening gestures as a way of manipulating the Sundanese for his own ends. Knowing that Sundanese prefer to avoid open conflict and overt aggressions, he acts as if he were angry as a ploy even though he does not feel anger; of course, he must be careful not to go too far. The Sundanese, too, learn to manipulate Batak, sometimes against the Javanese, by appealing to the Batak as a strong and aggressive person, and by flattering him in ways that appeal to his inner conception of himself.

Although manipulative behaviour is frequently employed, the Bandung Batak realize that in the long run it is much more effective to play the game by Sundanese rules. More as an outward accommodation than an inner transformation, the Batak acquire a working knowledge of Sundanese culture, learn to predict how the Sundanese will act, and modify their own behaviour in accord with Sundanese standards. This is the very first step in the process by which ethnic labeles and what we call "culture" changes in the course of social interaction. But the process accelerates over time and has unanticipated consequences.

A Batak from Sumatra who had spent four years in a city in Java returned to Medan and described his experiences. In Java he said, he ate less, became thinner, and his voice got softer, but after he returned to Medan he became strong again. He ate more, began to talk loud, and he regained his strength and "Batakness". This man's revealing observation suggests that, to be Batak is to be crude but also stroag and masculine, and that upon returning to Sumatra he regained his true self. But those who reside permanently on Java and who raise a family there cannot have this experience of a self regained, because on Java they are not fully aware of a self lost.

The most extensive change occurs among Batak children who have been born and raised in Bandung. They play and attend school with Sundanese children, and they grow up learning the rules of Sundanese cultur not as a superficial secondary accommodation but as their first learning experience. The first three grades of the public primary school in Bandung use the Sundanese language as the medium of instruction; in Medan the language of instruction is Indonesian because the school population is so ethnically heterogeneous. In high school in Bandung there are classes in Sundanese culture and all students are expected to write stories and poems in Sundanese. As a consequence the Batak families in Bandung speak Sundanese or Indonesian to their preschool children, so as to better prepare them for school. Almost all Batak adults in Bandung speak Sundanese, as it is necessary for the men in business and for the women in the market and in the neighborhood. One Batak educator confided to me with considerable apprehension that he and other adults were very concerned, as most Batak families in Bandung speak Sundanese and Indonesan at home and there were now many Batak children who were barely able to speak their own language. It is a dilemma, he said, but what can we do?

An essential component of Batak adat rituals is the sharing of a common meal. In Medan the participants sit on mats on the floor and eat with their fingers; in Bandung they sit at tables and use silverware. In anthropological terms we would say that all participants at the ceremonies in both Medan and Bandung are equally "Batak;" that both bariations are equally part of "Batak culture;' and that the Bandung pattern is an adaptation to the Sundanese and to the position of the Toba Batak minority in the urban system of ethnic group relations on Java. For ethnographic completeness we must add that in Bandung before a wedding there is a small private part of the ceremony for the close family, primarily representatives of the wife-giving and the wife-receiving groups, at which food is shared. At this private ritual the participants do sit on the floor and eat with their fingers but it is always held indoors and Sundanese are never present. At the larger public ceremony to which hundreds and even thousands of guests may be invited, including Sundanese, the Bandung Batak use tables and silverware.

The Batak, too, see the difference as an adaptation to existing circumstances, and they give a basically situational explanation, in terms very similar to the theoretical positions of Max Gluckman and Clyde Mitchell. When in Bandung follow Bandung practice, and when in Medan follow Medan practice. An adult Batak ftom Bandung who returns to Sumatra for an adat ceremony feels quite at ease with the Medan pattern of sttting on the floor and eating with his fingers in public. As a child in Sumatra he grew up in that tradition and despite his many years on Java, it is still natural to him. But the striking change in attitude and feeling tone occurs among the Java born Batak who go to Sumatra for the first time. One Batak youth said that the practice of sitting with a group of men eating together with ones fingers from a common bowl was rather primitive and probably unsanitary. He commented that even though he was a Batak he really felt like a "tourist" in Batakland, and he soon returned to more familiar surroundings in Java.

To summarize thus far, what begins in Bandung as a conscious accommodation takes on a deeper significance in the second generation and goes beyond a Gluckman-Mitchell type of situational flip-flop, as the Java born Toba Batak begin to evaluate themselves and other Batak by Sundanese standards. The process of becoming Sundanese-like and of learning the rules of the local game is transformed as the urban Sundanese rules become part of the Batak definition of proper conduct. But the situation in Indonesia is such that the process does not go to completion: Batak rarely become Sundanese. In Barth's terms, they maintain ethnic group boundaries but the cultural content changes. They retain their Toba Batak identity, live in Bandung, speak mostly Sundanese and Indonesian, and practice a culture that is at least partly Sundanese. They are Bandung Batak.

Medan and Bandung Compared: A Summary

In Medan there is no one ethnic group that is a majority, no one culture is dominant, and there is competition among ethnic groups for economic and political power. In Bandung, on the other hand, the Sundanese are a numerical majority, are the dominant culture in their home area, and have a virtual monopoly of political power. The three conditions which I label the dominant culture hypothesis structure the larger urban context and give rise to two different processes of ethnic group relations. In Medan the cleavages between ethnic groups are sharply defined, relationships are tense, and each group tends to stay together. In Bandung the relationships between ethnic groups are more relaxed and there is more interaction between groups than in Medan. In Bandung, compared to Medan, there is more intermarriage between members of different groups and the cultural and attitudinal differences between the older and the younger generation within each group are greater.

In Medan there is no common cultural code and no widely shared rules to follow making it somewhat difficult for the different ethnic groups to relate to one another. They have little basis for predicting each other's behaviour so they tend to remain apart. In Bandung, all migrant groups adapt to Sundanese standards, follow Sundanese rules, and thus share a common code which facilitates interaction. At jehnese, Minangkabau, and Batak in Bandung relate to one another in Sundanese terms.

What we have done thus far is to state which conditions give rise to which societal consequence and to isolate two different process of ethnic group relations. We have established firm links between urban ecology and the larger social system on the one hand, and strategies of adaptation on the other. We have provided models of intergroup relationships guided by symbolic interaction theory. At this point, however, it will be appropriate to introduce two qualifications.

The first qualification is that we have reluctantly but purposely ignored individual variation. Although well aware that persons within any one ethnic group occupy different niches in the urban occupational structure, have different social networks, and interactional strategies based on varying degrees of sophistication, our objective has been to isolate the larger context within which individual adaptations are defined. The second qualification is related to the above in that, depending up-on one's position in the system, the consequences that we have described for Bandung occur in Medan and vice versa. To take one example, in Medan there is a top elite consisting of the very wealthy businessmen, high government officials and military personnel, and professionals such as medical doctors. Many of this social class have been overseas for training or business. They speak foreign languages, interact with the local foreign community, and relate, to one another in some contexts by what might be called an international common code. It must be emphasized, however, that they neither renounce their ethnic ties nor appreciably diminish their participation in ethnic affairs. These data would represent a contradiction of our major thesis if we were attempting to domonstrate that Medan is one "kind" of city and Bandung another "kind", or if our objective were to construct mutually exclusive classes as part of a rigid typology. But as our aim is to isolate social processes and to specify the prior conditions which generate them, the example is consistent with the hypothesis advanced and, indeed, serves to strengthen it.

Identity Change and Intermarriage

Previously we said that Batak rarely become Sundanese. But there are circumstances in which the members of one Indonesian ethnic group do change their identity and become something else. We next consider a varity of ways this occurs.

The Mandailing Batak are an example of a group that defines itself very differently, depending upon the context. In Sumatra they refer to themselves by the single term Mandailing and choose not to be known as Batak. They are a Moslem people and they want to disassociate themselves from the crude and Christian Toba, even though the Mandailing and the Toba dialects of Batak are very close. In Sumatra the Mandailing preference for separation is widely known and respected but in Bandung the dominant Sundanese lump the Mandailing, the

Toba, and the other subgroups together in the larger category Batak.

The peoples of Java are not sensitive to all of the finer ethnic distinctions relevant on the outer islands. The Mandailing are then placed in the position of having to explain what kind of people they are to the Sundanese and sometimes they do so by saying that they are really like the Minangkabau, a Sumatran Moslem group located south of the Batak highlands. But on other occasions, especially during periods of political tension in Bandung, it is advantageous for the Mandailing to stand together with the Toba. Then they say to the Toba and to themselves that as all Batak have a common ancestor and share the same adat, they are thus one people. A Mandailing may be a Batak or not, depending on the situation. And although this is a particularly clear-cut example it is not an unusual one, for indeed the phenomenon depicted of presenting oneself differently depending on the context is universal.

As there are large military and educational establishments in and near Bandung many Toba Batak men enter the city as soldiers or as students. According to one estimate, the ratio of unmarried Batak men to women is seven to one. The consequence is that Batak men frequently marry Sundanese women. In most of these cases the Sundanese wife will "become" Batak in that she learns to speak Batak, converts to Christianity, is adopted into her husband's mother's clan, attends the adat rituals, and raises her children as Batak. To become Batak in this case does not mean an identity change, for if the wife is asked her ethnic affiliation she will reply that she is a Sundanese married to a Batak. If her children are asked, however, their first response is that they arc Batak, and if prodded slightly they may say they are Batak with a Sundanese mother.

At the same time that the wife is becoming Batak and being incorporated into the Bandung Batak community, the husband and children are progressively becoming Sundanese, not in identity but in culture, and at a faster rate than would otherwise be the case because they have a Sundanese within the primary unit of socialization. The two processes occur simultaneously and while they are not contradictory, they are not identical either. The Sundanese woman, by accepting the differentiating and visible symbols of "Batakness", becomes Batak quite consciously and all at once. Becoming Sundanese by virtue of residence in a Sundanese city is a longer term and more subtle process in which unconscious identification with the dominant power group plays a significant role. To put it in another and somewhat oversimplified way, the child inherits his ethnic identity from his Batak father but most of his culture patterns from his Sundanese mother as well as from his Sundanese peer group.

For centuries, Javanese men have been migrating to Bandung and have taken Sundanese wives. As a rough generalization, if the man is an upper-class aristocrat the children become Javanese but if the man is lower class, isolated from his Javanese relatives, and landless in his home area, then he becomes dependent upon his wife's family and the children become Sundanese. If asked, the children say they are Sundanese with a Javanese father. Indeed, there are many Sundanese in West Java who have had Javanese ancestors whom they acknowledge.

Marriages in the other direction in which Batak or Javanese women marry Sundanese men do occur, but less frequently, probably because most migrants to Bandung are men. Each group, however, has its own cultural explanation. The Batak say that if a woman marries out of the Batak community the children are lost to it because they have no clan (which is passed patrilineally) and no wife receiving relatives which makes it impossible to perform the Batak adat rituals, When a Batak man marries ont of the ethnic group, his wife is adopted into his mother's clan as if it were a matrilateral cross cousin marriage; his mother's father and brothers become the core of the wife giving group and his own lineage relatives the wife receiving group. The pressure to prevent Batak women from marrying out is considerable. Even if the woman runs off with a Sundanese man, her clan relatives do not accept the union but will make every effort to bring her back to the Batak community. The Javaneses; on the other hand, explain that they are "older", that is superior to the Sundanese, and that it is not appropriate for an "older" higher status woman to marry a "younger" man of lower status. As a concomitant, it is said that Javanese women find Snndanese man too feminine and sexually unattractive. Sundanese society is characterized by others and by Sundanese themselves as open and tolerant and although they appear to give their women away quite freely, they gain in the long run by incorporating and assimilating the lower class Javanese who, as the most numerous migrant group in West Java, provide many of the spouses.

One theoretically significant finding is that the offspring of intermarriages become neither Indonesian nor mestizo, but rather they take the ethnic affiliation of either the father or the mother. They choose one as their primary ethnic identification and acknowledge the other affiliation. In Moslem-Christian inter-marriages the family usually settles on one religion, especially after there are children, and therefore, do not remain mixed. If pressed to specify the most important factor influencing the choice of ethnic and religious identification, a first approximation would be that children take the affiliation of the higher status parent, but there are innumerable exceptions. The evidence also suggests that children are not given a real choice in this matter, that the choice is made for them by their parents.

Although Indonesian intellectuals and foreign academicians use the term Indonesianization, its meaning is not entirely clear. Those who migrate to the cities do not lose their ethnicity nor does intermarriage in Bandung result in the merging of separate ethnic affiliations into a larger Indonesian identity. Former President Sukarno frequently called for increased intermarriage as a partial solution to Indonesia's problems but if our tentative findings prove to be more generally applicable his proposal appears less effective than he might have anticipated.

Another implication of our data, relevant to an understanding of larger patterns of urbanism in Indonesia, is that Bandung urban culture is a regional Sundanese variant and not a generalized metropolitan Indonesian superculture. It might be anticipated, that in the central Javanese city of Jogjakarta the rules of the local urban game will be Javanese and that in urban Den Pasar on the island of Baii they will be Balinese. Although we have not conducted research in other regions, we feel that the Bandung pattern may be generalized to other Indonesian cities located in ethnically homogeneous home areas in which migrants adapt to the dominant culture group, while the Medan pattern may hold in other new cities characterized by extensive migration of whom are in a dominnat power position. If this is indeed the case, then generalizations about of the regional variations and of the diverse social processes which occur in what on superficial examination may appear to be seemingly similar urban centers.

One pervasive influence on ethnic relations among all groups throughout the Indonesian archipelago is the role of the Javanese, for it is widely felt that efforts of the central government to foster a national Indonesian identity are in reality a plot to further Javanese political control. Being Indonesianixed is equated with being Javanixed, with the result that people hold fiımly to thnic cultures to avoid being submerged in what they perceive as a Javanese mainstream. To some, and this is an extreme view, the Javanese are equated with the Dutch as an alien colonial power imposing decisions that are made neither in terms of local categories nor in terms of the local situation.

The Javanese in Bandung

Nowhere is the opposition to the Javanese experienced as strongly as among the Sundanese of West Java. Within the city of Bandung there are almost sixty Sundanese ethnic associations; some are genealogical groups consisting of the Sundanese within one family line; others are designed to advance Sundanese art and dance and to revive Sundanese folk culture; and still others are primarily political in orientation and work civic improvement. We expect to find ethnic associations among migrant peoples but not among the dominant host population. The explanation is that these groupings were created with reference to the Javanese. The Sundanese are vehement in their opposition to the Javanese. They trac the origin of their confiict with them in mythological terms to a fight between the Javanese kingdom of Modjopahit and the Sundanese kingdom of Padjadjaran in the year 1357. Six hundred years later almost all Sundanese children can recount the story of this battle, which the Javanese won, with visible affect and bitterness. As the second largest Indonesian ethnic group, the Sundanese, of course, are reminded daily of the overwhelming Javanese political power and numerical superiority.

To racapitulate, with approximately one-half of Indonesia's total population, the Javanese are the dominant culture in the country. The Sundanese, however, are the dominant group in Bandung so that the migrant gronps to that city orient their behaviour with reference to them. The Sundanese in turn, although the local power group, see themselves in opposition to the nationally dominant Javanese. And the Javanese do not really understand what what ethnicity is all about; they are the WASPS of Indonesia.

The Javanese and the Batak perceive other Indonesians quite differently, and they have different conceptions of Indonesia as a nation. To summarize briefly a position presented in more detail elsewhere,[19] whenever one Batak confronts another human being a decision is made that the other is either a Batak like oneself or a non-Batak different than self. The most fundamental binary opposition is between Batak and non-Batak; the differentiation is made on the basis of ethnicity. Indonesians are skilled in distinguishing ethnic identity by such criteria as hair style, skin color, facial contour, body mannerisms, name, and speech pattern. Although the Javanese are aware of ethnicity their basic binary opposition is between others as more or less civilixed, refined or crude, of higher culture and status or lower culture and status. When one Javanese confronts another he first determines who is higher and who lower, and he selects from a vast repertoire of respect behavior that which is most appropriate. This initial distinction is the one utilized and appled to members of other ethnic groups when a Javanese moves outside his home area.

To the Batak the ethnic groups of Indonesia are structurally similar to patrillineal clans. In the Batak highlands the members of a descent unit have a common male ancestor and constitute a biological group, are localized in a geographical area, share traits of temperament and character, and have their own variant of Batak culture and language which is somewhat unique and which has symbolic items of distinctiveness. In the Batak view, Indonesia consists of a number of structurally similar ethnic groups each of which is also a biological unit, is localized in a home territory, and has its own temperament, culture, and language. Just as patrilineal descent groups are little nations within the Batak highlands, so the various ethnic groups are separate nations within the Republic of Indonesia.

The Javanese, of course, do not share this view. They see a homogenous Indonesia consisting of separate persons who are more or less civilized, and at least in the traditional conception, the most cnltured and refined were the Javanese nobility. Ethnicity is confusing to the Javanese who point out that members of all ethnic groups in Indonesia have high positions in the government, that all have equal opportunity, that considerable economic development occurs in the outer islands, and that Javanese language or culture has never been imposed on the national scene. An outer islander might counter that, nevertheless, national power is in the hands of the Javanese with the ineuitable consequence that key national decisions are made from a Javanese perspective and on the basis of Javanese logic.

Despite the feeling against the Javanese, there is little sentiment to break up the unitary repblic by creating separate states. The rebellions in Sumatra, Celebes, and elsewhere were designed to change the national Indonesian government, not to establish separate governments. There have been severe struggles for power on the national level, especially between the Moslems and the Bommunists, but only an insignificant minority of Indonesians would want to see their national fragmented into smaller politicnl units.

Ethnic particularism and exclusiveness is almost universally disapproved if too blatantly expressed, even though everyone is well aware of the strength of ethnic ties. In North Sumatra political parties do represent ethnic groups but the Toba Batak, for example, join the Parkindo, a Chrtstian party, and there is no Toba Batak ethnic party as such. Explicitly ethnic political movements have generally been unsuccessful in Indonesia. In Medan there are three Toba Batak newspapers, owned by Batak, whose news coverage and editorial policy are biased in favour of the Batak. The papers, however, are published in the Indonesian language, although all Batak in Medan speak and read their own language. According to one editor, the Batak in Medan would not buy a newspaper published in the Batak language.

Indonesians rarely talk about ethnicity in mixed groups, although they do so frequently and freely in private among members of their own ethnic group. Thə census of 1970, moreover, did not gather information on ethnic group affiliation and the Central Bureau of Statistics does not publish data on ethnic population distributions, not because such information is deemep unimportant, but because, in the words of one official, it is "too sensitive". Political leaders who represent a local ethnic group must participate in ethnic affairs internally within the group and represent their constitutents in the national arena. At the same time, however, they cannot alienate other groups by being too openly ethnic. There are two ways for a leader to commit political suicide; one is to deny his ethnicity and the other is to be too obviously ethnic. In Indonesia, ethnicity must be expressed, but it must be disguised.

Conclusion

To write about the expression of ethnicity in such a vast nation as Indonesia based on only 21 months of field work may appear both bold and presumptuous, particularly as we have ranged so widely from Sumatra to Java and to the entire archipelago. I fully realize and indeed expect that future research will correct the inevitable overgeneralizations. But my treatment of the subject is based on the firmly held theoretical position that we must raise our sights to deal with the larger system. I agree with my colleague Lehman[20] that members of ethnic categories take positions in culturally defined systems of inter-group relations, and that while we must describe interactions in context, for indeed this is the heart of our subject matter, the interpretation of the interactions is dependent upon an analysis of the larger system qua system.

The expression of Sundanese ethnicity in Bandung requires a simultaneous appreciation of the demography, the dominant culture, and the locus of power both within the urban system and within the national system, for the Sundanese face in both directions. And Indonesian ethnicity simply cannot be understood from the perspective of Java alone, but must be viewed in the larger context of Java and the outer islands taken as a whole. To deal with systems within systems is a complex matter. But the Indonesians do so every day, and their national motto "unity in diversity" expresses their aspiration for the solution of the ethnic predicament in which they find themselves.

NOTES

1. M. Gluckman, "Tribalism in Modern British Central Africa," *Cahiers d' Etudies Africaines* 1, 1960.
2. M.G. Smith, "Social and Cultural Pluralism", *Annals, New York Academy of Science*, 83, 1960: A. Cohen, *Custom and Politics in Urban Africa: A Study of Hausa Migrants in Yoruba Towns* (Berkeley: University of California Press, 1969); F. Barth, *Ethnic Groups and Boundaries* (Boston: Little, Brown, and Co., 1969.
3. J. Furnivall, *Colonial Policy and Practice* (Cambridge: Cambridge University Press, 1948).
4. H. Geertz, "Indonesian Cultures and Communities", in R. McVey (ed.), *Indonesia* (New Haven: Human Relations Area Files, 1963); K. Pelzer, "Physical and Human Resource Patterns", McVey, *Ibid.*
5. E. Bruner, "Kinship Organization Among the Urban Batak of Sumatra", *Transactions, New York Academy of Sciences* 22, 1959; "Urbanization and Ethnic Identity in North Sumatra", *American Anthropologist*, 63, 1961; "Medan: The Role of Kinship in an Indonesian City", in A. Spoehr (ed.), *Pacific Port Towns and Cities* (Honolulu: Bishop Museum Press, 1963).
6. L. Wirth, "Urbanism as a Way of Life", *American Journal of Sociology* 44, 1938.
7. P. Milone, *Urban Areas in Indonesia: Administrative and Census Concepts* (Berkeley: Institute of International Studies, University of California, Research Series 10, 1966).
8. R. Redfield and M. Singer, "The Cultural Role of Cities", *Economic Development and Cultural Change*, 3 (1), 1954, and A. Southall, "Introductory Summary", in A. Southall (ed.), *Social Change in Modern Africa* (London: Oxford University Press, 1961).
9. G. Sjoberg, *The Preindustrial City* (New York: The Free Press, 1960).
10. J. Furnivall, *op cit*. Also, J. Furnivall, *Netherlands India: A Study of Plural Economy* (Cambridge: Cambridge University Press, 1939).
11. *op. cit.*, (1939), p. 447.
12. P. Mercier, "On the Meaning of Tribalism in Black Africa", in P. van den Berghe (ed.), *Africa: Social Problems of Change and Conflict* (San Francisco: Chandler Publishing, 1965), and A. Southall, "Determinants of the Social Structure of African Urban Populations, with Special Reference to Kampala (Uganda)", in D. Forde

(ed.), *Social Implications of Industrialization and Urbanization in Africa South of the Sahara (Paris: UNESCO, 1956).*

13. R. W. Liddle, *Ethnicity, Party and National Integration: An Indonesian Case Study*, (New Haven and London: Yal University Press, 1970), pp. 277, 187.
14. *Ibid.* p. 207
15. *Ibid.* p. 227
16. A. Epstein, *Politics in an Urban African Community* (Manchester: Manchester University Press, 1958).
17. Bruner, *op. cit*, (1959, 1963).
18. N. Braroe, *Change and Identity: Patterns of Interaction in an Indian-White Community* (Unpublished Ph. D. dissertation, Department of Anthropology, University of Illinois, 1970).
19. E. Bruner, "Kin and Non-Kin", in A. Southall (ed.), *Urban Anthropology* (London: Oxford University Press, 1972).
20. F. Lehman, "Ethnic Categories in Burma and the Theory of Social Systems", in P. Kunstadter (ed.), *Southeast Asian Tribes, Minorities, and Nations*, (Princeton: Princeton University Press, 1967).

Index